WOMEN WRITING LATIN

Volume 1

WOMEN WRITERS OF THE WORLD
Katharina M. Wilson, *Series Editor*

WOMEN WRITERS IN PRE-REVOLUTIONARY FRANCE
Strategies of Emancipation
edited by Collette H. Winn

RUSSIAN WOMEN WRITERS
edited by Christine D. Tomei

WRITINGS BY PRE-REVOLUTIONARY FRENCH WOMEN
From Marie de France to Elizabeth Vige-Le Brun
edited by Collette H. Winn and Anne R. Larsen

WOMEN WRITING LATIN
From Roman Antiquity to Early Modern Europe
edited by Laurie J. Churchill, Phyllis R. Brown,
and Jane E. Jeffrey

WOMEN WRITING LATIN
FROM ROMAN ANTIQUITY TO
EARLY MODERN EUROPE

VOLUME 1
Women Writing Latin in Roman Antiquity,
Late Antiquity, and the Early Christian Era

Edited by
LAURIE J. CHURCHILL
PHYLLIS R. BROWN
AND
JANE E. JEFFREY

In Three Volumes
Volume 1

Routledge
Taylor & Francis Group

NEW YORK AND LONDON

Published in 2002 by
Routledge
270 Madison Avenue
New York, NY 10016
www.routledge-ny.com

Published in Great Britain by
Routledge
2 Park Square, Milton Park
Abingdon, Oxon OX14 4RN
www.routledge.co.uk

Library of Congress Cataloguing-in-Publication Data

Women writing Latin : from Roman antiquity to early modern Europe / edited by Laurie J. Churchill, Phyllis R. Brown, and Jane E. Jeffrey.
    p. cm.—(Women writers of the world ; 6)
   Includes bibliographical references.
   Contents: v. 1. Women writing in Latin in Roman antiquity, late antiquity, and the early Christian era—v. 2. Medieval women writing Latin—v. 3. Early modern women writing Latin.
    ISBN 0-415-94247-0 (set)—ISBN 0-415-94183-0 (v. 1)—ISBN 0-415-94184-9 (v. 2)—ISBN 0-415-94185-7 (v. 3)
    1. Latin literature, Medieval and early modern—Women authors—History and criticism. 2. Latin literature—Women authors—History and criticism. 3. Women and literature—Rome—History. 4. Women and literature—History. I. Churchill, Laurie J., 1948- II. Brown, Phyllis Rugg, 1949- III. Jeffrey, Jane E., 1954- IV. Series.

PA8030.W65 W66 2002
870.9'9287—dc21

2002024703

Women Writing Latin: From Roman Antiquity to Early Modern Europe is dedicated to the women who taught us Latin when we were girls, those who first gave us the words that made this book possible. They include Frances Abramowitz, St. Margaret's School, Waterbury, Connecticut; Eleanor C. Bailey, St. Margaret's School, Waterbury, Connecticut; Virginia Brunson, Whitehaven High School, Memphis, Tennessee; Elizabeth Schleyer, Monroe High School, Rochester, New York; and Mary Shults, Monroe High School, Rochester, New York. To all young women currently studying Latin: may this book enable you to know more fully the traditions of which you are a part.

Contents

Acknowledgments

Thanks to the National Endowment for the Humanities for funding two summer institutes that catalyzed this project. "New Perspectives on Classical Antiquity: Teaching Classics in the Twenty-first Century," directed by Bella (Zweig) Vivante at the University of Arizona, provided the context for exploring more fully ideas long brewing on the gendered dimensions of Latin pedagogy, on women's relation to and their uses of Latin in social-historical perspective, and on the possibilities of revisioning the Latin curriculum from new perspectives. The three editors of *Women Writing Latin* met at an NEH summer institute in 1997, this time on "The Literary Traditions of Medieval Women," directed by Jane Chance at Rice University. Here we worked (and played) with a group of incredibly spunky, imaginative, and intelligent peers on whose collective energy this book is founded. Several of these colleagues also contributed their work to *Women Writing Latin*. We had the pleasure of working with Katharina Wilson at the Rice NEH. Her kind encouragement inspired us to move forward with *Women Writing Latin* for the series Women Writers of the World. Thanks are due to all the participants in "The Literary Traditions of Medieval Women" for stimulation, collegiality, new directions, and good times.

We also thank the friends, family members, colleagues, libraries, and universities that supported us in various ways. Ohio Wesleyan University provided funding for a research leave and West Chester University for release time, without which *Women Writing Latin* simply would not have been written. The Canterbury Program in the English Department at Santa Clara University funded an internship that provided invaluable assistance of many kinds; Santa Clara University sophomore Thomas Garvey, the Canterbury Intern, repeatedly demonstrated his intelligence, excellent language skills (including knowledge of Greek and Latin), proofreading skills, and meticulousness, as well as his ability to outsmart Microsoft Word, especially during the final process of printing the copy to submit to the press. George Hardin Brown (Professor of English and Classics at Stanford University) generously assisted us with some of the thorniest challenges of post-classical Latin and guidance on some medieval theological issues. The public library in Truth or Consequences, New Mexico, afforded a quiet space and Internet access in times of need.

Women Writing Latin: An Introduction

Latin literacy, the ability to write as well as to read Latin, has usually been understood to be fundamental to institutions of male power and authority in the period extending from Roman antiquity to early modern Europe. As such, Latin has been understood as the language of empire, scholarship, and the church—the language of patriarchal power—for two thousand years. Recently, however, scholars have begun to recognize ways women have participated in the institutions associated with power and authority. With this recognition comes a growing awareness of women's roles in Latin literacy and the roles Latin literacy have played in women's lives. The writers represented in the three volumes of *Women Writing Latin* are bound not by geography or time or vernacular language but by their connection to Latinate cultural literacy, which has influenced Western culture from the classical era through the European Christian Middle Ages and beyond.

Divided into three volumes—*Women Writing Latin in Roman Antiquity, Late Antiquity, and the Early Christian Era; Medieval Women Writing Latin*; and *Early Modern Women Writing Latin*—*Women Writing Latin* brings together nearly thirty named and several anonymous women whose writings give witness to the historical reality that Latin was a language of women as well as of men: a language of homes, nurseries, and brothels as well as of communities of religious women. The writings of the women relate in complex ways to the development of Latin in the ancient, classical, and early Christian worlds as a spoken, literary, and imperial language; its role as the foundational language of the Christian Church in the West and in various European social and political systems; and its role as the language of early modern humanists.

Scholarship has been slow to recognize women's uses of Latin as viable areas of inquiry. One purpose of *Women Writing Latin* is to provide an overview of Latin texts and their contexts and thereby contribute to an increasingly percep-tible dimension of Latin literacy—namely, that surprisingly large numbers of classical, medieval, and early modern women were literate and that a significant number of them read and wrote Latin. Although *Women Writing Latin* does not include all the Latin writings of women or even all the most important women (note, for instance, the absence of Dhuoda, Gertrude of Helfta, and Maddalena Scrovegni, to name some of the better known), the work nevertheless grew to require three volumes.

During the Middle Ages, while European vernacular languages and litera-tures rapidly developed, Latin stabilized and standardized the written tradition. It has been usual to associate women with the development of the vernaculars and men with the uses of Latin that survived well into modernity. The etymology of the word *vernacular*, deriving from *vernaculus*, "of or belonging to homeborn slaves," suggests an opposition to rather than a shared participation in literacy, a term itself derived from *litteratus*, meaning "learned, accessible only to the let-tered." *Litterator*, a masculine noun meaning "philologist or grammarian," comes closest to its English derivative, *literacy*, while the adjective *litteratus*, "under-standing Latin morphology and syntax," emphasizes the exclusivity of Latin liter-acy.[1] The women and texts represented in *Women Writing Latin* contribute to a more complicated understanding of the relationship between Latin literacy and the development of the European vernaculars, partly because they illustrate a wide variety of uses of Latin literacy but also because they demonstrate that Latin literacy was less exclusive than has generally been believed.

Even if Latin literacy actually includes far more women than have been rec-ognized, however, the cultural values associated with literacy in general and Latin literacy in particular nevertheless derive from beliefs about literacy as a male enclave. Therefore, the three volumes of *Women Writing Latin* contribute to a larger endeavor of rethinking assumptions about literacy based on conventional gender ideologies. In *The Implications of Literacy: Written Language and Models of Interpretation in the Eleventh and Twelfth Centuries*, Brian Stock defines the *literate* as those

> who could read and write a language for which in theory at least there was a set of articulated rules, applicable to a written, and, by implication, to a spoken language. Even today, such terms as *preliterate* and *illiterate*, which are commonly used to describe earlier phases of culture, imply a semantic norm linked to the use of texts.[2]

Work such as Stock's invites scholars to rethink the relationships between Latin and vernacular literacy. Some of the women represented in these volumes, who wrote in Latin as well as in Greek, Hebrew, and often in more than one vernacu-lar, illustrate a complex form of literacy modern linguists call code switching; they also remind us how difficult it can be to reconstruct the rules and values of earlier cultures without distortion by our own beliefs, values, and especially assumptions about what constitutes literacy.

The slowness of scholarship to recognize women's roles in the Latin tradition results not only from outmoded gender ideologies but also, in part, from a narrow understanding of the meanings of *author, culture,* and *literature.* Theoretical awareness cultivated by feminism, cultural studies, and new historicism has revealed the extent to which our understanding of Western culture has been shaped by the exclusion of texts considered nonliterary, often at least partly because they were written by women.[3] Moreover, literary historians and critics are increasingly aware that the idea of authorship has changed significantly over time in response to various cultural pressures.[4] Some of the texts in *Women Writing Latin in Roman Antiquity, Late Antiquity, and the Early Christian Era* and *Medieval Women Writing Latin* extend our understanding of authorship to include writing by women cited in male-authored texts; anonymous voices in graffiti, epigraphy, marginalia, and mortuary rolls; and, perhaps most complex of all, women who collaborated with scribes. The writing in these volumes also contributes to broader understanding of the cultures that allowed these works of literature to be written and preserved. What is important, therefore, is that the barriers that restricted women's full participation in Latin culture—prohibitions against receiving a formal education, teaching outside the home or convent, and speaking or preaching in public—were, while not overcome, dealt with in various ways by the women represented in the three volumes of *Women Writing Latin.*

Paradoxically, however, these textual examples also contribute to a realization that a dependence on a surviving written record for information about literacy may, in fact, distort our understanding. Stock writes, "One can be literate without the overt use of texts, and one can use texts extensively without evidencing genuine literacy. In fact, the assumptions shared by those who can read and write often render the actual presence of a text superfluous."[5] At the same time, since surviving texts provide most of the evidence available to shape our knowledge of the interrelationships of literacy and culture in the past, the breadth of authorship and subject matter exemplified in this collection simultaneously confirms and qualifies our understanding of the power of Latin to conserve and sustain Roman social, moral, and ethical values. In his study of medieval language and culture, Michael Richter argues that medieval Latin, though primarily a written language, a *Schriftsprache,* controlled by an elite group, and mainly used for administrative purposes, nevertheless transmitted to post-Roman societies values implicit in the Latin language.[6] Increasingly it is possible to recognize the tension between Richter's observations and evidence that Latin was used more widely and by a more varied group of authors than has previously been believed.

Attitudes toward medieval Latin itself have probably also restricted our understanding of women's contributions to Latin literacy. Earlier scholars have faulted postclassical authors for simplifying inflectional and phrasal structures, but Harrington writes that it is "a mistake to assume that Medieval Latin is always easier . . . ; in fact much that was written in Medieval Latin was linguistically and stylistically very complex. But the language remained very definitely Latin, and Cicero, Caesar and Virgil would readily have understood most Medieval Latin, even though the vocabulary in specialist fields would have puzzled them."[7]

New studies of medieval European vernacular literacy and literature have opened up vast areas for scholarship and criticism on women; these three volumes join a few others in exploring women's contributions to Latin literacy, what came to be called, in the sixteenth century, *Res Publica Litteraria*, or the Republic of Letters.[8] Thus, the extant Latin texts, some of which are included in this volume, provide us with more information about women's lives and their linguistic presence and in doing so replenish contemporary consciousness with the manifest reality that women not only wrote, but wrote in Latin on virtually every topic men addressed in the same periods.

Women Writing Latin in Roman Antiquity, Late Antiquity, and the Early Christian Era opens with fragments of a letter from the noblewoman Cornelia, wife of Tiberius Sempronius Gracchus, consul in 177 B.C.E., to her son Gaius Sempronius Gracchus. Although the only extant manuscripts of these fragments date to a full century after Cornelia died, references in Cicero's essays and Quintilian's *Institutes* confirm the circulation of letters like the one included here during the years immediately after Cornelia's death. Furthermore, as Judith Hallett demonstrates, evidence from both Cicero and Quintillian confirms the testimony of the letter included here that Cornelia had taken an active part in shaping her sons' education and political careers. Judith Hallett's, Jane Stevenson's, and Elizabeth Woeckner's contributions demonstrate that fuller information about women's uses of Latin, even when fragmentary, can enrich our understanding of Roman antiquity.

In addition, a good deal of women's writing in Latin dates from the late Roman–early Christian period, 300 C.E.–800 C.E. Early Christianity seems both to have afforded opportunities for women to write in Latin and for those writings to have been valued enough for them to survive. New work (including Hallett's and Erhart's contributions to this volume on Claudia Severa and Fabia Aconia Paulina) qualifies Patricia Wilson-Kastner's statement that Sulpicia's poetry is the only non-Christian writing to survive after the Augustan Age.[9] At the same time, works such as Perpetua's diary of martyrdom, Proba's adaptation of Virgil's Latin to Christian themes, and Egeria's epistolary account of her pilgrimage to the Holy Land attest to the importance of women's voices as the early church began to transform what had been the Roman Empire into early European Christian culture.

The chronological range of volume 2, *Medieval Women Writing Latin*, extends from the sixth-century queen, nun, abbess, and saint Radegund to the fourteenth-century mother of eight, widow, nun, founder of a religious order, prophetess, and reformer Birgitta Birgersdotter, also known as Saint Bride of

Sweden. Although volumes 1 and 2 of *Women Writing Latin* demonstrate that the tradition of female literacy did not begin in religious communities of women, as Margaret L. King has asserted, nevertheless, "the root of the modern female intellectual experience"[10] probably is to be found in those communities. During the early Middle Ages, in addition to the better-known Irish and Northumbrian monastic centers were the Merovingian, Carolingian, and Ottonian convent cultures, where girls and women heard Latin read, sung, prayed, and taught not only every day, but conceivably every hour. Hearing words, phrases, and sentences over time amounted to training in the Latin language. Even so, when these women would engage in the composing process, they would encounter problems similar to those M. T. Clanchy describes in his biography of Abelard:

> For a medieval writer the difficulties of getting the text on to parchment were rela-
> tively simple compared with the initial problem of converting one's thoughts into
> Latin. This required years of training. Because it was nobody's mother tongue and
> its rules of style and construction had been established more than a thousand years
> earlier, Latin tended to take over anyone who began to write it. To the rhetoric of the
> classical authors (Virgil, Cicero, Ovid, and so on) had been added the even more
> powerful models of the Latin Bible and the Latin liturgy, with which every monk
> and nun was in daily contact through chanting and hearing readings.[11]

Women writers such as Hrotsvit, Hildegard, and Heloise offer relatively familiar examples of women's success in meeting the challenges Clanchy describes. Authors such as the ninth-century schoolgirl discussed by Steven Stofferahn in *Medieval Women Writing Latin* provide new glimpses of the various ways women expressed themselves in Latin.

Also represented in volumes 2 and 3 are writings from a highly literate Spanish culture, which, according to Harvey J. Graff, had preserved much of Roman culture:

> In contrast to Gaul, there seem to be no regions in Spain in which writing was
> totally absent. Clerical and monastic schools contributed to the preservation of lay
> education; some monks and clerics placed themselves in private homes to tutor chil-
> dren who were not preparing for a religious career. A rich cultural life surrounded
> the Spanish Visigothic court, as kings and princes adhered more closely to classical
> traditions than did the Merovingians. Grammar and rhetoric instruction continued,
> although both kings and laymen were actively involved in religious culture, too.[12]

Linda McMillin's contribution of documents from the Benedictine convent of Sant Pere de les Puelles provides the earliest example included in this collection of literate Iberian culture; Edward George's essay on Luisa Sigea evinces

women's participation in the highly literate culture of Spain well into the early
modern period.

Although Italian women dominate *Early Modern Women Writing Latin*, as
seems appropriate given Italy's role in fostering humanist scholarship and writing, the northern European women's somewhat later writings perhaps speak even
more eloquently of women's active participation in the humanistic community
Erasmus named *Res Publica Litteraria*. These Renaissance women were not only
important contributors to the neo-Latin revival that characterizes the sixteenth
century, but also many of them were extraordinary polyglots who wrote letters to
one another in Greek and Hebrew as well as in Latin and a variety of vernacular
languages. For example, the Dutch woman Anna Maria van Schurman, whose
writings conclude volume 3, had learned fourteen languages by the middle of her
adult life, and she even wrote a grammar of Ethiopian. In her essay on van Schurman, Pieta van Beek points out that learned Renaissance women had a significant
network of their own to complement the male-dominated *Res Publica Litteraria*.
For example, van Schurman exchanged letters with the Irish-British Dorothea
Moore (in Latin and Hebrew), the British Bathsua Makin (in Greek), the French
Marie Jars du Gournay and Marie du Moulin (in French, Latin, and Hebrew), the
German Elizabeth of Bohemia (in Latin and French), and the Swedish queen
Christina and Danish Birgitte Thott (in Latin). These letters testify to the intellec-
tual exchange, support, and encouragement these women offered one another.

In an essay about linguistic and literary influences on medieval women writers, Katharina Wilson and Glenda McLeod discuss the difficulty of ascribing "traditions" to the variety of languages and literary models that women used. What
cannot be underestimated, argue Wilson and McLeod, is that some women chose
to write and chose Latin when any number of vernaculars were available:

> Scanning women's writing by what one might think the simplest principle possi-
> ble—the languages used—unveils the level of complexity facing any surveyor of
> medieval literature. Like men, women wrote in a wide assortment of languages; to
> understand the importance of this variety, however, one must recognize that linguis-
> tic choice for medieval writers, as for some modern writers in multilingual areas,
> carried philosophical and political implications.[13]

Indeed, studies of the effects of colonial and postcolonial politics and policies on
patterns of literacy and literature have led to an awareness that cultural minorities
respond to political and social hegemonies in a variety of ways, including assimi-
lation through mimicry, creative transcendence that simultaneously affirms the
mainstream culture and the minority culture, and writings that are subversive in
some way. However, now as in the past, the hegemonic policies generally exclude
and silence nonconformists.[14] Presumably, women writing in the ancient,
medieval, and early modern periods, though privileged in many ways that make

their lives fundamentally different from those of racial minorities and the poor in the United States, faced situations something like those that students of color encounter in composition and rhetoric classrooms in the United States, where, Victor Villanueva suggests, "traditional ways of teaching literacy have not only forced particular languages and dialects upon America's people of color, but have forced particular ways with language—rhetorical patterns—patterns that help to maintain American racial, ethnic, and cultural stratification, as well as gender and class."[15]

Modern studies of early Europe tend to fall into two broad approaches: those that concentrate on philological study of sources and textual transmission and those that explore the historical, social, and cultural dimensions of history and literary production, though increasingly critics recognize that close study of texts is fundamental to cultural critique. A common point of contact between the two is the *subtextual* status of the writing studied here, for its language falls into a category of textual history that Gilles Deleuze and Felix Guattari define as a literature written by a minority group in a major language.[16] What Deleuze and Guattari admire most about a minor literature is its political concerns, not the politics of government, religion, or, even, language, but, as in the Greek *polis*, communities of people. It is the communal that ultimately marks a literature as minor: "its cramped space forces each individual intrigue to connect immediately to politics. The individual concern thus becomes all the more necessary, indispensable, magnified, because a whole other story is vibrating with it."[17] Women who learned to write in Latin engaged a language established through history and by convention as a canonical language. In part because of their status as a writing minority, women writing in Latin question, sometimes consciously, sometimes not, the self-perpetuating structures and themes of major texts, such as long-held beliefs about the very physical and hardly intellectual nature of women. Furthermore, many of the barriers that excluded women from positions of power in the Roman and Christian empires nevertheless provided a way for them to influence the development of literary language and patronage, especially an elaborate network of women educating other women at home, in the convent, and through letters. While most of the women in these three volumes clearly honored the classical and patristic texts through which they achieved Latin literacy, nevertheless some of the writers represented here clearly helped undermine the exclusiveness and authority of Latinity through their work in translation and through their education of other women who did not have access to Latin literacy.

Scholarly study of women's writing, like the production of women's writing itself, has been a disparate, halting activity. Even among classicists, women writing Latin are usually considered accidental and anomalous. These volumes do not attempt to be exhaustive but to demonstrate the value in more sustained study. Some of the writers who first occurred to the editors, such as Dhuoda, the Helfta nuns, St. Clare, Maddalena Scrovegni, Queen Elizabeth, and Sor Juana Inéz de la

Cruz, are not included, nor are some of the most familiar works of well-known authors, such as Heloise's so-called personal letters to Abelard or Hildegard's lyric poetry. A goal of *Women Writing Latin* is to contribute to our knowledge of women writers, thereby complementing Peter Dronke's *Women Writers of the Middle Ages*, Marcelle Thiébaux's *Writings of Medieval Women*, and Katharina Wilson's *Medieval Women Writers*.[18]

The approach *Women Writing Latin* takes, while chronological, is bilingual and contextual; each chapter includes a Latin text, an English translation, a brief introductory essay sketching the author's life and describing important cultural influences, especially familial, religious, and political, to the extent that they are known, together with a select bibliography. *Women Writing Latin* presents the Latin texts with English translations in order not to perpetuate the exclusivity of Latin literacy. The contributors represent numerous disciplines: classics, history, literature, religion, and women's studies. Likewise, the texts representing women's writing in Latin are rich and varied: graffiti; petitions; wills; letters to children, friends, and patrons; saints' lives; poetry; plays; visions; encyclopedia; scriptural commentary; scientific treatises; and philosophical dialogues.

Because *Women Writing Latin* exemplifies the range and variety of ways in which women engaged Latin, it opens the door to further inquiry and study not only of the texts themselves but also of the social-historical contexts that allowed them to be written and preserved. Perhaps even more important, through its engagement with undervalued texts from the history of Western culture, *Women Writing Latin* can contribute to the changing dimensions and goals of Latin studies, women's studies, cultural studies, literary studies, historical studies, rhetorical studies, and composition studies, adding to our understanding of the interplay of literacy and education in the shaping of cultures.

NOTES

1. Herbert Grundmann, "*Litteratus-illitteratus*: Der Wandel einer Bildungsnorm vom Altertum zum Mittelalter," *Archiv für Kulturgeschichte* 40 (1958): 1–15.

2. Brian Stock, *The Implications of Literacy: Written Language and Models of Interpretation in the Eleventh and Twelfth Centuries* (Princeton, N.J.: Princeton University Press, 1983), p. 6.

3. Stephen Greenblatt has pointed out that "Western literature over a very long period of time has been one of the great institutions for the enforcement of cultural boundaries through praise and blame." "Culture," in *Critical Terms for Literary Study*, 2d ed., ed. Frank Lentricchia and Thomas McLaughlin (Chicago: University of Chicago Press, 1995), p. 226.

4. In an overview of the meaning of the word *author*, Donald E. Pease notes the word's original associations with founding rules and conservative principles (relevant especially to the medieval disciplines and moral authorities) and the tension between these associations and the word's later use to denote "writers whose

claim to cultural authority did not depend on their adherence to cultural precedents but on a faculty of verbal inventiveness." "Author," in *Critical Terms for Literary Study*, ed. Lentricchia and McLaughlin, pp. 106–7.

5. Stock, p. 7.

6. Michael Richter, "The Reality of Latin Civilization in Medieval Europe," in *Studies in Medieval Language and Culture* (Dublin: Four Courts Press, 1995), p. 155.

7. K. P. Harrington, *Medieval Latin*, rev. ed. (Chicago: University of Chicago Press, 1997), p. 11.

8. Two recently published studies add significantly to our understanding of women's roles in the *Res Publica Litteraria*. In her "Women Latin Poets in Britain in the Seventeenth and Eighteenth Centuries," *The Seventeenth Century* 16 (2001): 1–36, Jane Stevenson writes: "There is a substantial amount of evidence that seventeenth- and eighteenth-century England was well stocked with educated, more or less Latinate gentlewomen, familiar with the contents and diction of Classical texts. Besides the daughters of gentlemen, it also contained a number of schoolmasters' daughters and women of the middling sort who had been taught Latin" (p. 7). Stevenson continues, "The unusually high level of Latin literacy among women poets may indeed suggest that there is a relationship between Latin and the confidence to write, but it also shows that a number of women possessed both" (p. 8). Before exploring this more positive picture of "more or less Latinate gentlewomen" in the neoclassical period, Stevenson points out, "The impression which Kempe, Bercher and others give of an Elizabethan England replete with women classicists actually comes down rather rapidly to a small number of highly visible women, almost all at the court" (p. 2). In *Latin; or, The Empire of the Sign: From the Sixteenth to the Twentieth Century*, trans. John Howe (London: Verso, 2001) Françoise Waquet cites many sixteenth-century authors who argued that Latin was "a path to perdition for women" (p. 250) because Latin literacy would give women access both to dangerous subject matter (notably biology and sex) and, on account of its usual means of instruction, to male tutors.

9. Patricia Wilson-Kastner, "Introduction," in *A Lost Tradition: Women Writers of the Early Church* (Washington, D.C.: University Press of America, 1981), p. viii.

10. Margaret L. King, *Women of the Renaissance* (Chicago: University of Chicago Press, 1991), p. 175.

11. M. T. Clanchy, *Abelard: A Medieval Life* (Oxford: Blackwell, 1998), p. 14.

12. Harvey J. Graff, *The Legacies of Literacy: Continuities and Contradictions in Western Culture and Society* (Bloomington: Indiana University Press, 1987), p. 41.

13. Katharina M. Wilson and Glenda McLeod, "Wounding Trumpets, Chords of Light, and Little Knives: Medieval Women Writers," in *Women in Medieval Western European Culture*, ed. Linda E. Mitchell (New York: Garland, 1999), pp. 331–32.

14. In "Maybe a Colony: And Still Another Critique of the Comp Community," Victor Villanueva writes about the ways "internal colonization," a term Latin American sociologists use to describe Amerindian regions, can result in a "cultural mimicry that the other [America's people of color] is forced to undergo before creative transcendence is allowed expression." *JAC: A Journal of Composition Theory* 17.2 (1997): 186–87.

15. Villanueva, p. 184.

16. Gilles Deleuze and Felix Guattari, *Kafka: Toward a Minor Literature*, trans. Dana
     Polan (Minneapolis: University of Minnesota Press, 1986), p. 16.
17. Deleuze and Guattari, p. 17.
18. Peter Dronke, *Women Writers of the Middle Ages: A Critical Study of Texts from
     Perpetua (†203) to Marguerite Porete (†1310)* (Cambridge: Cambridge Univer-
     sity Press, 1984); Marcelle Thiébaux, *The Writings of Medieval Women: An
     Anthology*, 2d ed. (New York: Garland Publishing, 1994); Katharina M. Wilson,
     ed., *Medieval Women Writers* (Athens: University of Georgia Press, 1984); Katha-
     rina M. Wilson, ed., *Women Writers of the Renaissance and Reformation* (Athens:
     University of Georgia Press, 1987).

I

Roman Antiquity

Women Writing in Rome and Cornelia, Mother of the Gracchi

Judith P. Hallett

From the first decades of the second century B.C.E. onward, Latin literary works represent women as creators of written texts. For example, at lines 20–75 of his *Pseudolus*, a comedy that can be dated by its production notice to 191 B.C.E., the playwright Plautus portrays a lovesick young man named Calidorus as smitten by the courtesan Phoenicium. He is especially distressed by a letter he has just received from her. In the excerpts from this letter that Calidorus and his ingenious slave—the title character Pseudolus—read aloud, she proclaims her passion for Calidorus and complains that she has been sold to another man. To be sure, Pseudolus makes sarcastic remarks about Phoenicium's handwriting, style, and sentiments. Still, she is characterized as employing a sophisticated literary vocabulary and several poetic figures of speech. Such details, albeit in the portrait of a fictional character, imply that Plautus (and presumably his audience) thought women, even those of nonelite backgrounds, capable of writing as men do.

Many later Roman authors of the classical era, which extends from the time in which Plautus wrote to the early second century C.E., refer to the writings of several historical women from the first centuries B.C.E. and C.E. Unfortunately, most of these Latin texts by women have not survived to modern times. One such woman, Clodia, enjoyed close ties with some of the most politically powerful men in mid–first century B.C.E. Rome. Her controversial brother, Publius Clodius Pulcher, served as tribune of the people in 58 B.C.E. and was a candidate for higher office when he was assassinated by his foes six years later. Her more conservative husband, Quintus Caecilius Metellus Celer, served as consul in 60 B.C.E. after a military career that included commanding the province of Cisalpine Gaul in northern Italy.[1]

Scholars generally identify this Clodia as the lover of the poet Catullus (ca. 84–54 B.C.E.), a woman immortalized in his verses under the metrically equivalent name of "Lesbia." Catullus's choice of this particular pseudonym for his inamorata pays homage to the sixth-century B.C.E. Greek female poet Sappho of Lesbos. His high regard for Sappho took other forms as well: he translated some of her lyrics into Latin and adopted her distinctive meter in two of his poems. In calling Clodia "Lesbia," Catullus may also have implied that Clodia, like Sappho, not only wrote but also valued elegantly crafted poetry.[2]

Significantly, at *Pro caelio* 27.64, a lawcourt speech of 56 B.C.E. defending another young man with whom Clodia was romantically involved, the orator and statesman Cicero dismissively refers to Clodia by the Greek noun *poetria*, "female poet." Furthermore, several of Catullus's poems that represent "Lesbia" as speaking may be interpreted as alluding to her performances of poetry, some of it poetry that she wrote herself. Among these Catullan poems are two, 70 and 72, written in the elegiac meter. They portray her as voicing a memorable literary conceit: that she would prefer Catullus's affections even to those of the god Jupiter. In poem 51—which loosely translates lyrics by Sappho, retaining their original Sapphic meter—Catullus first speaks in his own person of "Lesbia" as "sweetly laughing"; later, he appears to assign "Lesbia" an entire, final, stanza in which she laughs at his idleness and self-preoccupation.

Clodia's own daughter, Caecilia Metella, would seem to have followed her mother's example. The poet Ovid represents her, at *Tristia* 2.437–38, as having written poetry, and at the same time as having been celebrated, pseudonymously, as "Perilla." In the early years of the first century C.E., Ovid also writes from exile on the Black Sea to another young female poet he calls Perilla, perhaps his own stepdaughter, at *Tristia* 3.7. Most noteworthy of these lost women writers is the younger Agrippina (15–59 C.E.), the sister of the emperor Gaius Caligula, wife of the emperor Claudius, and mother of the emperor Nero. Her memoirs are cited as an important historical source in the late first century C.E. by the elder Pliny at *Natural History* 7.46 and in the early second century C.E. by the historian Tacitus at *Annales* 4.53.3.

Nevertheless, a few writings in Latin by Roman women of the classical period have been preserved for posterity. The earliest dates from the second half of the second century B.C.E.: two fragments of a letter from a noblewoman named Cornelia to her son Gaius Sempronius Gracchus. This Cornelia was the daughter of Publius Cornelius Scipio Africanus, a military leader renowned for ending Rome's second Punic War against the North African city of Carthage when he defeated Hannibal at Zama in 202 B.C.E. But she is more often remembered as the mother of two politically radical sons, Gaius Sempronius Gracchus and his elder brother, Tiberius. Both of these men died at the hands of their enemies while serving as tribunes of the people, Tiberius in 133 B.C.E. and Gaius in 121.[3]

The letter urges Gaius not to seek the office of tribune, but to think of her sorrowful plight instead. It was likely to have been written ca. 124 B.C.E. Born ca. 195–190 B.C.E., Cornelia would have been in her late sixties or early seventies at the time she wrote it. According to Plutarch's biography of Gaius Gracchus, Cornelia for many years after Gaius died lived in her villa near the Bay of Naples, invariably "recalling the accomplishments and sufferings of her dead sons for her guests without any display of emotion."

According to Plutarch's *Life of Tiberius Gracchus*, Cornelia's husband Tiberius Sempronius Gracchus, consul in 177 B.C.E., had left her a widow in 153 B.C.E., shortly after she gave birth to the last of their twelve children. Plutarch also relates that after Cornelia was widowed, she rejected a marriage proposal from a Ptolemaic ruler of Egypt and devoted herself totally to rearing the three of her offspring who survived their childhood—Tiberius, Gaius, and a daughter, Sempronia.[4] Other Roman authors of later periods stress Cornelia's dedication to the upbringing of her children as well. In the *Dialogue on Oratory*, Tacitus has one of his characters maintain that the extensive role played by elite Roman mothers in their sons' education during the bygone republican era resulted in a superior breed of Roman political leader. Cornelia, mother of the Gracchi, is the first such woman Tacitus cites by way of illustration.

So, too, the first-century C.E. writer Valerius Maximus recalls an anecdote about Cornelia's emotional investment in her sons at *Memorable Deeds and Sayings* 4.4—namely, that when a woman staying at Cornelia's bayside villa insisted on displaying her own extremely beautiful jewelry, Cornelia detained her in conversation until Tiberius and Gaius returned from school, and then announced, "These are *my* jewels." Later in the same century the elder Pliny describes a celebrated statue of Cornelia at 34.31 of his *Natural History*. The inscription at its base—"Cornelia, daughter of Africanus, [mother] of the Gracchi"—survives to this day.[5] Pliny reports that in his own time the statue stood in the portico of Octavia, sister of the emperor Augustus, an edifice erected around 20 B.C.E. But Pliny also notes that the statue had originally been placed in the portico of Metellus, a structure built during Cornelia's own lifetime. Evidently Romans of later generations hailed Cornelia as a paragon of matronal and maternal excellence because her own contemporaries had inspired them to do so.

These two fragments of Cornelia's letter survive only in the manuscripts of the biographer and historian Cornelius Nepos. He is thought to have died in approximately 24 B.C.E., a full century after Cornelia would have written these words to her younger son. No other extant classical Roman source quotes from these fragments directly. Some scholars have found this fact disconcerting. Some also consider the unusual style of the letter, the self-absorption of its first-person speaker, the self-assertive stance adopted, the angry language employed, and the raw emotions expressed to be at strong variance with their own, modern notions of an admirable mother. As a result, there are those who would question Cornelia's authorship of this letter and even the female gender of the author.[6]

Yet both Cicero, in an essay of the mid–first century B.C.E., and the late first century C.E. oratorical authority Quintilian, at *Institutes* 1.1.6, provide evidence that letters of this sort were in public circulation after Cornelia's death, familiar to them and no doubt to others as well. At *Brutus* 211, Cicero portrays his friend Atticus as arguing for the powerful impact of fathers, teachers, and mothers on children's speech. To establish the beneficial influence of maternal speaking habits, he notes that he has read the letters of Cornelia and states that their style proves the Gracchi "to have been nurtured not so much in her bosom as in her speech." Quintilian invokes Cornelia for the same purpose, observing that "we have heard that their mother, Cornelia, had contributed greatly to the eloquence of the Gracchi, a woman whose extremely learned speech also has been handed down to future generations."

Echoes of Cornelia's letter also resonate in similarly indignant speeches assigned to mature women by Roman authors writing in the twenties and teens B.C.E. These echoes further suggest that Cornelia's letter is authentic, or at least that the letter was thought to be by Cornelia at around the time Nepos was writing. The earliest of these Latin texts that call Cornelia's letter to mind is the work of the historian Livy: in a speech delivered by the fictional Veturia—aged mother of the early republican leader Coriolanus—to dissuade her traitorous son from invading Rome in 488 B.C.E. It appears at chapter 40 of Livy's second book, which appears to have been completed around the time of Nepos's death.[7]

The other speeches are slightly later in date. Those of three other fictional figures—the Carthaginian queen Dido, the Latin queen Amata, and the mother of Euryalus—in books 4, 7, 9, and 12 of Vergil's epic *Aeneid* were written shortly before 19 B.C.E. The fictional speech that the love poet Propertius in his final elegy places in the mouth of a historical personage, Augustus's stepdaughter Cornelia, is generally dated to 16 B.C.E., the year of this woman's death.[8]

All of these texts resemble, and hence appear to echo, Cornelia's letter by utilizing—much as Cornelia does with Gaius—a series of rhetorical questions, two or more of them "anaphoric," that is, beginning with the same word. Several of these texts, like Cornelia's letter, emphasize the speaker's old age, characterizing it as wretched and sorrowful, and refer to old age with the word *senecta* (rather than with the more ordinary term *senectus*).[9] Several raise the prospect of the speaker's imminent death (indeed, Propertius's Cornelia is portrayed as already dead, and as speaking to her family from the grave). The speech that Livy gives to Veturia in particular recalls Cornelia's by using the conjunctions *nec . . . nec* to negate a pair of comparative adjectives that govern personal pronouns in the dative case. Cornelia proclaims *id neque maius neque pulchrius cuiquam atque mihi esse videtur*, "to no one does this seem either greater or more beautiful than it does to me" (with the alternative spelling *neque . . . neque*);

Livy's Veturia observes *nihil iam pati nec tibi turpius nec mihi miserius possum*, "I am able to endure nothing more shameful for you nor more miserable for myself."

Still, one peculiar feature of Cornelia's letter that it does not share with these later speeches assigned to women in Augustan literary works is its "genderless" style. There is no grammatical detail, such as an adjectival or pronomial form, in the first excerpt of Cornelia's letter that specifically identifies the author as a woman. Only two details in the second excerpt—the repeated use of the feminine adjectival form *mortua*, "dead"—make Cornelia's sex clear. Indeed, at one point Cornelia uses the grammatically masculine phrase *deum parentem*, "parent-god, parent who has become a god" (rather than the feminine *deam*, "parent-goddess"), when speaking of herself.

Cornelia also behaves in what might be regarded as a "male-identified" or "transgendered" Roman fashion, too.[10] She one-ups Gaius in the "patriotism department" by deprecating his defense of vengeance against enemies. She appropriates the role of father-protector by portraying the future without her parental guidance as a time of unrelieved misery for her son. The paucity of feminine grammatical forms, obviously, lends support to those who deny the authenticity of this letter, viewing it as a male forgery. So do Cornelia's efforts to adopt masculine conduct in competing with, disparaging, and asserting her irreplaceability for her son. So, for that matter, do her outspoken criticisms of an adult male child, whose formal rights and authority far surpass her own in a patriarchal society such as that of republican Rome.

But among the similarities between Cornelia's letter and several of these speeches by women in later literary texts of the early Augustan period is what would appear to be a distinctively "female" approach to family matters of political import. Cornelia evinces, and several of the women whose words call hers to mind are portrayed as evincing, a similar style of "motivational" political speech in their communications with their sons. In determining what is best for the state as well as for their sons, they accord priority to family ties and family members—feelings over abstract political rights and principles. They define themselves through their connections with rather than their separation from others and ground their actions in an ethic based on relationships and responsibilities rather than one based on abstract rights.

In this way Cornelia and these female figures in Augustan literary texts call to mind observations about women's morally freighted decision making by the psychologist Carol Gilligan—albeit observations about how most women, in contrast to most men, tend to make moral judgments and decisions today.[11] The family-oriented, emotionally grounded nexus of political values to which Cornelia and these "maternal" females in Augustan literary texts subscribe certainly stands in sharp contrast to the value system of various Roman men who lived several centuries prior to Cornelia, men remembered for their conduct in their role as fathers. These are men renowned for upholding abstractly defined principles of civic conduct at the expense of family solidarity and for engaging in punitive behavior against family members who do not adhere to these same principles.

The individual family headed by a *paterfamilias*, father in his role as family head, comprised the basic structural unit of the ancient Roman state, *res publica* (referred to by the Romans themselves as their "fatherland," *patria*). Correspondingly, the Romans of the classical era viewed the right of *patria potestas*—the supreme power invested in a Roman father over offspring and other dependents—as the foundational basis for Rome's system of law and order. Several legends about the early republican period featured *patres* who, in their capacity as high officeholders, publicly exercised their *patria potestas* by exiling or even executing traitorous or merely insubordinate sons for offenses against the state. Whatever their historical accuracy, these legends furnished Romans of later times with an acceptable rationale for unfeeling paternal severity.[12]

One is the story of Rome's first consul, Lucius Junius Brutus, who—as Livy relates at 2.3–5 of his history—ordered his sons slain when they conspired to overthrow the republican form of government that their father had established in 509 B.C.E. Another such tale is that of Titus Manlius Torquatus, consul in 340 B.C.E. At 8.7.15, Livy scripts for Torquatus a stern speech accounting for his decision to put his own adult son to death for military insubordination and thereby "set a painful but healthy example for the youth of the future." Livy portrays Torquatus as caught in a difficult situation, "having to forget either the Roman state or myself." Although Livy's Torquatus acknowledges that he is emotionally stirred by inborn affection for children, as well as by his son's display of manly excellence, he insists on having his son bound to the stake and hacked to death with an axe. He attributes greater importance to upholding, rigidly and inflexibly and by right, a single, abstractly defined principle of civic conduct—the necessity of adhering to military discipline—than to upholding the affective pull of family ties on him personally.

As a Roman woman, Cornelia—and, for that matter, the legendary Veturia—could not punish her son in the same way that Torquatus did his. She held no *patria potestas* and was ineligible to hold high political office. Nor was it in her interest for her son to leave Rome or even distance himself from their family. Women, even elite and privileged women like Cornelia, depended on their male kin for their social identity and personal validation far more than did a man like Torquatus. Thus, in instances where she and her son disagreed, she—like Veturia—was limited to motivational as opposed to punitive speech.

Admittedly, Cornelia's efforts in this letter at motivating Gaius to see things from her own point of view take the form of browbeating: angry, confrontational, demanding, egotistical, intimidating, and explicitly shame- (and implicitly guilt-) inducing rhetoric. She even compares the behavior of her son to that of a personal political enemy, *inimicus*. "Other than those who murdered Tiberius Gracchus," she says, "no *inimicus* has made my life as difficult as you have." Cornelia then proceeds to fault Gaius for failing to shoulder the responsibilities of his dead siblings, to minimize her anxieties in old age, and to make an adequate attempt at pleasing and obeying her. By associating her son's opposition to her own wishes with "destroying our country," she returns to the earlier theme of limiting revenge on personal enemies to activities that do not harm one's nation, suggesting that Gaius is not merely comparable to her enemies but also no better than his own.

So, too, Livy's Veturia engages in browbeating, referring to her son Coriolanus as an enemy (albeit *hostis*, an enemy of the state rather than a personal political foe, since he has in fact joined forces with the hostile Volscians). Like Cornelia, she confronts her son with a series of rhetorical questions to arouse his shame and guilt. Her guilt-inducing tactics additionally include blaming Rome's woes on herself because she gave birth to Coriolanus, and she comes across as angrier and more confrontational than Cornelia. But Coriolanus's more outrageous political conduct warrants as much—and Veturia, like Cornelia, proves successful in getting her son to do what she wants.

The first excerpt of Cornelia's letter implies that she has been asked by her son to endorse an abstractly defined mode of civic conduct: the principle of taking vengeance on personal enemies, *inimici*, in the political arena. And indeed Cornelia seems to voice agreement with Gaius in proclaiming this principle *pulchrum*, a beautiful thing. But at the same time she refuses to adhere to this principle rigidly and inflexibly. Instead, Cornelia asserts that such vengeance should not be pursued if it harms one's country. What is more, Cornelia does not view keeping the Roman state strong and harm-free as inimical to and incompatible with family loyalties or in conflict with the affective pull of family ties. Rather, a family-oriented, emotionally grounded ethos underlies her definition of appropriate moral, civic, and patriotic conduct.

For example, in voicing the expectation that Gaius would take the place of his dead siblings in the context of taking Gaius to task for mistreating her, Cornelia represents her son as derelict in his family duties and in turn seeks to exploit her son's own family feelings. She accuses their entire family of acting insanely, not just Gaius. Although she begs Gaius to postpone his campaign for tribune until she is dead and can no longer feel, she reminds him that he will eventually be praying to her as the god of his parent, and should feel shame at having abandoned ancestral deities when they were still alive.

Livy also portrays Veturia as linking what is politically consequential with what is best for a family and its feelings. Thus she emphasizes the emotional pain her son's conduct has caused her personally and underscores her son's emotional ties and obligations to both herself and his other family members. Strikingly, Livy has Veturia call attention to Coriolanus's wife and sons, whereas Cornelia says nothing about Gaius's wife and offspring.[13] Veturia goes further than Cornelia in another regard. In addition to citing her own role as Coriolanus's biological mother, she characterizes Rome itself as having given birth to and nurtured him (*te genuit atque aluit*). In so doing, Livy depicts Veturia as equating her son's native land with herself, recasting his *patria* as his "*matria*."

A similar emphasis on obligations to and emotions roused by family members informs various speeches by Vergil and Propertius that echo Cornelia's letter. At *Aeneid* 7.359–72, Vergil portrays the Latin queen Amata as angrily addressing her husband Latinus in protest of his political decision to betroth their daughter Lavinia to the Trojan exile Aeneas rather than to her nephew Turnus. She demands that family ties and family feeling be given pride of place in forging political alliances. At 12.56–63 Vergil has Amata address Turnus himself. Employing language that Vergil also has the mother of the Trojan warrior Euryalus use when addressing her fallen son at 9.473 ff., she characterizes him as "a source of respite for my unfortunate old age" (*senectae / tu requies miserae*). She then urges him not to engage in single combat with Aeneas for Lavinia's hand. Significantly, at 7.357, Vergil describes Amata's indignant expression of family-first sentiments as speaking *solito matrum de more*, "in the manner customary for mothers." He thus implies that her fierce display of emotion, insistence on sensitivity to family members' feelings, and privileging of blood family ties over other political goals are typical features of maternal motivational speaking.

At 4.11.87–94, Propertius has his newly dead Cornelia issue two sets of orders to her two young sons (both of whom grew up to become consuls, one in 1 C.E. and the other in 6).[14] Cornelia's commands to them merely concern the way in which she would like them to treat their father's next wife or—if their father does not remarry—their father himself. And it merits notice that she defines her sons' major obligations to their father as emotional in nature. At 65–68 this Cornelia may mention her husband's and her brother's high public offices and demand that her daughter imitate her own monogamous and moral lifestyle. Nevertheless, she wants her male children to lift their father's spirits in her absence, not follow his political example.

Consequently, these Roman literary portrayals of motivational speeches by mature, maternal women—speeches expressing family-oriented, emotionally grounded political values that resemble Cornelia's letter in striking ways—do not merely argue for the authenticity of Cornelia's letter, or at least its perceived authenticity during the Augustan era. They also suggest that this kind of motivational speaking and these political values were closely associated with Roman women. And this is because such speaking and such values were initially associated with a much scrutinized and admired woman like Cornelia.

The word *initially* warrants emphasis. Cornelia's letter to Gaius, which articulates Roman political values that include a concern for families and their emotional needs, is a radical document. Its author's priorities differ greatly from those inculcated by Roman patriarchal tradition, which pitted political against familial and emotional concerns. We should also note that these family-first political priorities are not limited in their later influence to speeches assigned by Augustan authors to female characters. The Roman literary figures and historical personages who gave voice to these priorities in the generations after Cornelia include men as well. At 6.817 ff. of the *Aeneid*, for example, Vergil portrays Anchises, the father of Aeneas, as deploring the behavior of several political leaders who endured and caused suffering as a result of paying insufficient heed to family feeling. Among these men are the legendary son-slayers Brutus and Torquatus. Anchises also hails the men kindred to Cornelia—Gracchi who were her husband and sons, Scipiones who were her father and son-in-law—but merely as illustrious men destined to lead the Roman state. While Cornelia's letter may not be a canonical Latin literary text, or even a well-known one, the radical views it voices seem to have exerted a significant impact on the most highly esteemed work of classical Roman literature.

NOTES

1. T. P. Wiseman, *Catullus and His World: A Reappraisal* (Cambridge: Cambridge University Press, 1985), pp. 35–53.
2. Wiseman, pp. 115 ff., 135, 138, and 152–55.
3. *Cornelius Nepos: A Selection, Including the Lives of Cato and Atticus*, trans. with introductions and commentary by Nicholas Horsfall (Oxford: Clarendon Press, 1989), pp. 125–26.
4. See also Horsfall, p. 125.
5. Horsfall, p. 42.
6. Horsfall, pp. 41–42, 104, 125–26.
7. R. M. Ogilvie, *A Commentary on Livy, Books 1–5* (Oxford: Clarendon Press, 1965), p. 2.
8. Horsfall, *A Companion to the Study of Virgil* (Leiden: E. J. Brill, 1995), pp. 20 ff.; *Propertius, Elegies Book IV*, ed. W. A. Camps (Cambridge: Cambridge University Press, 1965), p. 153.
9. P. G. W. Glare, ed., *Oxford Latin Dictionary* (Oxford: Oxford University Press, 1982).
10. For the concept of "transgendering," see Barbara McManus, *Classics and Feminism: Gendering the Classics* (New York: Twayne Press, 1997), pp. 91–118.
11. Carol Gilligan, *In a Different Voice: Psychological Theory and Women's Development* (Cambridge, Mass.: Harvard University Press, 1982), pp. 24–63.
12. See s.v. *"patria potestas"* by Barry Nicholas and Susan Treggiari in the *Oxford Classical Dictionary*, 3d ed., ed. Simon Hornblower and Antony Spawforth (Oxford: Oxford University Press, 1996), pp. 1122–23.
13. For Gaius's wife and son, see Plutarch, *Gaius Gracchus* 15, 17.5.
14. Judith P. Hallett, "Queens, *Princeps*, and Women of the Augustan Elite: Propertius' Cornelia-Elegy and the *Res Gestae Divi Augusti*," in *The Age of Augustus*, ed. Rolf Winkes (Providence, R.I.: Acta Archaeologica, 1986).

TWO EPISTOLARY FRAGMENTS ATTRIBUTED TO CORNELIA, MOTHER OF THE GRACCHI

Verba ex epistula Corneliae Gracchorum matris ex libro Corneli Nepotis de Latinis Historicis excerpta.

1. Dices pulchrum esse inimicos ulcisci. Id neque maius neque pulchrius cuiquam atque mihi esse videtur, sed si liceat re publica salva ea persequi. Sed quatenus id fieri non potest, multo tempore multisque partibus inimici nostri non peribunt, atque uti nunc sunt erunt potius quam res publica profligetur atque pereat.

Eadem alio loco.

2. Verbis conceptis deierare ausim, praeterquam qui Tiberium Gracchum necarunt, neminem inimicum tantum molestiae tantumque laboris, quantum te ob has res, mihi tradidisse; quem oportebat omnium eorum quos antehac habui liberos partis tolerare atque curare ut quam minimum sollicitudinis in senecta haberem, utique quaecumque ageres, ea velles maxime mihi placere atque uti nefas haberes rerum maiorum adversum meam sententiam quicquam facere, praesertim mihi cui parva pars vitae superest. Ne id quidem tam breve spatium potest opitulari, quin et mihi adversere et rem publicam profliges? Denique quae pausa erit? ecquando desinet familia nostra insanire? ecquando modus ei rei haberi poterit? ecquando desinemus et habentes et praebentes molestiis insistere? ecquando perpudescet miscenda atque perturbanda re publica? Sed si omnino id fieri non potest, ubi ego mortua ero, petito tribunatum; per me facito quod lubebit, cum ego non sentiam. Ubi mortua ero, parentabis mihi et invocabis deum parentem. In eo tempore non pudet te eorum deum preces expetere, quos vivos atque praesentes relictos atque desertos habueris? Ne ille sirit Iuppiter te ea perseverare, nec tibi tantam dementiam venire in animum. Et si perseveras, vereor ne in omnem vitam tantum laboris culpa tua recipias uti in nullo tempore tute tibi placere possis.

TRANSLATION BY JUDITH P. HALLETT

These words are excerpted from a letter of Cornelia, mother of the Gracchi, from the book of Cornelius Nepos on Latin Historians.

1. "You will say that it is a beautiful thing to take vengeance on enemies. To no one does this seem either greater or more beautiful than it does to me, but only if it is possible to pursue these aims without harming our country. But seeing as that cannot be done, our enemies will not perish for a long time and for

many reasons, and they will be as they are now rather than have our country be destroyed and perish."

The same letter in a different passage.

2. "I would dare to take an oath swearing solemnly that, except for those who have murdered Tiberius Gracchus, no enemy has foisted so much difficulty and so much distress upon me as you have because of all these matters: you who should have shouldered the responsibilities of all of those children whom I had in the past. You should have shown concern that I might have the least anxiety possible in my old age; that, whatever you did, you would wish to please me most greatly; and that you would consider it sacrilege to do anything of rather serious significance contrary to my feelings, especially as I am someone with only a short portion of my life left. Cannot even that time span, as brief as it is, be of help in keeping you from opposing me and destroying our country? What end will there finally be? When will our family stop behaving insanely? When will we cease insisting on troubles, both suffering and causing them? When will we begin to feel shame about disrupting and disturbing our country? But if this simply cannot take place, seek the office of tribune when I am dead; as far as I am concerned, do what will please you when I shall not perceive what you are doing. When I have died, you will sacrifice to me as a parent and call upon the god of your parent. Does it not shame you to seek prayers of those gods, whom, when they were alive and on hand, you considered abandoned and deserted, at that time? May Jupiter not for a single instant allow you to continue in these actions nor permit such madness to come into your mind. And if you persist, I fear that, by your own fault, you may incur such trouble for your entire life that at no time would you be able to make yourself happy."

BIBLIOGRAPHY

Primary Sources
Marshall, P. G., ed. *C. Nepotis vitae cum fragmentis*. Leipzig: Teubner, 1977.

Secondary Works
Camps, W. A., ed. *Propertius, Elegies Book IV*. Cambridge: Cambridge University Press, 1965.

Gilligan, Carol. *In a Different Voice: Psychological Theory and Women's Development*. Cambridge, Mass.: Harvard University Press, 1982.

Glare, P. G. W., ed. *The Oxford Latin Dictionary*. Oxford: Oxford University Press, 1982.

Hallett, Judith P. "Queens, *Princeps* and Women of the Augustan Elite: Propertius' Cornelia-Elegy and the *Res Gestae Divi Augusti*." In *The Age of Augustus: An Interdis-

ciplinary Conference, edited by Rolf Winkes. Providence and Louvain-La-Neuve: Acta Archaeologica, 1986.

Horsfall, Nicholas. *A Companion to the Study of Virgil*. Leiden: Brill Academic Publishers, 1995.

———. *Cornelius Nepos: A Selection Including the Lives of Cato and Atticus*. Translated with introductions and commentary by Nicholas Horsfall. Oxford: Clarendon Press, 1989.

McManus, Barbara F. *Classics and Feminism: Gendering the Classics*. New York: Twayne Press, 1997.

Nicholas, Barry, and Susan M. Treggiari. *"Patria potestas."* In *The Oxford Classical Dictionary*, edited by Simon Hornblower and Anthony Spawforth. Oxford: Oxford University Press, 1996.

Ogilvie, R. M. *A Commentary on Livy, Books 1–5*. Oxford: Oxford University Press, 1965.

Wiseman, T. P. *Catullus and His World: A Reappraisal*. Cambridge: Cambridge University Press, 1985.

An Introduction to Epigraphic Poetry

Jane Stevenson

Epigraphic poetry—verses carved on stone or written on other hard surfaces, mostly funeral inscriptions—is an often-neglected source for women's writing. Very large numbers of epigraphic poems survive from antiquity and the early Middle Ages, quite a few of which are attributed to women. They cover a wide range, from carved inscriptions on formal stone monuments for the dead (the great majority, and understandably so, since so many monuments have survived) to inscriptions written on walls, which survive only in a few highly unusual circumstances, and incised writing on small objects such as curse-tablets or votive offerings (though the latter are usually prose). It is widely assumed that the fact that fewer women were literate means that they *never* wrote inscriptions. This assumption needs examination, and this essay is a preliminary attempt to open the question up for debate. I will present a selection of poems written in a female voice, ascribed to women, for which a good case can be made. If my basic assumption that women could, and did, write verse on subjects of deep concern to them is accepted, then these poems, and others for which a similar case can be made, are very valuable. They introduce us to a wider social range of Roman womanhood than do the handful of aristocrats who have left poetry in manuscript, and they offer some insight into women's interests and values.

There is no way of being certain that these texts are by the women whose voices seem to speak in them. Roman literary culture included the possibility of writing in a female persona: Ovid's *Heroides* is the longest and most ambitious work in this mode, but Ovid is not unique in this respect. The poems of mourning included here are interestingly different from run-of-the-mill Roman elegies on the dead and show a number of similarities to each other: the concerns that emerge strongly include the speaker's emotional tie with the decedent and, quite often, the decedent's social status. Whether this means we are looking at a voice *for* women, or the voices *of* women, is debatable. Other literary sources provide evidence for the existence of women poets: the circles of Tibullus, Catullus, and Martial all included women. Martial, in fact, knew at least three female poets, Sulpicia (wife of Calenus), Theophila, and Pantaenis, as well as Polla Argentaria, wife of Lucan, who may also have been a writer. We also have more general evidence that women were some-times literate. So, if a proportion, even a small proportion, of women could write, and writing poetry was not a shocking, unheard-of practice for upper-class girls, but socially respectable, is it still necessary to assume that the poetry we actually have could reasonably have been written by the women to whom it is attributed?

Even if this is unacceptable, if the reader of this essay feels that this approach is lacking in academic rigor because the case is intrinsically unprovable, these poems still have something to tell us about Roman women, whom we see, for the most part, through the eyes of male lovers (or haters), such as Propertius, Ovid, Tibullus, and Juvenal. If women did not write these inscriptions, they were, at the very least, content that posterity should see them as they are presented here, which is more than we can say for Cynthia, Corinna, Nemesis, and Juvenal's female tar-gets, and the inscriptions therefore reveal something of women's self-image.

The literary sources for classical Rome supply the names of a number of woman poets, notably Sulpicia and Julia Balbilla. The latter's work is in Greek and survives only in epigraphic form, helping to explain why the first is far better known than the second.[1] But the poems of Julia Balbilla, not included here since they are not in Latin, serve as a reminder that in the Roman world, much poetry was inscribed rather than written, even poetry by very high-status people.

Though it is beyond the reach of historians, we may be certain that women of Late Antiquity had a popular culture of their own, one that did not involve writ-ing. John Chrysostom, patriarch of Constantinople in the late fourth century, is witness to women's culture in the Greek-speaking Eastern Empire, and what he says is probably true also of the Roman world:

> . . . by nature we take such delight in song that even infants clinging at the breast, if they are crying and perturbed, can be put to sleep by singing. This is how the nurses who carry them in their arms, walking them up and down many times and singing them childish ditties, make their eyelids close. . . . Again, women who are weaving, or disentangling the threads on their spindles, often sing: sometimes each of them sings for herself, at other times they all harmonize a melody together. . . .[2]

The same must surely have been the case in the Latin-speaking West, though the only possible evidence we have for this is in epigraphic texts. While this essay as a whole will be mostly dedicated to epigraphic poetry, I want to consider briefly how epigraphic evidence creates access to Roman women's popular culture by looking at subliterary texts, curses, and graffiti.

The numerically least significant, though not the least thought-provoking, category of epigraphic evidence for women's writing in antiquity is the curse-tablet (*defixio*): curses written on sheet lead and devoted to an appropriate deity. Here, since aggrieved individuals seeking redress in this fashion were mostly plebes, women's authorship is impossible to establish: it is probable that *defixiones* were mostly written by the magician to whom the injured party went to set the curse, but this evidence is particularly interesting, despite the difficulties which it presents, because it allows us a glimpse of the concerns of lower-class women. There is one such tablet that merits inclusion here because of its sinister force and its strongly rhythmical structure (though it is not, formally speaking, verse) and because, whether or not the woman who speaks wrote it, it provides a tiny glimpse into the world of the submerged ninety-five percent of the Empire's inhabitants.[3] It is one of a number of surviving Latin curses made by women.[4]

Side A	*Side B*
Nomina data	Silonia
mandata	Surum Caenum
ligata	Secundum
ad inferos	ille te
ad illos	sponsus pro[vo]cat
per vim conruant.	eum amo.

This *defixio* is from Kreuznach (Roman Crucinacum in the Rhineland), inscribed on a sheet of lead (A and B represent recto and verso). A *defixio* is a document in which a god or demon is invited to persecute someone whom the curser wishes to suffer. Despite the apparent nominative case of Silonia, the most probable reading is that the curse has been set by a rival of Silonia's. Since the first half should set the spell on those whose names are given, we should probably read *Silonia[m]*. We may conjecturally translate: "The names which are given, mandated, and bound are cast down by force to the infernal gods. Silonia; Surus Caenus Secundus: he, [my?] spouse, invites you: I love him." It seems to be addressed to Silonia: Surus is perhaps the writer's errant husband, who has been sweet-talking Silonia, or possibly Surus is married to neither, but seeks Silonia in marriage to the chagrin of the speaker. Syntax disintegrates into a series of fragmentary ejaculations; only raw emotion survives.

Of the verse that survives as graffiti, the most significant both in quantity and quality comes from Pompeii. Buried by the eruption of Vesuvius in 79 C.E., the city's excavation began in the eighteenth and nineteenth centuries, and one of the surprises the excavation revealed about the classical world was that the walls were covered with graffiti, suggesting a high level of popular literacy that was common to both genders. A particularly lively and attractive poem in iambic senarius, which may be by a woman, was found on the via Veneria:[5]

> Amoris ignes si sentires, mulio,
> Magis properares, ut videres Venerem.
> Diligo iuvenem venustum; rogo punge iamus
> Bibisti, iamus, prende lora et excute,
> Pompeios defer, ubi dulcis est amor,
> Meus est . . .

> If you have ever felt the fire of love,
> mule-driver, hurry up, so that you
> may see Love. I am in love with a
> lovely boy; I pray you, lay it on,
> let's go—you've been drinking!
> Let's go—take the reins and shake
> them. Bring the Pompeians to where
> sweet love is. [He] is mine . . .

This fragmentary poem has some of the freshness and charm of a popular song—I find myself thinking of "Long distance operator, get me Memphis, Tennessee"—the uncaring, workaday world forcibly co-opted by the joyful solipsism of love. The problem with it is, of course, that a Roman *man* in love with a *iuvenis venustus* would be no more ashamed to inscribe his passion on the via Veneria for all to see than a woman. I cannot, therefore, claim it as certainly a woman's work.

I now want to turn to some little-known epigraphic poetry that allows a strong case to be made for female authorship. The first I want to discuss is the Gentianus poem (no. 1). It forms an obvious link with the poetry of Julia Balbilla: like her work, it was composed to be carved on one of the great monuments of Egypt, and, as we will see, its author was of equal social status. As the poem itself proclaims, the grieving sister of Decimus Gentianus wrote a poem in his memory and had it carved on the pyramid at Memphis in Egypt after 116 C.E.[6] Its author seems to have been familiar with Horace: line 3 evokes *Odes* 3.2.50, "i secundo / Omine et nostri memorem sepulcro / Scalpe querellam." The original carving has presumably succumbed to the ravages of time, but, fortunately, it was copied twice in the late Middle Ages, once by a Lüneburg nobleman, Otto von Neuhaus (also known as Wilhelm of Boldensele), who in 1336 undertook a pilgrimage to the Holy Land (this is the version printed by Mommsen in *Corpus Inscriptionum Latinarum*) and a second time by Felix Fabri, a preacher and monk of Ulm, who twice made the same pilgrimage, in 1480 and 1483. His text is to be found in his

Evagatorium in Terrae Sanctae, Arabiae et Aegypti Peregrinationem.[7] The sister's own name was probably given in a colophon, but was not recorded by either Wilhem or Fabri: the family name Gentianus obviously formed part of it, so "Gentiana" can reasonably be used for convenience to refer to her.

There seems no a priori reason to doubt that the hexametric poem in the voice of Gentiana is by the sister of Decimus Gentianus. Many upper-class girls were capable of such a composition (the number of women poets referred to by her contemporary Martial is an indication of this), and hers was a very aristocratic family. We are probably in a position to identify its subject. One Terentius Gentianus, who had campaigned with Trajan in the Dacian wars, appears on a stone at Sarmizegetusa with a whole list of honors, including being *censitor* of Macedonia, consul, and pontiff.[8] Degrassi lists [D.] Terentius Gentianus as suffect consul in 116, thus giving us the earliest possible date for the poem.[9] Decimus Gentianus, whose honors included campaigning with Trajan, a consulship, the pontificate, and censorship, is most probably the same man: Decimus must then be his first name. Interestingly, Martial in *Epigrammata* 1.86, writing in the late '80s or '90s, associates a "Terentianus" with Egypt: just possibly Decimus Terentius Gentianus?—"but he is as far removed from me as Terentianus, who is now governor of Syene on the Nile." His Terentianus is a grandee, the sort of man Martial might have turned to for patronage, rather than an equal: this portrait would fit with our poem, one that might in turn suggest that Decimus Terentianus, in his younger days, had literary associations. Putting the two pieces together, we might suggest the possibility that Decimus Terentius Gentianus had a lengthy involvement with Egypt before his sister came to visit, only to find that he had died. The fact that Gentiana was visiting Egypt is a testimony to her extremely high status: an expedition that involved ladies was by definition complicated and costly.[10] Tacitus, a writer almost contemporary with Gentiana, shows that in his time, while it was more and more common, there was considerable hostility toward Roman officials traveling with their womenfolk.[11] While Romans increasingly accepted that a patrician serving abroad might want to have his wife or daughter with him, the argument for the considerable investment represented by having his sister visit was more tenuous.

This poem by Gentianus's sister is very much public verse. Obviously, it marks personal loss and speaks to the common experience of finding a longed-for adventure meaningless without the appropriate person by one's side. Yet it seems primarily concerned to inscribe Gentianus's status and relationship with Trajan and to be an assertion of family status, more than of private emotion within a family. As we shall see, expressions of status and family pride are frequent aspects of epigraphic poetry.

The known women poets whose social class we have evidence for are, like Gentiana, mostly of patrician rank: such is the case with Sulpicia I, Julia Balbilla, and Cornificia, whose poetry is praised by St. Jerome but is now lost. Opportunities for a literary education for women of lower social levels were a less certain matter. However, literacy was surprisingly widespread in the cities of the early empire (though far more common among men than women),[12] and we have no need to dismiss the possibility that some if not all of these women's inscriptions are what they appear to be.

A bereaved individual must surely have gone to a workshop, as many people still do today, to commission a stone from a monumental mason, constrained by considerations such as budget, fashion, propriety, personal taste, and availability. What we do not know is whether we may imagine such a person giving the workman a wax tablet or a piece of papyrus on which she had written the words she wished to have carved, or whether these were necessarily *always* commissioned from penny-a-line poets. Lattimore notes, "It seems, on the face of it, highly likely that the client who wanted a poem or phrase could dictate one which he had seen somewhere, or one which he had composed himself, or else fall back on the stonecutter for suggestions."[13]

Significantly, only a small number of epitaphs in which a woman speaks either for the deceased or for herself survive. The actual proportion of epitaphs in a woman's voice among the corpus that survives can be judged from the fact that, in the convenient collection of Bücheler, *Carmina Latina Epigraphica*, only about two percent of the poems are cast in the form of a woman commemorating her dead. Most epigraphic poems, for obvious reasons, are created for (if not by) people who can afford to commission tombstones, people, therefore, who are prosperous enough for literacy to be a possibility. So, although in his *Ancient Literacy* W. V. Harris is certainly correct in suggesting that a much smaller proportion of women were literate in antiquity than men, that does not necessarily cast doubt on the authorship of the inscriptions that we have, since they represent such a tiny proportion of the total surviving.

One example of a verse in a female voice, but almost certainly not written by a woman, is worth examining in this context. An inscription on a sarcophagus at Aquincum reads as follows in the Edward Courtney translation:

> Aelia Marcia, his mother to her dead son, and Aelia Apollonia his sister supervised the erection of this monument to the memory of Quintus Aelius Apollonius, soldier of new military cohort of Syrians; served for three years, lived for twenty.

> To a man is given life that is slippery, shaky, fleeting, fragile, good or bad, treacherous, hanging on a slender thread through a variety of chances with no clearly-marked finishing-post. Live to the full, mortal, while the Fates grant you time, whether the country embraces you or cities or a military camp or the sea. Love the flowers of Venus, pluck the benign gifts of Ceres and the generous gifts of Bacchus and the viscous gifts of Athena; cultivate a serene life, calm because of your clear conscience. Speedily a boy and a youth, speedily a man and then worn out by old age, you will be like this in the tomb, with no memory of the honours of men alive on earth.[14]

Since Quintus Aelius was no more than an infantry soldier, then we should not expect too much of the literacy level of his mother and sister who paid for this monument. But the real giveaway is that, as Courtney points out, there is a fragment of another sarcophagus, also at Aquincum, with the first halves of the lines of the same poem. But even without that, the formal impersonality of this verse is obvious: we learn nothing of this twenty-year-old except that his mother and his sister cared about him: the poem is to, and about, generic Man.

But an interesting aspect of the epitaphs in a first-person female voice as a group is that there are so many of which this is *not* true. One epitaph of special interest, for the level of concentrated emotion that it seems to express, is that of Salvidiena given below (no. 3), which explodes the distinction between public and private, breaking the decorum of public utterance with a scream of uncontrollable pain. Formulaic expressions of grief such as "may the earth lie light on you," "eternal sleep," and "farewell" are notably absent in this inscription. The sad specificity of years, months, days, and even hours bespeaks a culture in which parents had horoscopes made so that the hour of birth is precisely recorded:[15] here it adds to the raw, obsessive quality of the inscription. Many Latin epitaphs see a special pathos in the virgin snatched away by death;[16] but few lay such stress on the emotional state of the bereaved: consider the extraordinarily emphatic line *gementem plangentem plorantem*. The upbraiding of the dead by the living is a theme that has its parallels;[17] but the emphatic use of the word *mamma* (twice) is remarkable. *Mamma* is classical Latin for "mummy," or "mommy."[18] It appears in only a handful of inscriptions (*mater* is far more usual): all the other examples given in *Thesaurus Linguae Latinae* are inscribed by affectionate offspring—including the psychologically revealing *patri et mammae*: "to Father and Mamma."[19] This is the only surviving epitaph in which a speaker refers to *herself* as *mamma*.

Normally, the inscribed epitaph is by definition a public genre, but this particular example locates itself insistently in the private world of inconsolable personal grief, while placing the inscription itself in the public domain to be read by strangers. In general, many of the epitaphs that speak in a woman's voice are more immediate, more personal, and more directly focused on the relationship between the living and the dead than those that speak in the voices of men. The poem of Cornelia Galla, for example (no. 2), focuses vividly on her own sense of bereavement, on the way that the monument she has commissioned works not to perpetuate her husband's face and memory to succeeding generations (which is the reason usually given for monuments), but as a reminder to her alone of what he looked like. In order to make sense of this, we should remember the impressive, unidealized lifelikeness of surviving Roman funerary sculpture. We learn little of Frontonianus, but we learn a great deal about how his wife felt about him and how she proposed to ensure that his memory stayed fresh in her mind: again, these are unusual motifs in Latin epigraphic verse in general.

The Christian Roman world also produced epigraphic poetry by women. Constantia's epitaph for her husband Anastasius (no. 4), found on the via

Ardeatina in Rome, is internally dated to the year 355, when Flavius Arbitio was consul. They were a Christian couple: Anastasius means "Resurrection," and Constantia has been named after the first Christian emperor, Constantine. However, the content of the epitaph bespeaks just as much loss and pain as any of the pagan ones given here and makes no mention either of Christian consolation or the hope of resurrection, even though the stone itself, as well as the couple's names, demonstrates Constantia's Christianity. The letters preceding the poem (which is in hexameters) are alpha and omega (because Christ said "I am *alpha* and *omega*, the first and the last") while the X in the middle is a chi, the first letter of *Christos. In nomine Dei* at the end is also an obviously Christian formula. In spite of these Christian references, the sensibility of the poem is completely untouched by Christianity and closely resembles some of the earlier pagan epitaphs. It may perhaps be seen as a product of a transitional period of religious sensibility.

At about the same time, Augusta Constantina (d. 354), daughter of Constantine the Great and wife first of Hannibalianus then of Gallus Caesar, founded a church dedicated to the Roman martyr St. Agnes on the via Nomentana in Rome. The decorations on this monument include a fourteen-line poem in her name: however, it is always a moot point whether royal individuals do their own writing, so it is not included here.[20] But another woman of the fourth century, Taurina, names herself as a nun and is the author of an acrostic poem on four saintly ladies, Licinia, Leontia, Ampelia, and Flavia, whose niece (or close female relative: *neptis* is often imprecise) she is. Presumably a fifth sibling fell so far below the family standards of holiness as to marry and have children. Unlike the Constantia epitaph, this poem speaks of complete confidence in the next world—in which, evidently, the women of this family were hugely invested. The lives of nuns are described as active and triumphant; they subdue the devil as dragon or serpent, following the prophecy in Genesis 3:16. Their mother is proud of them (interestingly, no male family members are mentioned anywhere in this celebration of female solidarity and spiritually fecund virginity), and they stand close to the Virgin herself. This poem is a powerful celebration of relationships between women and offers an interesting insight into the rewards of monasticism.

The epitaph of Bishop Hesychius of Vienne (near Lyons) is another example of Christian funerary poetry and was written apparently by his sister Marcella. The sister of a near contemporary, Caesarius of Arles (Caesaria), was highly literate, and left letters to prove it. Nearer to home, Avitus of Vienne's dedication of a 666-line poem in praise of virginity to his sister Fuscina suggests that she was a woman of cultivation.[21] It seems likely that Marcella was a nun: in this period, brothers and sisters seem often to have gone into religion together; and in such cases, the sibling tie was often strengthened by their chastity, since it was unaffected by the requirements of clerical celibacy, and neither had the interests of wife and children to overlay memories of childhood affection.[22]

The last poem I want to discuss, the work of a husband and wife, is remarkably ornate in a way that recalls notable Gallo-Roman writers of Late Antiquity, such as Sidonius Apollinaris. It is an indication of the continuity of classical culture and also of the cultivation of the senatorial order, some time after the fall of Rome. In 474, under Julius Nepos (in the Western Empire), there was a *Quaestor sacri palatii* named Licianus. He was sent on a special mission to Euric, king of the Visigoths, and is described by Sidonius as able and trustworthy.[23] Since the poem appears (on palaeographical grounds) to date to the fifth century, it may be by this man and his otherwise-unattested wife. It is possible that Licinianus is related in some way to the family of nuns memorialized by Taurina, since they include a Licinia, and Roman names tend to go by families. This poem was found by the shore in Roman Dalmatia (Yugoslavia), near modern Zivogostje, at a point where a spring of sweet water emerges and makes its way to the sea. It was inscribed on the rock near the source.[24] The poem has some charm and is also interesting as a historical document. The style of both writers, leisurely, ornate, and euphuistic, characteristic of Late Antique Gaul, comes from the same world of elegant accomplishment as Sidonius Apollinaris, but its address to a *genius loci* is a testimony to the lingering paganism of the Roman upper class. The actual paganism of the authors cannot be assumed, since another notable Gallo-Roman poet, Ausonius, a Christian (indeed, a bishop), has left a similar address to a spring (*salve, fons, ignote ortu, sacer, alme, perennis*).[25] In the pagan period, of course, the devotion to springs had been a serious matter; as David Bright has observed, "The resident spirit of rivers and springs is more than mere metaphor: it is a crucial fact of local cult. A region is characterised—indeed it is personified—in the river flowing through it, or rising in it."[26] Similarly, Servius comments, *nullus enim fons non sacer* (there is no stream that is not holy).[27] But by the fifth century, an allusion to a stream evoked romantic or antiquarian, rather than seriously religious, sentiment. The poem is also a testimony to the continuation of affectionate, companionate marriage among the upper classes, especially since it was still far from automatic for wives to accompany their husbands to provincial posts.[28]

This essay offers only a tiny glimpse into four centuries' worth of epigraphic verse. What I hope to have done is to explore the question of epigraphy as an area that has something to offer to the study of women. The study of classical Latin poetry concentrates so overwhelmingly on a small number of authors that our one surviving woman Latin poet with an indentifiable oeuvre, Sulpicia I, was barely noticed before the 1980s. Here, again, epigraphic poetry is significant as an aspect of the history of women's culture. Epigraphic poetry was of deep interest to Renaissance scholarship and is therefore important to women's sense of their own literary history. The quantity of noncanonical Latin verse collected from inscriptions and read in the Renaissance is easy to overlook. Humanists were interested in epigraphic poetry: they collected it furiously and published it. The existence of quite a number of epigraphic poems attributed to women is unlikely to have been lost on such women as the Latin poet Anna von Pallandt (whose foster brother, Jan Gruter, published a major collection of epigaphic poems, *Inscriptiones Antiquae totius orbis Romani*, in Heidelberg in 1602–03) or Margaretha Welser, who collected the inscriptions of Augsburg in the early sixteenth century in her *Libellus de vetustis imaginibus et inscriptionibus Augustae Vind. repertis et de antiquissimis Caesarum titulis ac nominibus ex veteribus numismatis collectis.*[29] Despite its high visibility in the Renaissance, epigraphic poetry is noticed infrequently now—but it provides an underexplored and potentially rich field for the recovery of women's writing.

NOTES

1. She was of aristocratic birth; indeed, her paternal grandfather had been a king (Antiochus IV of Commagene), while her maternal grandfather may have been Tiberius Claudius Balbillus, a notable astrologer who served as prefect of Egypt from 55 to 59 C.E. Five Greek poems of hers were carved on the legs of the Colossus of Memnon—a reminder that many cultivated Roman writers of the first and second centuries preferred to use that language. See A. and E. Bernand, eds., *Inscriptions grecques et Latines de Colosse de Memnon* (Paris: Institut Français d'Archeologie Orientale, 1960), pp. 28–31. There is a single line of Latin prose appended: "Ego Julia Balbilla Memnonem audivi": "I, Julia, heard Memnon," referring to the mysterious noise the statue emits at dawn. A Latin iambic trimeter written on a wall in Rome may possibly represent an otherwise lost Latin oeuvre: *Balbilla votum debitum reddo tibi. Carmina Latina Epigraphica* (*CLE*), ed. Franz Bücheler, vol. 1 (Leipzig: Teubner, 1895), no. 847, p. 393; Katharina M. Wilson, *Encyclopedia of Continental Women Writers*, vol. 1 (New York: Garland, 1991), pp. 73–74.
2. John Chrysostom, *Sermon on the Psalms* (*Patrologiae Graecae* 55, 156–57).
3. Auguste Audollent, *Defixionum Tabellae quotquot innotuerunt* (Paris: Albert Fontemoing, 1904), no. 100, p. 153.
4. Others may be found in Audollent, *Defixionum Tabellae*, no. 131, p. 187; no. 220, p. 294.
5. *CLE*, vol. 1, no. 44, pp. 22–23.
6. Discussed by Ludwig Friedländer, *Roman Life and Manners under the Early Empire*, vol. 4, appendices and notes, 6th ed., trans. A. B. Gough (London: Routledge, 1913), pp. 137–38.
7. Felix Fabri's version is printed by Friedländer, see previous note.
8. *Corpus Inscriptionum Latinarum* vol. 3, no. 1463, "Terentio Gentiano, trib. militum, quaestori trib. pl. pr. leg. Aug. consuli pontif. cens. provinc. Maced. colonia Ulpia Traian. Aug. Dac. Sarmazegetusa patrono."
9. Attilio Degrassi, *I fasti consolari dell'impero Romano* (Rome: Edizioni di Storia e Letteratura, 1952), p. 34: L. Fundanius and Lamia Aelianus are given as principal consuls for the year, but three other sets are listed for 116.
10. In his "Roman Women and the Provinces," *Ancient Society* 6 (1975), A. J. Marshall states that in the first century C.E., "proconsuls, legates, procurators and even quaestors now took their wives and daughters with them as a regular practice" (121). Tourism in the form of pilgrimage becomes increasingly part of the Chris-

tian Roman world in the fourth century. See E. D. Hunt, *Holy Land Pilgrimage* (Oxford: Clarendon Press, 1982).

11. *Annales* 3.33.

12. On which see W. V. Harris, *Ancient Literacy* (Cambridge, Mass.: Harvard University Press, 1979), pp. 260–61. We should perhaps note that in Pompeii, some of the prostitutes (presumably drawn from the lower ranks of society) were literate: J. J. Franklin, "Literacy and the parietal inscriptions of Pompeii," in *Literacy in the Roman World*, ed. Mary Beard (Ann Arbor: University of Michigan Press, 1991), p. 97.

13. Richmond Lattimore, *Themes in Greek and Latin Epitaphs* (Urbana: University of Illinois Press, 1962), p. 19.

14. Edward Courtney, *Musa Lapidaria* (Atlanta, Ga.: Scholars Press, 1995), no. 199, pp. 186–87.

15. Lattimore, *Themes*: "In Latin inscriptions, the number of hours in the unfinished day is frequently stated, a practice which Cumont attributes to belief in astrology" (p. 16).

16. See Lattimore, *Themes*, pp. 192–94, and also *Aeneid* 6.305–7:

> huc omnis turba ad ripas effusa ruebat,
> matres atque viri, defunctaque corpora vita
> magnanimum heroum, pueri innuptaeque puellae.

17. Lattimore, *Themes*: "In three inscriptions from Numerus Syrorum, Africa, the dead are called *crudelis*" (p. 181). "A further Latin commonplace of mourning for the young is the statement that the dead never gave any cause for grief except by dying . . . [this is] peculiar to the Latin epitaph" (ibid., pp. 198–99).

18. Varro, *ap. Non.* 81.4, Martial I.101.1 (this last is about an affected lady who uses baby talk).

19. *Thesaurus Linguae Latinae*, s.v. *"mamma"*; *Corpus Inscriptionum Latinarum* 6, no. 10016; 9, no. 5228; 6, no. 38891, 6, no. 15585 (quoted).

20. *CLE*, vol. 1, no. 301, p. 146.

21. See Marcelle Thièbaux, *The Writings of Medieval Women*, for a thorough survey of educated women in Late Antique Gaul.

22. Her epitaph for her brother was copied into a Carolingian collection of similar poems, Paris, BN Lat. 2832 (s. viii), and also preserved by Renaissance humanist antiquarians: it does not, as far as I know, survive at Vienne. The manuscript is described by Ernst Dümmler, *Neues Archiv* 4, pp. 297–99.

23. *Epistolae* 3.7.2.

24. *Corpus Inscriptionum Latinarum* 3, no. 1894: *inter Macarscam et Narentae ostia ad vicum Zivogostje sub monasterio S. Crucis ad ipsum maris liturs in ima rupe non laevigata leguntur carmina haec scripta pravis litteris. . . . olim miniatis.*

25. *The Works of Ausonius*, ed. R. P. H. Green (Oxford: Clarendon Press, 1991), 2.20.30.

26. David F. Bright, *Haec Mihi Fingebam: Tibullus in His World* (Leiden: E. J. Brill, 1978), p. 56, and see further L. A. Holland, *Janus and the Bridge* ("The Powers of Rivers and Their Propitiation") (Rome: American Academy in Rome, 1961) Papers and Monographs of the American Academy in Rome 21.

27. Servius, *Ad Aeneadem* 7.84.
28. See Marshall, "Roman Women."
29. This survives in a Munich manuscript, Bayerische Statsbibliothek Clm 4018, and was edited by J. A. Mertens in 1778.

LATIN EPIGRAPHIC POETRY

1. *A woman's memorial poem for her brother Decimus Gentianus*[1]

Vidi pyramidas sine te, dulcissime frater,
et tibi quod potui, lacrimas hic maesta profudi
et nostri memorem luctus hanc sculpo querelam.[2]
sic nomen Decimi Gentiani pyramide alta
pontificis comitis tuis, Traiane, triumphis
lustra[que] sex intra censoris consulis exstet.[3]

2. *Cornelia Galla's epitaph for her husband Varius Frontonianus*[4]

Hic situs est Varius cognomine Frontonianus,
quem coniunx lepida posuit Cornelia Galla
Dulcia restituens veteris solacia vitae
marmoreos voltus statuit, oculos animumque
longius ut kara posset saturare figura.
Hoc solamen est visus. Nam pignus amoris
pectore contegitur memor[i] dulcedine mentis
nec poterit facili labsum oblivione perire,
set dum vita manet, toto est in corde maritus.
nec mir[um], quoniam tales quae feminae mores . . . [5]

3. *Salvidiena's epitaph for her daughter Vitilla*[6]

V[itilla] Salvidiena Q[uniti/ae] Libera Hilara
Salvidienae Faustillae
deliciae suae

---

[1]*CLE* 1, no. 270, p. 130.
[2]Horace, *Odes* 3.11.50–52, *i secundo / Omine et nostri memorem sepulcro / Scalpe querellam.*
[3]Probably meaning that he achieved the two highest honors of the Roman state by the early age of thirty.
[4]*CLE* 2.1, no. 480, p. 228, and *CIL* 8.434, p. 62. Note that this is from a second-century grave from Ammaedara, in Roman North Africa.
[5]The poem continues. Unfortunately, only a few words are extant from each of the lines in the second half.
[6]*CLE* 2.2, no. 1570, p. 578; *CIL* 6.4, no. 25808, p. 758. *CIL* notes that "it was found outside the Collatine gate (in Rome) in a vineyard."

eruditae omnibus artibus.
reliquisti mammam tuam
gementem plangentem plorantem.
    vixit an. xv
mensib. iii, dieb. xi, hor. vii
virginem eripuit Fatus malus.
destituisti, Vitilla mea
miseram mammam tuam.

4. *Constantia's epitaph for her husband Anastasius* (355)[7]

A   X   Ω

Tristis Anastasio Const[antia carmina scribit
coniunx, qui lucem t[enebris mutavit amaris.
Vita quater denis et q[unique annis fuit, eheu
quam cito praerept[us dilectae uxoris amori,
fletus duodecumum cum Ianus sumeret ortum,
conditus Arbitio co[nsul cum duceret annum.
                    in nomine Dei

5. *Taurina's Epitaph for Licinia, Leontia, Ampelia and Flavia*[8]

Lumine virgineo hic splendida membra quiescunt.
Insigneis animo, castae velamine sancto
Crinibus imposito caelum petiere sorores
Innocuae vitae meritis operumque bonorum.
Noxia vincentes Christo medicante venena
Invisi anguis palmam tenuere perennem,
Aspide calcato sponsi virtute triumphant

Letanturque simul pacata in secula missae
Evictis carnis vitiis, saevoque dracone
Obluctante diu subegunt durissima bella.
Nam cunctis exuta malis hic corpora condunt.
Tantus amor tenuit semper sub luce sacratas,
Iungeret[9]ut tumulo sanctarum membra sororum.
Alvus quas matris mundo emiserat una,

---

[7]*CLE* 1, no. 660, pp. 312–13. Found on the via Ardeatina in Rome.
[8]*CLE* 1, no. 748, pp. 357–58.
[9]Here, and with *accipiet* later in the poem, I translate as if it were *–ent*. Often in inscriptions the *n* is represented by a line over the vowel: this is easily omitted or effaced as the stone weathers.

Ad caelum pariter mittet domus una sepulcri.
Mirifico genetrix fetu, quae quattuor agnas
Protulit electas, claris quae quattuor astris
Emicuit castosque choro comitante Maria
Letatur gradiens germanis septa puellis.
Ingressae templum domini venerabile munus
Accipient, duros quoniam vicere labores,

Floribus et variis operum gemmisque nitentes
Lucis perpetuae magno potientur honore.
Adventum sponsi nunc praestolantur ovantes
Veste sacra comptae, oleo durante beatae,
Immortale decus numerosa prole parentes
Aeterno regi fidei pietate sacrarunt.

Nomina sanctarum lector si forte requiris,
ex omni versu te littera prima docebit.
Hunc posuit neptes titulum Taurina sacrata.

6. Epitaphium Sancti Hesicii [Episcopi][10]

Praesulis iunctum tumuloque Aviti,
Funus Hesici tegitur sepulchro,
Qui cluens olim micuit honore
           Pontificali.

Quique mundanis titulis peractis,
Quaestor et regum habilis, benignus
Ambiit demum habitare sacris
           Incola tectis.

Cultibus Christi sapienter haerens
Fautor et pacis studuit furentes
Reddere cives speciali votis
           Mentis amicae.

Temporum mensor numeros modosve
Calculo cernens strenuusque doctor
Unde fraterna docuit libenter
           Agmina tempus.

Septenum necdum peragens bilustrum
Corpus huic sedit posuit beatae

---

[10]Text from *Alcimi Ecdicii Aviti Viennensis Episcopi Opera*, ed. Rudolf Peiper, *Monumenta Germaniae Historiae. Auctores Antiquissimi* 6.2 (Berlin: Weidmann, 1883), pp. 187–88.

Mente cum iustis habitans refulget
    Luce perenni.

Quem soror Marcella gemens obisse
Ultimum praebens lacrimis levamen
Nomen hic scalpsit titulumque fixit
    Carmine parvo.

7. Pelagia and Licinianus, *To the Nymph of the Spring*[11]

Licinianus

Litorea praessus scruposae margine r[up]is
    inriguus gelido defluit amne latex,
cuius perspicuo per levi[a s]ax[a mea]tu
    praedulcis salsam per[luit unda Teth]yn,
indigenis gratus, preterlabentibu[s almus]:
    i[n]cola delicias, aduena laudat [opes.
salve Nymfa meos dignata inv[iser]e finis
    et celebrem cunctis conciliare locum:
nostra salutifero tu mactas pred[ia fo]nte,
    Licinianus ego carmine te dom[i]nus.

Pelagia

Diversum sortita capis finemq[ue caput]que
    Nymfa, caput cautes, term[inus unda] tibi est.
quid queat arcanum sap[iens pernosce]re fontis?
    nasceris e scopulis, fo[ns, moriture freti]s.
hoc Pelagia suos fontes epig[r]ammate donat,
    magne, tui pignus, lic[inian]e, tori.

TRANSLATIONS BY JANE STEVENSON

1. *A woman's memorial poem for her brother Decimus Gentianus*

I have seen the pyramids without you, dearest brother,
and I have done what I can for you.
Grieving, I have poured out my tears here,
and I carve this lament, a memorial of our grief:
thus, that the name of Decimus Gentianus stands on the high pyramid,
a celebrant and sharer in your triumph, O Trajan,
one who was censor and consul within the space of thirty years.

---

[11]*CLE* 2, no. 1531, pp. 728–29.

2. *Cornelia Galla's epitaph for her husband Varius Frontonianus*

> Here lies Varius, called Frontonianus
> whom his gentle wife, Cornelia Galla, laid to rest.
> To restore the sweet joys of her old life
> she ordered marble statues, so that she might sate
> her eyes and her mind for longer with his loved form.
> This sight is a consolation. For the pledge of love in the heart
> lasts by its sweetness in memory in the mind,
> and will not easily fall to oblivion, or perish;
> but while her life remains, her heart is full of her husband.
> Nor is it astonishing, since is feminine nature . . .

3. *Salvidiena's epitaph for her daughter Vitilla*

> Vitilla Salvidiena Hilara, Freedwoman of Quintus/a
> To Salvidiena Faustilla
> Her darling
> Skilled in all arts
> You have left your mamma
> moaning, weeping, mourning.
>   She lived 15 years
> 3 months, 9 days, 7 hours
> Bad fate snatched away the maiden.
> My Vitilla, you have left bereft
> Your wretched mamma.

4. *Constantia's epitaph for her husband Anastasius*

> A sad wife, Constantia, writes this poem for Anastasius,
> Who has changed the light for the bitter shades.
> His life lasted five-and-forty years, alas,
> How swiftly he was snatched from the love of his beloved partner,
> Lamented, when Janus overcame the twelfth month,
> In the year when Arbieto in the name of god governed as consul.

5. *Taurina's Epitaph for Licinia, Leontia, Ampelia and Flavia*[1]

> Limbs shining with virginal light rest here:
> Insignia mark them, and a holy mind, the chaste sisters
> Covering their hair with a veil, they sought heaven
> In their blameless lives and merits of holy works.
> Noxious poisons overcome, through the medicine of Christ,

---

[1]*CLE* 1, no. 748, pp. 357–588.

In safety they keep the eternal palm from the poisonous viper,
Asp trodden down, they triumph, through their Spouse's power.

Lightly they rejoiced embarked on the pacified world, the
Enemy, the fierce dragon, flesh's vices overcome,
Opposer conquered; long they warred against him.
Now here they trained their bodies, all evils shed
This love held them always consecrated during life,
In one tomb thus the holy sisters lie united
All given to earth by the womb of one mother.

A single house sent them all from the tomb to heaven
Mother of a wonderful birth, who brought for heaven
Pure elect lambs, four chaste lights amongst the shining stars
Encircling Mary in chorus: she rejoices
Led around the enclosure of the sister girls
In praise accepting the gift of entrance to the temple of the Lord
All harsh labors now she has conquered.

Flashing with gems, flowers, and all ornaments,
Light perpetual claims them as subjects with honor
Awaiting the Bridegroom's return they are praying,
Votaries in holy garments, with the everlasting oil of the blessed,
Immortal and numberless the offspring of the parents whom they consecrate
All in piety and faith, to the eternal King.

Reader, if you want to know the names of these saints,
It is given you in the first letter of each verse.
The nun Taurina, their niece, made this memorial.

6. *The Epitaph of Bishop Hesychius [of Vienne]*

The burial of Hesychius hides him in the grave,
Joined with the tomb of Bishop Avitus,
Who long ago, was reputed to shine
           with pontifical honor.

And who, having done with worldly titles:
The eminent magistrate of kings, a great man,
Went then to become an inmate
           under this holy roof.

Wisely clinging to the worship of Christ,
Promoter of peace, he strove to bring back
The warring citizens, through his special prayers,
           to a friendly mind.

Measurer of time in numerous ways,
An assiduous teacher, perceiving by computation
When the time was right, freely
              for a fraternal union.

He lived for seventy decades,
Whose body rests here, while he himself is with the blessed,
Living in the spirit,
              in the eternal light.

Whom his sister Marcella, mourning, describes,
offering with tears this final consolation:
She carves the name here, and places the inscription
              with a little verse.

7. Pelagia and Licinianus, *To the Nymph of the Spring*

Licinianus

The full spring, released by the seaward edge of the rough rock, flows in
      an ice-cold torrent,
whose sweet wave laves salt Tethys in its clear flow over smooth boulders,
generous to the people, bringing prosperity to the neighborhood:
a stranger-inhabitant praises its flow and its strength.
Hail, Nymph! worthy to look upon my lands
and to make the place universally known:
you bless our farms with a health-giving fountain,
so I, lord Licinianus, [bless] you with a song.

Pelagia

Nymph, fate has decreed that your end should be different from your
      beginning:
your beginning is in a rock, your end is in a wave.
How could even a wise man fathom the mystery of a spring?
You are born from the rocks, O spring, you are to die in the straits.
Pelagia gives to her waters, with this inscription,
a pledge (great Licinianus) to your bed.

BIBLIOGRAPHY

Primary Sources

Audollent, Auguste, ed. *Defixionum Tabellae quotquot innotuerunt tam in graecis orienti
      quam in totius occidentalis partibus praeter Atticas in corpore inscriptionum atticas
      editas*. Paris: Albert Fontemoing, 1904.

Bücheler, Franz, ed. *Carmina Latina Epigraphica*. 2 vols. Leipzig: Teubner, 1895.

Courtney, Edward, ed. *Musa Lapidaria: A Selection of Latin Verse Inscriptions*. American Classical Studies 36. Atlanta: Scholars Press, 1995.

Diehl, E., ed. *Inscriptiones Latinae Christianae Veteres* 2d ed. 3 vols. Berlin: Weidmann, 1961.

Le Blant, Edmond, ed. *Inscriptions Chrétiennes du Gaule antérieurs au xiiie siècle*. 2 vols. Paris: Imprimerie Impériale, 1856.

Peiper, Rudolf, ed. *Alcimi Ecdicii Aviti Viennensis Episcopi Opera*. Monumenta Germaniae Historiae. Auctores Antiquissimi 6.2. Berlin: Weidman, 1883.

Preussische Akademie der Wissenschaften, ed. *Corpus Inscriptionum Latinarum*. 16 vols.+ suppls. Berlin: Georg Reimer, 1862–.

Secondary Works

Franklin, J. J. "Literacy and the Parietal Inscriptions of Pompeii." In *Literacy in the Roman World*, ed. Mary Beard. Ann Arbor: University of Michigan Press, 1991.

Harris, W. V. *Ancient Literacy*. Cambridge, Mass.: Harvard University Press, 1979.

Lattimore, Richmond. *Themes in Greek and Latin Epitaphs*. Urbana: University of Illinois Press, 1962.

Marshall, A. J. "Roman Women and the Provinces." *Ancient Society* 6 (1975): 109–27.

Purdie, A. B. *Some Observations on Latin Verse Inscriptions*. Fribourg and London: Christophers, 1935.

The Eleven Elegies of the Augustan Poet Sulpicia

Judith P. Hallett

The collected works of the Latin poet Albius Tibullus are the source of Sulpicia's elegies and provide valuable literary context for her writings. He was born sometime between 55 and 48 B.C.E., and died in 19 B.C.E., the same year as Vergil. His poems, written in the elegiac meter, portray him as engaged in various love affairs: with women he calls Delia and Nemesis and with a young man he calls Marathus. The second-century C.E. Roman author Apuleius reports at *Apology* 10 that Tibullus's predecessor Catullus had used "Lesbia"—a metrically equivalent pseudonym alluding to the Greek female poet Sappho—for his beloved Clodia. In the same passage he states that Tibullus employed "Delia" as a metrically equivalent pseudonym of Greek derivation for the name of his own beloved Plania. Both "Nemesis" and "Marathus" are Greek as well, and presumably also have the same number of syllables and the same accentual pattern as the actual names by which these individuals were known.[1]

The pseudonym "Delia" apparently alludes to Apollo, god of poetry, and his birthplace on the island of Delos. In a similar vein, an elegiac poet contemporary with Tibullus, Sextus Propertius, calls his inamorata by the pseudonym "Cynthia," an allusion to Mount Cynthus on this same island. Yet "Delia" also means "clear" in Greek, and hence provides a literal translation of the Latin Plania. "Nemesis" is the Greek goddess of retribution, associated with the composition of love poetry by Catullus in 50.21–22. Though some scholars link "Marathus" with a Greek verb that means "to quench fire," the name may also come from the Greek word for "fennel stalk" and hence evoke an image of youthful male beauty as phallic-shaped vegetation of brief bloom.[2]

Tibullus does not, however, employ a pseudonym when paying tribute to his illustrious literary patron, Marcus Valerius Messalla Corvinus (64 B.C.E.–8 C.E.).

Rather, Tibullus refers to this man by his actual third name, or *cognomen*, Messalla. Consul in 31 B.C.E. and conqueror of the Aquitani during his governorship of Gaul a few years later, Messalla is also remembered for proposing the title *pater patriae*, "father of his country," for Augustus in 2 B.C.E.[3]

Our surviving manuscripts divide the poems of Tibullus into three books. Yet only two of the twenty poems in Book 3 are ascribed to Tibullus himself. The others appear to be the work of several of Tibullus's contemporaries who also benefited from the literary patronage of Messalla. Eleven of these eighteen elegies, eight of them written in the first person, chronicle the passionate love affair of a young woman. In two of these elegies she is identified by the name of Sulpicia. There is every indication that she is the author of these eleven poems and that Sulpicia—like the names by which Roman male elegists refer to themselves in their poetry—is her own name, not a metrically equivalent pseudonym.

One of the elegies that gives this woman's name, 3.16, also refers to her as the "daughter of Servius." Another elegy, 3.14, addresses Messalla and indicates that he is in a position to control where she spends her time. These two statements have led scholars to conclude that this Servius was most likely Servius Sulpicius Rufus, an eminent jurist who served as consul in 51 B.C.E. and died eight years later, or perhaps his similarly named and short-lived son. For the late fourth- and early fifth-century C.E. author Jerome, in *In Jovinianum* 1.46, p. 23, 288c, notes that the consul of 51 B.C.E. was married to Valeria, Messalla's sister, and that she refused to remarry after she was widowed.

Whichever Sulpicius Rufus was Sulpicia's father, therefore, Messalla was her close relation, either her maternal uncle or her late father's maternal uncle. Along with her father's male Sulpicii kin, he was certainly in a position to assume the legal responsibilities of guardianship over Sulpicia after her father's death. By the same token, Sulpicia's membership in Messalla's own family does much to explain why a collection of poems by Tibullus and other writers that Messalla patronized came to include her own elegies.

It is, moreover, precisely because of their inclusion in this collection that Sulpicia's elegies have been preserved for posterity, the only poems in Latin by a woman of the classical era that were bequeathed to later generations. Propertius may state at 2.3.19–22 that his Cynthia is a writer of learned verses. Cicero's characterization, at *Pro caelio* 27.64, of the woman whom Catullus called Lesbia may confirm the implication that she, too, composed poetry. Still, the writings of these two women have not managed to survive. Strikingly, Sulpicia's poems are neither quoted nor referred to by any other ancient writer.

These poems characterize Sulpicia's male lover, like Sulpicia herself, as surrounded with the trappings of privilege and affluence, and hence presumably a member of Rome's elite. He is referred to in five of these elegies by the name of "Cerinthus." This would appear to be a metrically equivalent pseudonym of Greek derivation like those which Catullus and Tibullus used for the women, and men, of whom they were enamoured. "Cerinthus" has literary associations just as "Lesbia," "Delia," and "Cynthia" do: it comes from the Greek word for wax, and most likely alludes to the wax tablets used for writing love poetry.[4] In referring to her beloved by a pseudonym, therefore, Sulpicia follows the standard poetic practice of male elegy writers.

Scholars are unanimous in viewing the final six of these elegies (3.13–18), all of them written in the first person, as the work of Sulpicia herself. Yet many scholars regard the first five (3.8–12) as a garland by someone else, presumably a male admirer and literary impersonator. They make this assumption for several reasons. First and foremost, even though two of these poems—3.9 and 3.11—are written in the first person, too, the other three—3.8, 3.10, and 3.12—are composed in the third person. These elegies thus speak of Sulpicia in what seems to be a detached manner, as observed rather than as an observer.

Another reason that scholars often deny that Sulpicia herself composed 3.8–12 is that each of these five poems is longer and contains more learned allusions than any of the other six. They are sprinkled not only with references to little-known titles of gods and names of faraway places, but also with relatively obscure words (such as the noun *indago*, a term for "hunting net" in 3.9, and *perlucida*, the adjective used to describe the Roman goddess Juno's radiance in 3.12).[5] Furthermore, scholars uncomfortable about crediting Sulpicia with authorship of 3.8–12 tend to assess all of Sulpicia's poems anachronistically: according to nineteenth- and twentieth-century Western notions about how a properly reared young woman of high social rank writes about and conducts herself. They consequently regard the speech and behavior attributed to Sulpicia in 3.8–12 as unwomanly, or at least as unbefitting an aristocratic maiden.

But a comparison of this sequence of love elegies to the series of love elegies written by Catullus a generation earlier argues for Sulpicia's authorship of all eleven. Various verbal and thematic similarities between the later six and first five elegies, some of which involve close resemblances between all eleven of these elegies and Vergil's epic *Aeneid*, encourage the same conclusion. So does a consideration of the social circumstances as well as the literary context in which Sulpicia wrote.

Catullus, whose full name was Gaius Valerius Catullus, appears to have been Sulpicia's distant kinsman on her mother Valeria's side.[6] Sulpicia seems to have endeavored to emulate and echo Catullus in several important ways: possibly because of their biological kinship, possibly because Catullus was the first Roman poet to write about his passion for a woman who wrote and responded appreciatively to erotic poetry herself. Sulpicia's most obvious means of homage is in her choice of the elegiac meter to chronicle, in a sequence of different poems, different aspects of her love affair. Our one surviving book of Catullus's poetry ends with a series of over fifty poems in the elegiac meter that depict, among other things, moments in his love affairs with both "Lesbia" and a male youth he calls by the Latin pseudonym "Juventius," "young man."

Obviously, Tibullus and Propertius also follow Catullus in choosing the elegiac meter to provide snapshots of their love affairs, taken from varying distances and offering different perspectives. But Sulpicia resembles Catullus in particular by doing so—in 3.8–12—through alternating distanced poems written in the third person with closely focused, self-revelatory poems composed in the first. After all, some of Catullus's elegies (like several of his other poems that employ other meters) refer to Catullus in the second or third person. For example, in poem 76, one of his most highly esteemed elegies, he addresses himself in the second person, as "you, Catullus." In poem 87, also in the elegiac meter, he talks about "Catullus" as "he," in the third.

To be sure, none of Catullus's elegies—nor any of his poems in other meters, for that matter—describe his own physical attributes or clothing directly and flatteringly, in the way that 3.8 and 3.12, both in the third person, describe the looks and garb of Sulpicia. Yet at 32.10, composed in the hendecasyllabic meter, Catullus claims that his sexually aroused organ pushes through his clothing when inviting one Ipsitilla to nine continuous copulations. And in such elegies as 69, 80, 89, and 97, Catullus criticizes other men for their flaws in appearance, grooming, and dress, thereby implying his own lack of physical shortcomings. Both he and Sulpicia testify to their physical desirability, albeit in different ways with different emphases.

In addition, Sulpicia seems to have emulated Catullus by writing elegies of greatly varying lengths to represent her own love affair. Catullus's elegies range from two lines to over one hundred lines long. Several are approximately the same length as are 3.8, 9, 10, 11, and 12, which contain 24, 24, 26, 20, and 20 lines, respectively. Catullus 76, for example, is twenty-six lines long; Catullus 65, the first poem in his elegiac sequence, twenty. Yet several Catullan elegies are four to six lines long, like Sulpicia 3.15, 16, 17, and 18. And Sulpicia 3.13 and 14, which are ten and eight lines long, respectively, have memorable Catullan elegiac counterparts of the same length, among them Catullus 101, an affecting address to the shades of his dead brother.

The difference between the number of learned allusions contained in Sulpicia's first five, and later six, elegies is not, moreover, grounds for attributing the first five poems to another, male, author. Catullus's briefer elegies, it should be emphasized, do not feature as many learned allusions as his longer ones. And Sulpicia's shorter elegies, 3.13–18, do display various indications of literary sophistication and erudition. Consider, for instance, the references to the Camenae, the Italian (as opposed to the Greek) muses who inspire Sulpicia's poetry, and to Venus as goddess of Cythera, in 3.13. Or the figurative use of the word *toga*—the garment worn by women who sold their sexual favors—to signify a woman of that type as well as of *torus*—a term for bed, to suggest Sulpicia's own sexual involvement with her lover in 3.16.

In addition to sprinkling both her long and short elegies with learned allusions, Sulpicia pointedly refers to herself as *docta*, learned, in 3.12. She thereby recalls efforts by Catullus, and indeed by Propertius, to praise the women they depict themselves as loving for their extensive learning. Catullus, to be sure, describes his Lesbia as *docta* in an indirect manner, and in a poem written in the hendecasyllabic rather than in the elegiac meter. In poem 35 he compliments an unidentified woman, who inspires her own lover's poetic efforts, as *doctior*, more learned "than the Sapphic muse." But since Catullus elsewhere associates his own beloved with Sappho through her pseudonym Lesbia, and since he himself imitates and evokes Sappho in various poems inspired by his beloved, the phrase "Sapphic muse" would seem a reference to his beloved herself. Propertius takes a more direct approach, referring to his Cynthia as *docta* at 2.3.19–22, when paying tribute to the poetry she writes, and when comparing her poetry favorably with that of two earlier Greek female poets, Corinna and Erinna.

Sulpicia 3.8 also recalls Catullus's efforts to praise the beauty of his beloved in his longest and most complex elegiac poem, 68. In 3.8 Sulpicia is described as magnificently arrayed (*culta*), exquisitely groomed, and erotically alluring enough to turn the eyes of the god Mars away from the charms of his lover Venus. Furthermore, the god of love is there said to kindle torches from Sulpicia's eyes when he wants to set the gods' hearts on fire (*exurere divos*, 3.8.5). Scholars have observed various similarities between this description of Sulpicia and several by Propertius and Ovid. But they might also have noted Sulpicia's statement that she inspires passion "gleaming white in a snowy robe" (*nivea candida veste*, 3.8.12) and Sulpicia's comparison between herself and the god Vertumnus on Olympus, who wears a thousand different outfits attractively. Both descriptions summon to mind Catullus 68.71, which speaks of his beloved as a "gleaming white goddess" (*candida diva*).

Nor have scholars paid sufficient heed to the Catullan resonances of the adjective *digna*, "worthy," in 3.8 and two other poems. Sulpicia first employs this word in 3.8 when claiming that she is unique among the girls (*sola puellarum digna*) in being worthy of Tyrian finery, fragrances from Arabia, and jewels from India. She utilizes the comparative form *dignior*, several lines later, to assert that no other girl is more worthy of the Muses, the goddesses who inspire poetry (*dignior nulla puella*). Catullus employs *digna* at 68.131 to liken his beloved to the mythic heroine Laodamia, when referring to her as "light of my life" (*lux mea*), a phrase that he repeats in the final line of 68.

In seeking, therefore, to legitimate herself as a divinely alluring *puella* worthy of representation in elegiac love poetry, Sulpicia 3.8 evokes Catullus's representation of his beloved in his most ambitious elegy as well as portrayals of physically desirable females in works by other elegiac poets. Her use of both *dignior* (*dignior illa viro*) at 3.12.10 and *digna* (*cum digno digna fuisse ferar*) at 3.13.10, both times to legitimate herself as worthy of her lover, and in the second instance to legitimate her lover as worthy of her, is thus doubly significant. It links her relationship with Cerinthus not only to her own claim to divinely favored apparel and literary appeal at 3.8, but also to Catullus's special, literary bond with his inamorata as well.

Like Catullus, Sulpicia also uses the phrase *lux mea* to describe her beloved, at both 3.9.15 and 3.18.1. Curiously, although the phrase *lux mea* frequently occurs in the elegiac poetry of both Propertius and Ovid, it does not turn up elsewhere in the three books containing the elegies of Tibullus and other poets in Messalla's circle. Sulpicia's use of the adjective *pia*, "devoted," to modify *cura*, "concern" for her lover, in 3.17 also harks back to Catullus 76, where he applies both this adjective and the noun formed from it, *pietas*, to describe devotion to a lover that merits recognition from the gods.

Sulpicia also echoes Catullus's description of love in using the adjective *mutuus*, "shared," "reciprocal," to represent the passion she would like to enjoy with Cerinthus, first at 3.11.6 and 7 (*mutuus ignis, mutuus amor*), then at 3.12.8 (*mutua vincla*). What is more, she not only characterizes their imagined love as "mutual" later in 3.11, when she asks Venus to enslave them both equally, but she also speaks of herself in 3.13.10 as having finally experienced love as "a woman worthy of having made love with a worthy man" (*cum digno digna*). Here, though, at 45.20, the Catullan description of mutual passion—they love and are loved with reciprocal affections" (*mutuis animis amant amantur*)—is not of the love between Catullus and his Lesbia, but of that binding a couple named Acme and Septimius. While mutuality is the hallmark of Sulpicia's love for Cerinthus, Catullus does not portray it as figuring in his relationship with Lesbia, nor do any of his fellow elegists represent their erotic liaisons as involving mutual passion.

Sulpicia devotes 3.16, a poem addressed to Cerinthus, to a complaint about a rival for his affections. Her complaint calls to mind numerous poems by her male elegiac predecessors and contemporaries, in which they wail over (and sometimes to) the women they love because these women are involved with men other than themselves. So, too, in 3.17, Sulpicia frets that Cerinthus is not sufficiently concerned about her suffering from a fever that wracks her body. Nevertheless, Sulpicia's other poems are more optimistic in tone: they celebrate her love and her commitment to writing poetry about it. In 3.13.5–8 she even offers the details of her affair for male and female readers who lack their own erotic experiences to savor as a substitute. Self-pitying laments about amatory disappointments occupy a far less prominent place in her poems than they do in the elegies of Catullus, Tibullus, and Propertius. Sulpicia hence differs from the male practitioners of elegy in her gender and in her generally and generously upbeat perspective on her love affair. She also contrasts with them in characterizing her relationship as one of equals who feel the same way about one another and for the most part treat one another in the same way.

These echoes of Catullus's poetry, which we find in both 3.8–12 and 3.13–18 and which often involve evocations of the same Catullan usage or theme by individual elegies in both groups, would suggest that Sulpicia wrote the first five poems in this series as well as the final six. Similarities between Vergil's *Aeneid* and several of Sulpicia's elegies also imply as much. These elegies include both 3.13–18, those that scholars agree to be Sulpicia's own work, as well as those often assigned to the admiring male imitator who wrote the "garland" of 3.8–12.

In a recent essay Alison Keith has called attention to several striking resemblances between Sulpicia 3.13–18 and Vergil's representation of Dido in the first and fourth books of Vergil's *Aeneid*. Keith focuses much of her attention on Sulpicia 3.13 and its use of the nouns *pudor*, which can mean "chastity" as well as "shame," and *fama*, which can mean "reputation" as well as "rumor."[7] Both Latin words loom large in Vergil's text.

Keith notes, "At the outset of *Aeneid* 4 Dido swears an oath to Pudor (4.27) in which she undertakes to respect the sexual proprieties dictated by modesty and regard for her good name by remaining faithful to the memory of her dead husband rather than succumbing to passion (*Aeneid* 4.18–29). Her oath accords with the Roman ideal of the 'one-man woman,' *univira*, the widow who refuses to remarry out of steadfast loyalty to the memory of a dead spouse. Dido breaks her oath, however, first in her sexual communion with Aeneas, and then, without regard for her good name, *fama* (4.170), in her open assertion of their union as *coniugium*, marriage (4.172)."[8]

Keith also observes that after the scandalous relationship of the lovers excites malicious gossip, *fama* (so 4.173–74, 189–95, and, I would add, 296–99, 665–66), Dido herself is represented as lamenting her loss of *pudor* and *fama*, good name, when she reproaches Aeneas for abandoning her at lines 320–23.[9]

There are key distinctions between the ways in which the words *pudor* and *fama* are used about Dido and by Sulpicia. To quote Keith again:

> Vergil represents Dido striving to conduct herself in accordance with the dictates of *pudor* despite her growing love for Aeneas (4.27, 55, 322); moreover, her downfall originates in the ill repute, *fama* (4.170, 323) arising from her neighbors' gossip, *fama* (4.170–197, 219–221, 296–299, 665–666) about their sexual relationship. In Sulpicia's poem, likewise, the constraints of *pudor* (3.13.2) are closely associated with the maintenance of her reputation, *fama* (3.13.9), as is particularly clear in the reference to composing a mask for rumor, *fama*. But Sulpicia, as the author of [her] literary destiny, can both contest Roman suspicion of female sexuality and redefine the terms of moral judgment. She tacitly suggests that deception (*texisse*, 3.13.1) is a frequent companion to *pudor*, and deftly reorients the sphere of *pudor* from dissimulation to openness. The regulation of female sexuality by innuendo and rumor (3.13.2), so injurious to Dido in the *Aeneid* (4.170–97) is rejected outright. Instead, [Sulpicia] emphasizes her extraordinary distance from Roman norms of female propriety through the pervasive sexualization of the process of poetic composition in the use of sexually charged verbs denoting covering and uncovering (*texisse, nudasse*), in the imagery of "pelvic" reception (*attulit in nostrum deposuitque sinum*), and in the claim of misbehavior (*peccasse*) to describe, proudly, her writing as well as her physical conduct.[10]

Keith also ascertains a parallel between Sulpicia's claim in 3.13.10 that she and her lover are worthy of bestowing erotic favors on one another—*cum digno digna*—and what is said maliciously about Dido and Aeneas at *Aeneid* 4.191–92: "To Libya had come Aeneas, a man whom beautiful Dido deemed worthy (*dignetur*) of union." These lines, Keith stresses, distort what Dido has said earlier, at 1.628 ff., about the similarities between her plight and that of Aeneas. Keith concludes her comparison between Sulpicia 3.13 and Dido in the *Aeneid* by remarking: "Sulpicia has sympathetically reimagined Dido's ignorance of the divine machinery of the *Aeneid* in her own informed personal relation with the Muses and Venus, and has recast Dido's pursuit of a love undertaken against the will of Rome's gods as a love fully in accordance with divine will. Like the Vergilian Dido, who does not conceal her fault (*culpa*, 170–172), but calls it marriage, Sulpicia delights in her fault (so *peccasse*) and revels in its publication. Where Dido is the object of rumors purveyed by Fama, however, Sulpicia publishes her transgressive passion to gain a literary reputation."[11]

According to Keith, the five short elegies that follow 3.13 also contain details that call to mind Dido's representation in the *Aeneid*. For example, Keith views Messalla's separation of Sulpicia from her beloved in 3.14 as similar to Jupiter's insistence that Aeneas leave Dido (although in contrast to Aeneas, who submits to Jupiter, Sulpicia defies Messalla's order and then gets a reprieve in 3.15). So, too, Keith regards Sulpicia's rebuke to Cerinthus for his faithlessness in 3.16 as comparable to Dido's angry reaction to Aeneas's departure. She links Sulpicia's portrayal of erotic passion as a fever in 3.17 and 18 with the way in which Dido is portrayed as suffering from a *cura*, as nourishing a wound, and as consumed by flame, at the very beginning of *Aeneid* 4. In this context Keith notes that Sulpicia "conflates the Vergilian imagery of Dido's love as at once flame and wound in the metaphor of love as a feverish illness."[12]

On the basis of these similarities, then, Keith views 3.13–18, Sulpicia's final six elegies, as a unified group of poems by Sulpicia. Together, she maintains, these poems respond to the Dido narrative in Vergil's *Aeneid* and redefine not only how a woman in Dido's situation should express and conduct herself but also how her lover should act. It is, however, by no means difficult to find similarities between each of Sulpicia's first five poems and Dido's portrait in the *Aeneid* as well. These similarities then allow us to view 3.8–18, and not merely 3.13–18, as a unified group of poems responding to Vergil, and implicitly insisting that Dido's tragic scenario is capable of a happy outcome. Let us look briefly at each of these elegies in turn.

In 3.8, the references to the gods Venus and Amor, and to Sulpicia's Tyrian *palla* and Tyrian wools, as enhancing Sulpicia's desirability immediately recall—and reverse—the situation that Vergil ascribes to Dido. Vergil, after all, represents Dido as the victim of both divinities, and as a refugee from her murderous Tyrian brother. So, too, the positively charged words *digna* and *dignior* in 3.8, as in 3.13, call to mind both the mutual worthiness of Dido and Aeneas, and its negative portrayal by Carthaginian gossips in *Aeneid* 4.191–92.

Most important, Dido—like Sulpicia—is also described as physically beautiful and resembling a divinity. At *Aeneid* 1.496 ff. Vergil calls her *pulcherrima* and likens her to the goddess Diana. In the hunting scene at 4.137 ff. he mentions her gold-knotted *crines*, hair (much as 3.8 asserts that Sulpicia's *crines* are lovely in any arrangement). What is more, here Vergil emphasizes—as part of the "mutual worthiness" theme—that Aeneas possesses physical beauty equal to that of Dido by terming him, superlatively, *pulcherrimus*. This hunt, however, is disrupted by a storm. After seeking shelter in the same cave, Dido and Aeneas consummate their passion without benefit of legal marriage. Vergil then characterizes "that day" as "the first day of her doom" and "the cause of her misfortunes." "That day" could not be more different from the first of March, the holiday on which 3.8 is set: a joyous celebration at which Sulpicia proudly testifies to her own beauty and asks the Muses to sing of her.

In 3.9, where Sulpicia envisions Cerinthus hunting, she uses the rare word *indago*. Vergil also employs this term at *Aeneid* 4.121, in the divine announcement of the hunt in which Dido and Aeneas take part. Sulpicia here portrays herself as willing to pursue stags, *cervi*, like those described as hunted animals at *Aeneid* 4.154 ff. She also refers to Cerinthus as a boy, *puer*; tries to dissuade him from hunting a boar, *aper*, and asks him to leave the hunting to his father. With these details she calls to mind Vergil's portrayal of Aeneas's son, the *puer* Ascanius, at the hunt, since Ascanius is said to be hoping to catch a boar as well.

But even these evocations of Vergil's Ascanius carry erotic associations. Vergil inextricably links Dido's passion for Aeneas to her desire to be with Ascanius: after all, at 1.657 ff. we are told that he is the god Amor in disguise. And perhaps the most important difference between the narrative about Dido in the *Aeneid* and the scenario in this poem is that Sulpicia proclaims a wish to be seen making love in the open amid the hunting nets, not hidden in a cave.

3.10 depicts Sulpicia as ill, in a state resembling that of the dying Dido at the end of *Aeneid* 4 and that of the lovesick Dido at the beginning of the book as well. There, Vergil says at 62 ff., sacrifices before the images of the gods at the *foci*, hearths, and prayers, *vota*, do not help. Here, though, the *vota* of Sulpicia and her beloved at the hearths are sought—and prove successful.

In 3.11 Sulpicia's passion for Cerinthus, like Vergil's representation of the love that Dido feels for Aeneas, is described metaphorically as "fire" and "burning." Sulpicia's reference to their prospective lovemaking as *furta*, secret couplings, also recalls Vergil's statement in *Aeneid* 4.172 that Dido hides her *furtivum amorem*. Nonetheless, the emphasis in this elegy on the mutual love of Sulpicia and Cerinthus is positive and celebratory, in contrast to the way in which the reciprocated passions of Dido and Aeneas are disparaged by ill wishers in *Aeneid* 4. At 191 ff. Dido and Aeneas are accused of neglecting their *regna*, political kingdoms, in favor of erotic dalliance (and at 4.267 ff. the god Mercury informs Aeneas that his affair has caused him to forget his political responsibility, *regnum*). Here, though, the erotic power of Cerinthus over Sulpicia is itself termed his *regna*. So, too, at *Aeneid* 4.103 ff. the goddess Juno, conceding defeat to Venus, merely allows Dido to be a slave to (*servire*) a Trojan husband. Here, though, Sulpicia rejoices in the new *servitium*, slavery of love, that Cerinthus imposes upon women.

Finally, in 3.12 Sulpicia prays to Juno as a beneficent deity, a goddess supportive of mutual love—not as Vergil's vindictive divinity. Here Sulpicia uses both the verb *servire* and the comparative adjective *dignior* in a positive sense to exalt her passion for Cerinthus and express the hope that it will be mutual. As we have just seen, Vergil has Juno utilize the former word grudgingly to describe her erotic agenda for Dido and Aeneas; mean-spirited Carthaginians, as noted above, employ a verb derived from *dignus* to deride their queen's mutually gratifying affair with Aeneas. The purple *palla* that Sulpicia claims Juno wears is noteworthy because Dido dresses in purple for the hunt in *Aeneid* 4. Sulpicia's insistence that she does not wish to be *sana*, mentally healthy, resembles Dido's recognition at *Aeneid* 4.595 that, as a result of her abandonment by Aeneas, she has become *insana*. Most significantly, Sulpicia voices a wish that her *vetus amor*, a love of long standing, will also prove long-lasting. Her choice of adjective evokes Dido's claim at Aeneid 4.23 that, in reawakening to physical passion, she recognizes *vestigia veteris flammae*, the traces of a long-standing passion.

Modern scholars who have viewed the first five of Sulpicia's elegies as the work of "some sympathetic poet and friend," possibly Tibullus himself, have largely taken this stance for "social" reasons, rooted in assumptions about what constitutes appropriate ladylike, and indeed appropriate gentlemanly, comportment in their own milieux. While admitting that Sulpicia possessed "remarkable literary ability," for example, Kirby Flower Smith nonetheless feels it "fair to suspect that she was somewhat willful and, let us confess it, a trifle spoiled." Labeling her "frank, ardent, impulsive," he attributes both her frankness and "naïveté" to her "youth, sex, and her essential innocence." Furthermore, he assumes that the male poet who wrote 3.8–12 displayed "grace, delicacy, and good breeding . . . exquisitely blended."[13]

Scholars such as Smith cannot bring themselves to believe that what he judges an "attractive young person" with "one of the longest pedigrees in the Empire" might boast of her own beauty and array, not to mention her torrid sexual relations with a man not her husband. But such scholars should have first taken a closer look at our ancient Roman evidence about the actual conduct tolerated by other privileged women in Sulpicia's social circle. To be sure, in the year following Tibullus's death in 19 B.C.E., Augustus issued a flurry of moral and marital legislation. It penalized adulterous relationships and rewarded marriage and childbearing by exempting from legal guardianship freeborn mothers of three children and freedwomen who had given birth to four. But, even so, at this very time Augustus's own daughter and only child, Julia, was apparently engaging quite flagrantly in precisely the kind of behavior her father had outlawed. In 25 B.C.E., when Julia was fourteen, Augustus had her wed to his seventeen-year-old nephew and heir, Marcus Claudius Marcellus, who died two years later. In 21 B.C.E. he again gave her away in marriage, this time to his friend Marcus Vipsanius Agrippa, a man over twenty years Julia's senior. While Julia bore Agrippa five children in quick succession, it was well known that she dallied with other partners during those years.[14] The later Latin author Macrobius reports, at *Saturnalia* 2.5.9, that she asserted, to those knowledgeable of her misdeeds and hence amazed that these children resembled her husband, "I never take on a passenger unless I have a full cargo," wittily implying that she only engaged in love affairs when already pregnant.

After Agrippa's death in 12 B.C.E., Augustus married Julia to his stepson, and eventual successor, Tiberius. But, as Suetonius reports at *Tiberius* 2, within a few years Tiberius and Julia became estranged. When Augustus eventually exiled Julia in 2 B.C.E. for her adulteries with a number of men, he only did so because they posed a threat to him politically. Among them—we are told by Velleius Paterculus at 2.100 of his *Roman History*—was the son of Augustus's archenemy Mark Antony. Julia is also remembered by Macrobius at *Saturnalia* 2.5.5 and 7 for her concern with her own physical appearance. Macrobius relates that she responded wittily to critical comments from her father about her risqué garb and that she was the object of his witty criticism when he discovered that she was having gray hairs plucked by her cosmeticians. Our information about Julia, however meager, renders Sulpicia's vocal pride in her looks and lover more credible.

In arguing that Sulpicia 3.13–18 constitute a unified group of poems, responding to Vergil's representation of Dido in the *Aeneid*, Alison Keith assumes that Sulpicia wrote after the *Aeneid* was published, during the years immediately following Vergil's death in 19 B.C.E. Expanding this unified group of poems to include 3.8–12 also requires the assumption that these poems, too, postdate the *Aeneid*. But such an assumption in turn raises serious questions about how old Sulpicia was when she wrote these elegies. If Sulpicia is in fact the daughter of a man who died in 43 B.C.E., then she could not have been born much later than the following year, 42 B.C.E. And in that case, she would have been at least in her mid-twenties, perhaps even her thirties, at the time she composed her poetry. Since Roman women of her social class were usually wed by their mid-to-late teens—Julia, as we have seen, married for the second time at age eighteen—it is highly unlikely that Sulpicia would have been a never-married maiden at that point in her life.

It is, of course, possible that Sulpicia wrote her elegies in the early twenties rather than in the early teens B.C.E., as a sexually and literarily precocious teenager, and that Vergil is responding to Sulpicia's poetic self-disclosures in his portrayal of Dido. Should that be so, then what is Vergil's message? That no woman, anywhere—even a foreign independent queen with greater financial resources and political power at her disposal than the aristocratic, well-connected and materially privileged Sulpicia—should attempt to follow Sulpicia's example. For such a woman risks her reputation, her well-being, and ultimately the survival not only of herself but also of her country if she engages in passionate liaisons outside of marriage, especially with men who should be spending their energies on their nation's welfare. It is possible, too, that Sulpicia's elegies depict an earlier period in her own life rather than a contemporary situation, that she chose to write about a youthful passion at a time when her youth was long spent.

But it would seem most likely that Sulpicia is in fact writing in response to Vergil, rather than vice versa, about contemporary events, and that she is writing well after her youth—or at least her maidenhood—was a thing of the past. It appears most plausible, too, that the love affair she celebrates was not her first sexual experience. Like Julia, like Vergil's Dido, she may well have been married at least once, and was at this point in her life a widow or a divorcée. The high manpower losses and socially divisive political behavior among Rome's elite during the decade leading up to Messalla's consular year bear special relevance to Sulpicia's situation. According to the Roman historian Sir Ronald Syme, even Messalla's own first marriage "ended in death or divorce . . . perhaps in the season of Actium."[15] The civil strife of the late thirties B.C.E., or Messalla's shifting political alliances, might also have led to the dissolution of his niece's union by death or divorce if she had been born in, say, 50 B.C.E., to the consul of fifty-one, and married by thirty-five. And, once Sulpicia became husbandless, her own widowed mother's refusal to remarry may well have inspired her to follow suit, although not necessarily disavow love altogether.

Sulpicia would have needed to remain under the control of a legal guardian even as a widow in her twenties or early thirties. But we still need to consider why her mother's brother Messalla seems to have assumed this role. He may well have been selected over her father's male relations (including her own brother) because he was also the guardian of her widowed mother. In this context, we should note that Sulpicia characterizes Messalla as sharing her mother's anxious overprotectiveness. For, at 3.12.15, when describing her mother's instructions to her at her birthday celebration, Sulpicia refers to her with the adjective *studiosa*, "attentive," the same word she uses when addressing Messalla at 3.14.5 and requesting that he cease to be so agitated and interventionist about her love affair with Cerinthus. And the support that Messalla proffered to Sulpicia as a writer of Latin poetry seems to have amply compensated her readers such as ourselves, who owe her poems to his literary patronage, if not necessarily Sulpicia herself.

NOTES

1. See the article on Tibullus by R. O. A. M. Lyne in *The Oxford Classical Dictionary*, 3d ed., ed. Simon Hornblower and Antony Spawforth (Oxford: Oxford University Press, 1996).
2. For the meaning of "Delia" and "Marathus," see, for example, Kirby Flower Smith, *The Elegies of Albius Tibullus* (1913, reprinted Darmstadt: Wis-

senschaftliche Buchgesellschaft, 1964), pp. 44, 289; see also s.v. μαραθον in H. G. Liddell and R. Scott, *A Greek-English Lexicon*, 9th ed. (Oxford 1940).

3. See the article on Valerius Messalla Corvinus, Marcus by Christopher Pelling in the third edition of *The Oxford Classical Dictionary*.

4. David Roessel, "The Significance of the Name *Cerinthus* in the Poems of Sulpicia," *Transactions of the American Philological Association* 120 (1990): 243–50.

5. See *The Oxford Latin Dictionary*, ed. P. G. W. Glare (Oxford: Oxford University Press, 1982), s.v. *"indago,"* and s.v. *"perlucidus."*

6. So T. P. Wiseman, "Sirmio, Sir Ronald, and the *Gens Valeria*," *Classical Journal* 88.3 (1993): 223–29.

7. Alison Keith, *"Tandem Venit Amor*: A Roman Woman Speaks of Love," in *Roman Sexualities*, ed. Judith P. Hallett and Marilyn B. Skinner (Princeton, N.J.: Princeton University Press, 1998), pp. 295–310.

8. Keith, p. 298.

9. Keith, p. 298.

10. Keith, pp. 300–301.

11. Keith, pp. 301–2.

12. Keith, pp. 303–6.

13. Smith, pp. 77–86. See also Niklas Holzberg, "Four Poets and a Poetess or Portraits of a Poet as a Young Man? Thoughts on Book 3 of the *Corpus Tibullianum*," *Classical Journal* 94.2 (December-January 1998–99): 169–91. Holzberg argues that "Sulpicia" is not a "historical female author who wrote those poems in Book 3 of the *Corpus Tibullianum* in which a woman of this name talks to us in the first person," but a male-authored fictional autobiography of someone who never existed. While his arguments are not grounded in "presentist" social assumptions, he claims that social pressures to "recover" women writers led scholars of earlier generations, up to and including the 1970s, to take the Tibullan text at face value rather than seek more ingenious literary explanations. Holzberg maintains that the author of these eleven poems was eager to "fill in a blank" in Tibullus 2.2, which wishes that one Cornutus may experience the faithful passions of a wife. Identifying this Cornutus with Sulpicia's Cerinthus, Holzberg contends that there is a single, male, author of Book 3 who invented a "premarital romance" for Cornutus. Such a thesis enables Holzberg, like earlier generations of scholars, to deny that Sulpicia is celebrating a physically consummated love affair outside of marriage, and recast her as "Cerinthus'" future and faithful wife.

14. See the article on Julia (3) by T. J. Cadoux and Robin J. Seager in *The Oxford Classical Dictionary*.

15. "A Great Orator Mislaid," *Classical Quarterly* 31.2 (1981): 421–27.

SULPICIA THE ELEGIST: THE ELEVEN POEMS

3.8

Sulpicia est tibi culta tuis, Mars magne, Kalendis
   spectatum e caelo, si sapis, ipse veni.
hoc Venus ignoscet: at tu, violente, caveto
   ne tibi miranti turpiter arma cadant.

illius ex oculis, cum vult exurere divos,   5
    accendit geminas lampadas acer Amor.
illam, quidquid agit, quoquo vestigia movit,
    componit furtim subsequiturque Decor.
seu solvit crines, fusis decet esse capillis;
    seu compsit, comptis est veneranda comis.   10
urit, seu Tyria voluit procedere palla;
    urit, seu nivea candida veste venit.
talis in aeterno felix Vertumnus Olympo
    mille habet ornatus, mille decenter habet.
sola puellarum digna est cui mollia caris   15
    vellera det sucis bis madefacta Tyros,
possideatque, metit quidquid bene olentibus arvis
    cultor odoratae dives Arabs segetis,
et quascumque niger rubro de litore gemmas
    proximus Eois colligit Indus aquis.   20
hanc vos, Pierides, festis cantate kalendis,
    et testudinea Phoebe superbe lyra.
hoc sollemne sacrum multos haec sumet in annos;
    dignior est vestro nulla puella choro.

3.9
Parce meo iuveni, seu quis bona pascua campi
    seu colis umbrosi devia montis aper,
nec tibi sit duros acuisse in proelia dentes;
    incolumem custos hunc mihi servet Amor.
sed procul abducit venandi Delia cura.   5
    o pereant silvae deficiantque canes!
quis furor est, quae mens densos indagine colles
    claudentem teneras laedere velle manus?
quidve iuvat furtim latebras intrare ferarum
    candidaque hamatis crura notare rubis?   10
sed tamen, ut tecum liceat, Cerinthe, vagari,
    ipsa ego per montes retia torta feram,
ipsa ego velocis quaeram vestigia cervi
    et demam celeri ferrea vincla cani.
tunc mihi, tunc placeant silvae, si, lux mea, tecum   15
    arguar ante ipsas concubuisse plagas;
tunc veniat licet ad casses, inlaesus abibit,
    ne veneris cupidae gaudia turbet, aper.
nunc sine me sit nulla venus, sed lege Dianae,
    caste puer, casta retia tange manu;   20

et quaecumque meo furtim subrepit amori,
    incidat in saevas diripienda feras.
at tu venandi studium concede parenti,
    et celer in nostros ipse recurre sinus.

3.10
Huc ades et tenerae morbos expelle puellae,
    huc ades, intonsa Phoebe superbe coma.
crede mihi, propera: nec te iam, Phoebe, pigebit
    formosae medicas applicuisse manus.
effice ne macies pallentes occupet artus,   5
    neu notet informis languida membra color,
et quodcumque mali est et quidquid triste timemus,
    in pelagus rapidis evehat amnis aquis.
sancte, veni, tecumque feras, quicumque sapores,
    quicumque et cantus corpora fessa levant;   10
neu iuvenem torque, metuit qui fata puellae
    votaque pro domina vix numeranda facit.
interdum vovet, interdum, quod langueat illa,
    dicit in aeternos aspera verba deos.
pone metum, Cerinthe; deus non laedit amantes.   15
    tu modo semper ama; salva puella tibi est.
at nunc tota tua est, te solum candida secum
    cogitat, et frustra credula turba sedet.
Phoebe, fave. laus magna tibi tribuetur in uno
    corpore servato restituisse duos.   20
nil opus est fletu; lacrimis erit aptius uti,
    si quando fuerit tristior illa tibi.
iam celeber, iam laetus eris, cum debita reddet
    certatim sanctis tutus uterque focis.
tunc te felicem dicet pia turba deorum,   25
    optabunt artes et sibi quisque tuas.

3.11
Qui mihi te, Cerinthe, dies dedit, hic mihi sanctus
    atque inter festos semper habendus erit.
te nascente novum Parcae cecinere puellis
    servitium et dederunt regna superba tibi.
uror ego ante alias. iuvat hoc, Cerinthe, quod uror,   5
    si tibi de nobis mutuus ignis adest.
mutuus adsit amor, per te dulcissima furta
    perque tuos oculos per Geniumque rogo.

mane Geni, cape tura libens votisque faveto,
   si modo, cum de me cogitat, ille calet. 10
quod si forte alios iam nunc suspirat amores,
   tunc precor infidos, sancte, relinque focos.
nec tu sis iniusta, Venus; vel serviat aeque
   vinctus uterque tibi vel mea vincla leva.
sed potius valida teneamur uterque catena, 15
   nulla queat posthac quam soluisse dies.
optat idem iuvenis quod nos, sed tectius optat;
   nam pudet haec illum dicere verba palam.
at tu, Natalis, quoniam deus omnia sentis,
   adnue: quid refert, clamne palamne roget? 20

3.12

Natalis Juno, sanctos cape turis acervos,
   quos tibi dat tenera docta puella manu.
lota tibi est hodie, tibi se laetissima compsit,
   staret ut ante tuos conspicienda focos.
illa quidem ornandi causas tibi, diva, relegat; 5
   est tamen, occulte cui placuisse velit.
at tu, sancta, fave neu quis divellat amantes,
   sed iuveni quaeso mutua vincla para.
sic bene compones: ullae non ille puellae
   servire aut cuiquam dignior illa viro. 10
nec possit cupidos vigilans deprendere custos
   fallendique vias mille ministret Amor.
adnue purpureaque veni perlucida palla:
   ter tibi fit libo, ter, dea casta, mero,
praecipit et natae mater studiosa quod optet: 15
   illa aliud tacita tam sua mente rogat.
uritur ut celeres urunt altaria flammae,
   nec, liceat quamvis, sana fuisse velit.
sis Juno, grata, ut veniet cum proximus annu
   hic idem votis iam vetus adsit amor. 20

3.13

Tandem venit amor, qualem texisse pudori
   quam nudasse alicui sit mihi fama magis.
exorata meis illum Cytherea Camenis
   attulit in nostrum deposuitque sinum.
exsolvit promissa Venus: mea gaudia narret, 5
   dicetur si quis non habuisse sua.
non ego signatis quicquam mandare tabellis,

ne legat id nemo quam meus ante, velim,
sed peccasse iuvat, vultus componere famae
    taedet: cum digno digna fuisse ferar.   10

3.14

Invisus natalis adest, qui rure molesto
    et sine Cerintho tristis agendus erit.
dulcius urbe quid est? an villa sit apta puellae
    atque Arretino frigidus amnis agro?
iam, nimum Messalla mei studiose, quiescas: 5
    non tempestivae saepe, propinque, viae.
hic animum sensuque meos abducta relinquo,
    arbitrio quam vis non sinit esse meo.

3.15

Scis iter ex animo sublatum triste puellae?
    natali Romae iam licet esse meo.
omnibus ille dies nobis natalis agatur,
    qui nec opinata nunc tibi sorte venit.

3.16

Gratum est, securus multum quod iam tibi de me
    permittis, subito ne male inepta cadam.
sit tibi cura togae potior pressumque quasillo
    scortum quam Servi filia Sulpicia:
solliciti sunt pro nobis, quibus illa doloris,   5
    ne cedam ignoto, maxima causa, toro.

3.17

Estne tibi, Cerinthe, tuae pia cura puellae,
    quod mea nunc vexat corpora fessa calor?
a ego non aliter tristes evincere morbos
    optarim, quam te si quoque velle putem.
at mihi quid prosit morbos evincere, si tu   5
    nostra potes lento pectore ferre mala?

3.18

Ne tibi sim, mea lux, aeque iam fervida cura
    ac videor paucos ante fuisse dies,
si quicquam tota commisi stulta iuventa
    cuius me fatear paenituisse magis,
hesterna quam te solum quod nocte reliqui,   5
    ardorem cupiens dissimulare meum.

TRANSLATIONS BY JUDITH P. HALLETT

3.8

Great god Mars, Sulpicia is arrayed for you on the Kalends, the first day of March, your month. If you have any discernment, come down from heaven to look at her yourself. Venus will pardon this: but you, god of brute force, beware that your weapons do not fall shamefully from your arms as you marvel at Sulpicia. From her eyes, when he wishes to set the gods on fire, fierce Love lights his twin torches. Whatever she does, wherever she wends her way, Attractiveness stealthily grooms her and follows behind her. If she loosens her hair, it is attractive for her to wear flowing tresses; if she arranges it, she must be revered with tresses arranged. She sets hearts aflame, if she has wished to go out in a Tyrian gown; she sets hearts aflame, if she comes out gleaming white in a snowy robe. In this way, on eternal Olympus, the bountiful god Vertumnus wears a thousand modes of dress, and wears a thousand attractively. She is unique among girls in being worthy to receive from Tyre soft wools twice dipped in expensive dyes. Let her possess whatever the wealthy Arab, who tills the scented crop, reaps from his nicely smelling fields, and whatever jewels the black Indian, close to the waters of Dawn, gathers from the red sea. Sing of her on these holiday Kalends, Pierian Muses, and Phoebus Apollo, proud with your tortoise-shell lyre. Let her welcome this traditional holy rite for many years; no girl is more worthy of your choir.

3.9

Spare my young man, boar, whether you control the fine pastures of the plain, or whether you frequent the remote places of the shady mountain, nor may it be your lot to have sharpened hard tusks for a struggle: let the guardian god Love keep him unharmed for me. But Diana, goddess of Delos, leads him far away with a passion for hunting. O, if only the woods would perish and the hunting dogs disappear! What madness is it, what a state of mind, to wish to wound delicate hands circling the closely packed hills with a hunting net. Or why is it pleasing to enter, stealthily, the lairs of savage beasts and mark white legs with barbed brambles? But nevertheless, so that I may be allowed to wander with you, Cerinthus, I myself will bear twisted nets through the mountains, I myself will seek the tracks of the swift stag and I will remove the iron chains from the quick-darting hound. Then, then would the forests please me, if, light of my life, I should be proven to have bedded down with you in the presence of the very hunting nets. Then, although the boar may come to the nets, he will depart uninjured, so that he may not disturb the pleasures of desiring passion. Now, without me, let there be no passion, but according to the law of Diana, chaste young man, touch the nets with chaste hand; and whatever woman stealthily creeps up upon my beloved, let her fall, to be torn to pieces, among fierce beasts. But you leave the desire for hunting to your parent, and quickly return yourself to my embrace.

3.10

Be present and banish the illness of the tender girl, be present, Phoebus Apollo, proud with your unshorn hair. Believe me, make haste: nor will it now cause you disgust, Phoebus, to have laid your healing hands on a lovely woman. See to it that wasting disease does not take hold of her limbs that grow pale, and that no hideous color deface her legs that are limp and weak, and whatever of evil there is and whatever gloomy thing we fear, a river with whirling waters drives into the sea. Holy one, come, and may you bring with you whatever fragrances and whatever charms relieve weary bodies; nor torment the young man, who fears that death is ordained for this girl, and makes vows for his mistress, too many to enumerate. Sometimes he vows, sometimes, because she is weak from illness, he says harsh words to the gods everlasting. Put aside your fear, Cerinthus, the god does not harm lovers. Only you love always: your girl is safe. But now she is yours entirely, the luminous girl thinks to herself of you alone, and a trusting throng sits at her side in vain. Phoebus Apollo, show your favor. Great praise will be granted you for having brought two back to health by saving one body. There is no need for weeping: it will be more fitting to use tears, if at any time she will be rather gloomy about you. Then you will be famous, then happy, when each lover, safe, will vie to give back what he owes you on the hallowed hearths. Then the devoted throng of the gods will say that you are fortunate, and each will also desire your healing arts for themselves.

3.11

Whatever day, Cerinthus, gave you to me, this day will have to be blessed by me and always celebrated among the holidays. When you were born, the Fates sang of a new form of love's slavery for women and gave you proud realms of power. But I am set on fire more than all other women. This thrills me, Cerinthus, that I am ablaze, if there is a shared fire in you that has spread from me. Let love that we share be on hand, I beg you, by our most delectable secret moments, by your eyes and by the spirit of your birthday. Birthday Spirit, stay, gladly receive offerings of incense and look favorably upon my vows, if only, when he thinks of me, he is heated with passion. But if by chance he already sighs for another love, then, I pray, holy one, abandon his faithless hearth. And may you not be unfair, Venus; either let each of us submit equally in bondage to love's slavery or remove my own bonds. But rather let us both be held in a powerful chain, which no day to come may be able to loosen. The young man wishes for the same thing that I do, but he wishes more secretly; for it causes him shame to utter these words openly. But you, Birthday Spirit, since—as a god—you feel all things, nod favorably: what does it matter if he seeks me secretly or openly?

3.12

Juno of birthdays, receive hallowed heaps of incense, which a learned girl gives to you with her tender hand. Today she is all yours, most joyously she has groomed herself for you, so that she might stand before your hearth to be gazed upon.

Indeed she credits her reasons for adorning herself to you, goddess; she is, however, the sort who wishes to have pleased secretly. You, hallowed goddess, show favor, so that no one may tear lovers apart. But prepare for the young man, I beseech you, chains that bind him in the same way. In this way you will match them well: to no girl is he, to no man is she, more worthy to be a slave of love. Nor let a watchful guard be able to catch them fulfilling their desires, and let the god Love furnish them with a thousand ways of deceiving. Nod favorably, and come, radiant in a purple robe: three times with a cake, three times with wine, chaste goddess, honor is paid you. Her attentive mother also teaches her what she should wish: she now asks for something different in her silent mind. She is set on fire as rapid flames set the altars on fire, nor although it may be possible, would she wish to have been of sound mind. May you, Juno, be pleased, so that when the next year will come, this same love, now old, may be present to their vows.

3.13

Love has finally come, of such sort that the rumor of having hidden it from anyone would cause me more shame than the rumor of having laid it bare. Won over by the poems that my Roman Muses inspired, Venus of Cythera brought him to me and dropped him in my embrace. Venus has fulfilled her promises: let anyone tell of my joys if they will be said to have been without joys of their own. Nor would I wish to entrust anything to sealed tablets: may no one get to read what I feel before the man that I love. But I delight in having misbehaved: it wearies me to wear a false expression for the sake of rumor. May I be said to be a woman worthy of having made love with a worthy man.

3.14

My hateful birthday is here, which must be celebrated as a gloomy occasion, in the troublesome countryside and without Cerinthus. What is more delightful than the city? Or is a country place—and the chilly river in the field of Arretium—suitable for a girl? Now, Messalla, excessively attentive to me, would you calm down. Often journeys are at the wrong time, kinsman. Although I have been led away, I leave behind my heart and my emotions, although he does not allow me to exercise my own judgment.

3.15

Do you know that the gloomy journey has been lifted, like a weight, from the girl's heart? Now I have permission to be at Rome on my birthday. Let that birthday be celebrated by all of us, which has now come to you by a chance you never thought would happen.

3.16

I am thankful that you, free from any care about me, are now so indulgent to yourself, in order that I, clumsy as I am, may protect myself from suddenly taking a bad fall. May your caring for a woman shamefully clad in a whore's toga and a partner-for-hire loaded with a wool-basket be stronger than Sulpicia, daughter of Servius. Still, men are anxious about me, to whom it is the greatest cause of sorrow that I may yield my position in your bed to a total nobody.

3.17

Cerinthus, do you possess devoted concern for your girl, seeing that now feverish heat attacks my exhausted body? Alas, I would not have wished to overcome gloomy illnesses if I did not think you wanted me to as well. But what is the benefit to me of conquering illnesses if you are able to endure my misfortunes with an unresponsive heart?

3.18

Light of my life, may I not now be to you as passionate a care as I seem to have been a few days earlier. Let your care for me subside if I, stupidly, have done anything in my entire youth of which I would admit to have regretted more than having left you alone, yesterday night, desiring to hide my blazing passion.

BIBLIOGRAPHY

Cadoux, T. J., and Robin J. Seager. "Julia" (3). In *The Oxford Classical Dictionary*, edited by Simon Hornblower and Antony Spawforth. Oxford: Oxford University Press, 1996.

Glare, P. G. W., ed. *The Oxford Latin Dictionary*. Oxford: Oxford University Press, 1982.

Holzberg, Niklas. "Four Poets and a Poetess or Portrait of a Poet as a Young Man?: Thoughts on Book 3 of the *Corpus Tibullianum*." *Classical Journal* 94.2 (1999: 169–91).

Keith, Alison. "*Tandem Venit Amor*: A Roman Woman Speaks of Love." In *Roman Sexualities*, edited by Judith P. Hallett and Marilyn B. Skinner. Princeton: Princeton, N.J. University Press, 1998.

Liddell, H. G., and R. Scott. *A Greek-English Lexicon*, 9th ed. Oxford: Oxford University Press, 1940.

Lyne, R. O. A. M. "Tibullus." In *The Oxford Classical Dictionary*, edited by Simon Hornblower and Antony Spawforth. Oxford: Oxford University Press, 1996.

Pelling, Christopher. "Valerius Messalla Corvinus, Marcus." In *The Oxford Classical Dictionary*, edited by Simon Hornblower and Antony Spawforth. Oxford: Oxford University Press, 1996.

Roessel, David. "The Significance of the Name *Cerinthus* in the Poems of Sulpicia." *Transactions and Proceedings of the American Philological Association* 120 (1990: 243–50).

Smith, Kirby Flower. *The Elegies of Albius Tibullus*. Darmstadt: Wissenschaftliche Buchgesellschaft, 1964.

Syme, Sir Ronald. "A Great Orator Mislaid." *Classical Quarterly* 31.2 (1981).

Wiseman, T. P. "Sirmio, Sir Ronald and the *Gens Valeria*." *Classical Journal* 88.3 (1993: 223–29).

Women's Graffiti from Pompeii

Elizabeth Woeckner

In view of the paucity of women's writing in Latin that survives from the classical period, I am particularly excited to be able to contribute the following graffiti recovered during the nineteenth-century excavation of Pompeii. As most people know, Pompeii and several neighboring towns in the Campanian countryside were destroyed by an eruption of Mt. Vesuvius in 79 C.E.[1] Today Pompeii is one of the most important resources for the study of Roman history and archaeology, not least because its walls were literally covered with writing of all kinds: from formal dedicatory inscriptions and election notices to graffiti, the subject of this discussion. Here I focus on two examples published in the *Corpus Inscriptionum Latinarum*, volume 4.[2]

Surprisingly, given recent interest in women in antiquity, to date there has been no systematic effort to identify women's graffiti from Pompeii.[3] As part of a larger project I have collected about a dozen graffiti that were almost certainly written by women, and, by and large, nearly all of them relate to the sex industry. Some are advertisements that list prices, services, and locations where available women would have been found.[4] In others, women who were presumably prostitutes salute the sexual prowess of their customers.[5] The problem is to differentiate between actual, if rather earthy, advertisements and insults. If we stop to recall the graffiti in modern bathrooms, it immediately becomes evident that not every notice is a bona fide offer of sexual activity. This effort is further complicated by our ignorance of the organization of the trade: did the prostitutes themselves create the advertisements or did the pimps?

CIL 4.8873: *TIBICINA*

CIL 4.8873, written as I shall argue by a *tibicina*,[6] the Roman female who played the *tibiae*, the double-pipe reed instrument,[7] has received scant scholarly attention since its publication by Della Corte in 1927.[8] It was found near 3.5 (no doorway number could be ascertained), an area located on the northwestern edge of the city between the Porta di Nola and the Porta Urbulana that has yet to be fully excavated. This graffito was scratched on a red column that was part of a balcony or garret on the second floor of the building. At the time of its discovery in 1918, the entire second storey had collapsed onto the via Dell'Abbondanza, the busiest street in Pompeii. The graffito itself does not survive. To the right of the text was a drawing of a quadruped with a long neck, possibly the *camelopardus* mentioned in line 3.

As can be seen from the emendations, any discussion of the metrical scheme is tendentious at best because of the difficulties associated with restoration.[9] Although the unsteady cursive writing includes numerous spelling errors, the minute letters are relatively similar in size.[10] Even if we cannot be certain about genre or form, we can recover the basic structure of sense. The *tibicina* (line 2) is the only possible subject for the first person constructions in lines 2 and 4. She scorns the opponent to whom she has lost a contest (line 1), notes the multiple talents of Apollo, and claims her status as a *tibicina* (line 2). In line 3 she questions the talent of her rival and ends with an expression of fury, calling upon the wrath of the god Volcanus. The translation is more or less straightforward with the exception of *pantorgana* (line 1).

Pantorgana is a neologism, occurring only in this inscription, and almost certainly a compound of the Greek *pan* and *to organon*. In this context *to organon* means "musical instrument" and indeed the phrase *ta panta organa*, meaning "many musical instruments" is found numerous times in Greek.[11] I offer by way of Latin parallel *topanta*, a neologism from the Greek *to panta*, found in the *Satyricon* of Petronius, meaning "the one and only."[12] So, too, *babaecalus*, meaning "yes-man," from the Greek *babai kalos*.[13]

Just as the Greek *pankration*[14] required multiple athletic skills, the *pantorgana* may have required its participants to demonstrate the ability to sing and play several musical instruments, or it may have been a musical contest that allowed a performer to bring in any musical instruments. Since this graffito came from the second storey of the building, by definition a private space,[15] it is possible that the *pantorgana* was a domestic musical competition that may have provided an evening's entertainment. Indeed, the *cenaculum* (dining room) was often located on the second storey over either a workshop or a business.

A bit of background about musical contests is appropriate at this point. Greek musical competitions can be traced back as far as the seventh century B.C.E., when citharodes, musicians who sang and accompanied themselves on the cithara, competed at the Pythian festival at Delphi and the Karneia in Sparta. The Panathenaea at Athens featured competitions for citharodes and *auletes*, the male musicians who played the *auloi*, the Greek version of the *tibiae*. The Romans were quick to adopt Greek musical competitions, but, as ever, they put their own unique spin on them.[16] In fact, the Roman ruling establishment seems to have had unusual ideas about musical competition; Polybius gives us a revealing picture in his description of the triumphal games of Lucius Anicius in 166 B.C.E.[17] Anicius had imported four professional Greek *auletes* to perform and, being dissatisfied with their efforts, ordered his lictors to compel the performers to fight amongst themselves using their flutes as weapons. The Roman audience applauded the mêlée that followed as the performance degenerated into a tumultuous battle between the musicians. Later competitions were probably more sophisticated. In imperial times musical competitions took place at the Juvenalia, Neronia, and the Capitoline games.[18]

The *tibicina* and her Greek counterpart, the *auletris*, were low-status females in the employ of higher-status males. We have come to know them through stereo-typed characterizations created by men. These entertainers are closely associated with the symposiastic traditions both at Rome and in Greece.[19] Popular tradition tells us that her duties were twofold; she provided musical entertainment and offered her sexual services to the male guests. She was often a slave or a concu-bine; in several places she is referred to as a prostitute.[20] The *tibicina* was associ-ated with the pleasures of the wine-shop and she was often portrayed as inebriated and inclined to drink any alcohol not under lock and key.[21]

Great importance was attached to her physical appearance. In the *Aulularia* of Plautus we find a fat *tibicina* rejected by a potential employer and several oth-ers praised for their physical charms.[22] Most telling is the comment of a soldier in the *Poenulus*, who, in refusing a *tibicina*, says: "I don't care for the *tibicina*, you wouldn't know which of the two were bigger, her cheeks or her breasts" (1415). While this may be a blunt description of aged, sagging breasts and jowls, the ref-erence to her enlarged cheeks emphasized the fact that she was considered unat-tractive when she puffed out her cheeks to blow air through her instrument. In fact, so much effort was required that some performers wore a halterlike device called the *phorbeia,* which helped to support their lips and cheeks while they played.[23] We learn from Cicero that the *tibicina* had the power not only to arouse young men to such an extent that they pursued (sexually) virtuous women, but also to soothe men by playing a slow and stately melody on her instrument.[24]

This graffito is particularly important because it gives us a rare first-person statement by a female performer. The *tibicina* should not be confused with her male counterpart, the *tibicen*. As far as I can determine, their roles were com-pletely different. The *tibicen*, in addition to playing at funerals, games, and plays, had the important duty of playing during a sacrifice.[25] So important was the music of the *tibicen* that the entire ceremony became ritually flawed if he stopped play-ing.[26] Furthermore, while the *tibicen* was a member of a *collegium* or professional guild, the female *tibicina* was principally characterized as a drunken and promis-cuous party girl.[27] Moreover, because of her status as a performer, she could be prosecuted on a charge of *infamia*, the legal term for public disgrace.[28]

There are, however, several indications that not all *tibicinae* fit the stereotype. According to Ovid, both male and female *tibiae* players participated in the famous strike of 312 B.C.E., which took place in response to an edict limiting the number of *tibiae* players who could accompany funeral processions.[29] In the *Adelphoe* of Terence, we find that the *tibicina* is a necessary participant in the wedding ceremony. In another passage in this same work the *tibicina* is included in the bustle of preparations that precede the marriage ceremony.[30] Some caution is required in using these passages since Roman comedy closely imitated Greek New Comedy. Such imitation begs the question, How Roman was this ceremony? The answer is most likely that it was Roman enough not to surprise the audience. Her Greek counterpart, the *auletris*, may also transcend the stereotypical characterization. In the *Symposium* of Plato, we find the *auletris* providing musical entertainment for women[31] and from Athenaeus, almost six hundred years later, we learn that the *auletris* was the only female permitted to enter the town hall at Naucratis during a religious festival.[32] Indeed, at Roman religious rites that were restricted to women, a *tibicina* would have been necessary. The *tibicina* and the *auletris* share one further similarity: while they are both discussed in the most pejorative terms, they could command extraordinarily high fees for their services. In fact, the *auletris* became so expensive that the Athenians passed a law to limit her wages. As such it is the first example of wage fixing in antiquity.[33]

Clearly, the status of the *tibicina* was ambiguous. This should lead us to wonder just how a *tibicina* might respond to the stereotypical view of her occupation and status, and I suggest that this graffito gives us some answers. At the beginning of line 1, the *tibicina* indignantly says, in effect: "Themis prefers the company of the gods to that of mortals; she left the earth and there is no fairness left these days." The *tibicina* here evokes the mythological doublet of Themis, the personification of right, and her daughter Dike, the personification of justice.[34] According to the *Phaenomina* of Aratus, Dike left the earth at the end of the golden age because of mankind's degeneration.[35] This particular tradition is found in Latin literature as well, in the sixth *Satire* of Juvenal.[36] Yet in Catullus 68 and the first eclogue of the third-century poet Calpurnius Siculus, it is Themis who fled at the end of the golden age, suggesting that the myths of Themis and Dike had become fused to a certain extent.[37] It follows then, that the absence of Themis, that is, that she prefers the company of the gods, may be understood as a comment about unfairness on the earth.

The *tibicina* then angrily concedes the victory to her rival, Talus. I have suggested the restoration to the male name Talus for several reasons. First, the name is attested twice at Pompeii.[38] Moreover, Apollo, in line 2, and Achilles and the giraffe, the *camelopardus* in line 3, are all masculine gender. Indeed, this is the only instance of the masculine form *camelopardus* as opposed to *cameloparda* or the Greek form *camelopardalis* in all of Latin.[39] This last point is especially important, for if, as I will argue, she uses this animal to make an ironic statement about her rival, it is sensible that his sex be reflected in the animal to which he is compared.

In the second line she evokes the mythological tradition of the contest between Marsyas the *tibiae* player and Apollo the citharode in which the gods served as judges. In every version of this myth Apollo defeats Marsyas, in one case by singing as he played the cithara and in another case by turning the cithara upside down and playing.[40] Notice that these are things a *tibiae* player could never do.

In Apuleius's version there are somatic descriptions of the contestants. Marsyas is described as ugly, bestial, dirty, and monstrous and *arte tibicen*, "in skill, a *tibicen*." Apollo, on the other hand, is described as fair and handsome and *arte multiscius*, "in skill, multitalented."[41] In no version is there any attention paid to the actual musical talents of the performers. Indeed, the fact that the citharodes received the largest prizes and the lion's share of the audience's interest at the Panathenaea further demonstrates the strong cultural preference for the cithara over the *tibiae*.[42] This cultural preference stems in part from the versatility that the cithara affords its players, especially the opportunity to sing while playing.

Line 2 offers a striking contrast between the divine male citharode and the mortal female *tibicina*. On one side we have the versatile and respected male citharode who is associated with the civilized and stately music of the paean; he is contrasted with the relatively limited female *tibiae* player who is associated with the wild and barbaric music of the Dionysiac revel.[43] Furthermore, the *tibicina* is judged on the basis of appearance—ironic since she plays an instrument that makes her look unattractive. Indeed, in one variant of the myth of Marsyas, Minerva throws the *tibiae* away and flees in embarrassment when she perceived that she was *foeda visu*, "horrible to look upon," as she puffed out her cheeks to blow the instrument.[44] It would seem that there was no attention paid to the respective talents of the musicians in either the mythical contests or possibly in the one in which the Pompeian *tibicina* competed. Rather, we see the cultural preference for the cithara over the *tibiae*.

I suggest that line 3 is an ironic comment about the *tibicina*'s rival. The heart of Achilles is easily understood as a reference to bravery. The story of the *Iliad* was widely known, and references to the bravery of Achilles occur throughout Latin literature.[45] *Claritas* ought to be understood to mean "distinctiveness." There are ample parallels for this usage; in fact, Pliny the Elder uses the word in precisely this way at the beginning of his discussions on the distinguishing characteristics of plants and, subsequently, of animals.[46]

The distinguishing characteristic of the giraffe, its *claritas*, is obviously its unusual appearance. This animal is encountered infrequently in Latin literature and is most often connected either with the *spectacula* or parades in honor of Roman emperors.[47] When the giraffe was introduced into the arena, the Romans quickly discovered that its appearance was more remarkable than its ferocity. Consequently it became known as the "wild sheep."[48] So the giraffe is not brave because of its *claritas*, its distinctive appearance. In fact, it is quite the opposite of what it appeared to be at first glance. So, too, I would argue, was the Pompeian *tibicina*'s loss in the *pantorgana*. She seems to suggest to us, by her use of the giraffe as a metaphor for deceptive appearance, that she lost not for lack of talent, but rather because she played an instrument and occupied a role to which Roman society attached little value.

In line 4 the *tibicina* expresses her anger, presumably at the outcome of the contest her rival has won. Her use of the word *medicina* is highly ironic and in this context ought to be understood to mean "cure." Indeed, *medicina* is construed as a remedy for agitated emotions in Vergil, Ovid, and Propertius.[49] Seeking a cure for her anger, she would appear to suggest that the most appropriate remedy is the fire of Volcanus. Volcanus was of course the Roman god of destructive fire, and as such he was worshipped and propitiated so that he would keep his destructive fire away from Rome.[50] Volcanus is further associated with death in a very interesting way, namely, by human sacrifice. The Romans sacrificed live fish to him at the Volcanalia. And, in fact, Varro makes it clear that it was thought the fish were a substitute for human beings, writing that "the people sent animals into the fire *pro se*, instead of themselves."[51] Not surprisingly, Volcanus functions as a metonym for volcanoes.

The final line of this graffito raises several questions. Was the *tibicina* so disgusted at the outcome of the contest that she wished to burn her instrument in anger and despair? Or did she call upon the destructive power of Mt. Vesuvius, as personified by Volcanus? The latter is not far-fetched, especially in a graffito from Pompeii, situated as it was below the rumbling mountain. This interpretation begs the question of whether the intended target of the wrath of Volcanus was her rival or the society that created the contest, or whether the *tibicina* considered suicide. In any case, she got her wish in 79 C.E.

I suggest that we understand this graffito as the response of the *tibicina* to the culture that devalued her and, in a very literal sense, defeated her. She responded to her defeat during what was presumably an evening's entertainment with the only weapon at hand, namely, the writing of this graffito. Probably of humble or servile origin, certainly semiliterate, nevertheless she seems to demonstrate some understanding of mythology and sufficient cultural awareness to make use of an animal from the *spectacula* in a sophisticated and humorous way. These four lines, shot through with bitterness and irony, offer invaluable insight into the status of the *tibicina*. In her, a woman who plays an instrument to which the culture accords low status, we see the clash of gender, sexuality, and the cultural preference for the citharode. The *tibicina* recognized the conflicts inherent in her profession and she expressed her anger at them in writing.

CIL 4.1679: THE BAR GIRL

This graffito was scratched on the south wall of the interior of the doorway to the *caupona* (a shop that served food and drink and possibly provided lodgings) located at 7.2.45, which was itself part of the larger Casa dell'Orso Ferito, located at 7.2.44. This large house was situated on the corner of the via Stabia and the via degli Augustali, a comparatively small street running parallel to the busy via del' Abbondanza. The *caupona* was located across the street from the *lupanar* or brothel.

This graffito has been subject to several different restorations. Its numerous orthographic errors combined with the inconsistent cursive writing make it nearly impossible to provide a metrical reconstruction.[52] We are on firmer ground for sense however. In lines 1–3 the bar girl Hedone salutes Castrensis, most probably a member of a popular pantomime troupe.[53] In lines 4–6 Hedone salutes both herself and those who will read the graffito. The prices of various kinds of wine available at the *caupona* are given in lines 7–13, and line 13 ends with another salute to Castrensis.

As indicated in the textual commentary, there is disagreement about whether this is one graffito or several. Admittedly there is a gap of 2.165 inches between lines 6 and 7 and a slightly larger one of 2.559 inches following *bib‹es›* in line 13. Such gaps need not force us to treat parts rather than the whole. In fact, this graffito, read in its entirety, demonstrates its own internal logic. The salutation of Castrensis begins and ends the graffito, linking the first line with the last. The second and third salutations of Castrensis (lines 3 and 13, respectively) demonstrate his importance to the author. References to Hedone in line 5 and line 7 provide a logical linkage between lines 1–6 and 7–13. The salutation *calos*, applied to both Hedone and Castrensis, also links lines 1–6 with line 13. It should also be noted that, with the possible exception of line 13, each section of the graffito seems to be written by the same hand.[54]

Since a good part of this graffito is a price list, it is reasonable to assume that Hedone worked at or owned the *caupona* in which the graffito was discovered. The Roman bar girl, like the *tibicina*, could be prosecuted on a charge of *infamia* because of the low repute of her occupation.[55] Literary sources lead us to believe that the bar girl was often available for sex. One of the most interesting examples of this tradition is the *Copa*, in the *Appendix Vergiliana*. This rather florid work of dubious authorship gives us a charming picture replete with the stereotypes associated with the bar girl: she is foreign, trained to dance and the play the castanets, drunken, and lustful.[56] The 38 lines of the *Copa* include five references to wine, two direct references to sex with the bar girl, one reference each to Amor, Bromius, and Priapus, and an overarching theme of living for immediate sensual pleasure. In this graffito Hedone's name, a transliteration of the Greek noun meaning "pleasure," emphasizes the connection between the bar girl and easy virtue.[57]

Graffiti such as *CIL* 4.8442 ("I screwed the bar girl") strengthens the connection between sexuality and this occupation. An even stronger piece of evidence that supports this stereotypical linkage is a document from Aesernia that lists the expenses of a guest at an inn: the bill reflects charges of three *asses* for bread, wine, and radishes and a charge of eight *asses* for sex with a bar girl.[58]

There is no evidence either in the graffito or in the *caupona* proper that Hedone acted as anything more than a wine server and hostess.[59] While this would seem to go against the traditional stereotype of the activities of the bar girl, we do have some evidence that not all bar girls were prostitutes. For instance, in *CIL* 14. 3709, a female innkeeper is described by her husband as a "chaste wife."

The *tibicina* and the bar girl show an interesting parallel. Recall that, according to Cicero, the *tibicina* was capable of inspiring men to a violent sexual frenzy with the music of her instrument. Apuleius tells the story of a middle-aged barmaid who not only seduced a man who stopped in her establishment, but caused him and many others to fall violently in love with her. Apuleius credits her with, among other things, the power to turn men into animals.[60] This tradition may show something of the unease that men must have felt about women who in some way, especially by virtue of their participation in activities that society at once condemned and took pleasure in, contravened the norms of female behavior. Paradoxically, the *tibicina* and the bar girl are simultaneously deprecated and invested with a mysterious, and potentially fearsome, power over males.

The fervor that surrounded theatrical performers and thus, by extension, Castrensis is crucial to an understanding of this graffito. As mentioned above, Castrensis was most probably a member of a popular pantomime troupe that performed at Pompeii and Herculaneum. Based on the evidence in other graffiti, it appears that Actius Anicetus was *dominus scaenicorum*, or the leader of a troupe that included Castrensis, Chloe, Mysticus, Echio, Iuvenis, Horus, Antica, and possibly Crestus. Actius Anicetus and members of his troupe are attested at both Pompeii and Herculaneum, and the graffiti in which they are named are clustered together in Pompeii. It is this clustering that argues most forcefully for the composition of the troupe.

I suggest that Hedone's salutation of Castrensis is an indication of the enthusiasm with which the Romans in general and the Pompeians in particular embraced their popular entertainers. In fact, Pompeii achieved quite a name for itself, and the notice of the Senate, when tensions between rival groups of theatrical fans led to a riot in 59 C.E. The subsequent ban on performances was entirely reasonable given the lawless disorder and loss of life.[61] Two groups of theatrical fans, calling themselves the *Paridiani* and the *Anicetiani*, identifying themselves with substantival adjectives derived from the name of the performer they supported (*Paridiani* = the supporters of Paris), are attested at Pompeii. The fans of Paris are mentioned in a graffito in which the owner of a *caupona*, one Purpurio, asks that people support Gaius Cuspius Pansa for aedile.[62] It seems likely that this *caupona* was a meeting place for these fans. In fact, the fans are also attested in a cluster of four other inscriptions in which they are linked with Triaria, possibly a fan or the proprietor of an establishment used as a meeting place.[63]

Hedone herself is linked quite intimately with the entertainer Pylades in *CIL* 4.10233: "Hey, Hyginus, Hedone sucked off Pylades." Although this could simply reflect malice or jealousy, whatever the truth of this graffito, the association is fascinating. Pylades was one of the most famous pantomimists of the early empire and is said to have introduced the tragic dance at Rome in 22 B.C.E.[64] He is featured in the inscription at Pompeii of A. Clodius Flaccus, one of the quinquennial duoviri sometime before 3 B.C.E.[65] This inscription, *CIL* 10.1074d, tells us that A. Clodius Flaccus gave games and spectacles of all sorts, including recitations "with all the pantomimists and Pylades." Note that he alone of all the performers is mentioned by name, in hopes surely of capitalizing on his "box office draw." If this is indeed the same man, it is unclear whether he competed at Pompeii before his debut at Rome. Whether the Pylades associated with Hedone is the original famed performer or a later imitator (as was very common) is of less importance than the strong association it provides between Hedone and the theater.

In view of this, it seems that Hedone has chosen to represent herself as a fan of Castrensis for several reasons. Her use of the salutation *calos*, widely attested with theatrical performers, may be informative. It would appear that she sought to derive status from her enthusiastic support for a popular entertainer. Recall that she congratulates both herself and Castrensis with this salutation. Further, all the occurrences of this salutation have been found in the ambit of persons liable to charges of *infamia* based on their occupations (a potential problem for Hedone as well).[66] This may point to the existence of a loose band of people who shared similarly low social status and who may have banded together, both socially and geographically, for mutual support. Lastly, aside from the fact that Hedone was quite probably a genuine fan of Castrensis, I suggest that she hoped to gain attention and material profit by identifying herself with a popular entertainer. Such an identification would have been good for business especially if the *caupona* became known as a meeting place for the fans of Castrensis. In fine, then, we have a small, personal, and unique picture of a star-struck bar girl, consumed by her passion for the performer Castrensis, with one eye on pleasure and the other eye on business.[67]

What conclusions can be drawn from such slender, tendentious evidence? First and foremost, that women, even low-status, uneducated women, were sufficiently literate to participate in the tradition of writing on the walls. The immediacy of graffiti preserves for us the emotional reaction of the *tibicina* as she struggles to negotiate the complexities of gender and status. Hedone's somewhat more elliptical graffito shows us the adaptive strategy of a working woman who uses the Roman passion for theatrical performers to increase her business and possibly her social standing with her peers. What unites these graffiti are the women's unique responses to the social pressures they faced, and the value of the graffiti lies in the fact that these same immediate and unique first-person responses can arguably increase our understanding of women's lives in ancient Pompeii.

NOTES

All citations of Latin and Greek texts, unless otherwise noted, refer to the
Loeb Classical Library (Cambridge: Harvard University Press). I wish to
thank T. Corey Brennan, Edward Champlin, Elaine Fantham, and the
editors of this volume for the helpful insights that have greatly improved this
discussion.

1. Prior to its destruction Pompeii was a thriving community of roughly 20,000
   people with a vigorous economic base of trade, agriculture, and service to luxury
   villas in Campania. To be sure, its monumental public architecture, markets,
   fora, and splendid private homes were rightly a source of civic and personal
   pride in antiquity, but its greatest claim to fame is modern: the peculiar nature of
   volcanic destruction preserved it to an astonishing degree. For a good overview
   of Pompeii (with references for further reading), see *The Oxford Classical Dictionary* (New York: Oxford University Press, 1996), s.v. *"Pompeii,"* and John B.
   Ward-Perkins, and Amanda Claridge *Pompeii A.D. 79*, (New York: Knopf,
   1978).

2. *Corpus Inscriptionum Latinarum: Inscriptiones Parietariae Pompeianae, Hercu-
   lanenses, Stabianae*, vol. 4, ed. C. Zangemeister (Berlin: Georg Reimer, 1871);
   Supplementi Pars Posterior, ed. A. Mau and C. Zangemeister (Berlin: Georg
   Reimer, 1909); *Supplementi Pars Tertia*, ed. M. Della Corte (Berlin: Georg
   Reimer, 1952); *Voluminis Quarti Supplementi Pars Tertia*, ed. M. Della Corte
   (Berlin: Georg Reimer, 1970). The reader should also be acquainted with the
   Pompeian reference system. At the beginning of modern systematic archaeological study of the site in the nineteenth century, Pompeii was divided into nine
   regions, numbered 1–9. The blocks, or *insulae*, were numbered, and each doorway in an *insula* was assigned a number. Therefore, the location of a graffito consists of three numbers: 5.7.3, for example. Although many inscriptions or graffiti
   have perished or been moved to museums, this text would have been located
   originally in region 5, *insula* 7, doorway 3. For locations and orientation see
   H. Eschebach, *Die stadtebauliche Entwicklung des antiken Pompej* (Heidelberg:
   F. H. Kerle, 1970), the standard reference work used to determine the location and
   name of a building. Its map is exhaustive and comprehensive. For several useful
   maps of Pompeii, see also Ray Laurence, *Roman Pompeii: Space and Society*
   (London: Routledge, 1994).

3. Women writers from Pompeii have been studied piecemeal: women who were
   named as supporters in the *programmata*, the election advertisements, have been
   treated by L. Savunen, "Women and Elections in Pompeii," in *Women in Antiquity:
   New Assessments*, ed. R. Hawley and B. Levick (London: Routledge, 1995), pp.
   194–206. Savunen concludes that women did indeed have a role as producers of
   political posters and, thus, an involvement in the political life of the city. The public
   role of Pompeian women has been treated by F. S. Bernstein, *The Public Role of
   Pompeian Women*, diss. (University of Maryland, Ann Arbor: UMI Dissertation
   Information Service, 1989). A useful prosopography may be found in the appendix.

4. *CIL* 4.5372, 1751, 8356.

5. *CIL* 4.2260, 2253.
6. See P. G. W. Glare, ed., *Oxford Latin Dictionary* (Oxford: Clarendon Press, 1968–82), s.v. "*tibicina*," invariably a female.
7. The *auloi* were double pipes with finger holes and a double-reed mouthpiece. Most often the pipes were played two at a time, with one in each hand. The majority were cylindrical in shape and had two or more sections that fit together or were bound by metal. Made from reed, bone, ivory, wood, metal, or some combination of these materials, they ranged in size from 20–25 cm. to 49–57 cm. For further discussion, see M. L. West, *Ancient Greek Music* (Oxford: Clarendon Press, 1992), pp. 81–94 and passim.
8. Matteo Della Corte, *Notizie degli scavi di antichità* 5 (1927): 107. See also by Della Corte, *Case ed abitanti di Pompei*, 3d ed. (Naples: Faustino Fiorentino, 1965), p. 368.
9. If the emendations in the first line are sound and we have lost no more than one syllable (if *Tal*[*us*] is correct), the line may be an example of iambic septenarius. Line three may also conform to this pattern as well. Line two may be either anapestic dimeter or a combination of ionics and choriambs. The fourth line is iambic. All these metrical schemes are common in Roman drama, either in the spoken dialogues (the *diverbia*) or in the *canticae*, which presumably were sung. The main problem here is that iambic septenarius in very close to everyday speech; the combination of metrical errors and orthographical difficulties raise the possibility that this is prose rather than verse. See also James W. Halporn et al., *The Meters of Greek and Latin Poetry* (London: Methuen, 1963), pp. 59–90.
10. No measurements were given by Della Corte (1927), but the piece of plaster on which the graffito was scratched was easily contained in a pair of cupped hands for photographing.
11. See *Greek-English Lexicon*, ed. Henry George Liddell and Robert Scott, 10th ed. (Oxford: Clarendon Press, 1996), s.v. "*organon*."
12. See Petronius *Satyricon* 37.8–9: "Now without why or wherefore she has ascended sky-high, and she's Trimalchio's one and only" (translation mine). See also the discussion in L. R. Palmer, *The Latin Language* (Norman: University of Oklahoma Press, 1954), p. 152.
13. See Petronius *Satyricon* 37.22–23: "In short, he could throw anyone of those yes-men into a teacup" (translation mine; the Latin *in rutae folium*, "into a leaf of rue," is a proverbial and untranslatable expression for "a small place"). See, again, L. R. Palmer, p. 152.
14. See *The Oxford Classical Dictionary*, s.v. "*pankration*."
15. See A. Wallace-Hadrill, *Houses and Society in Pompeii and Herculaneum* (Princeton, N.J.: Princeton University Press, 1994), pp. 17–37.
16. Most of the Roman tradition bears the trace of Greek influence. Nor is this surprising since after the defeat of Corinth in 146 B.C.E. and during the Imperial period, numerous Greek musicians and artists came to Rome, now the undisputed power of the Mediterranean. See G. Comotti, *Music in Greek and Roman Culture*, trans. R. Munson (Baltimore: Johns Hopkins University Press, 1989), pp. 48–55.
17. Polybius *History* 30.22 ff.

18. For the *Neronia*, the tripartite contest of athletic, equestrian, and musical events, established by the emperor Nero in C.E. 60, see Tacitus *Annals* 14.20; Suetonius *Nero* 12.3. On the Capitoline games, established by Domitian (81–96 C.E.), see Suetonius *Domitian* 4.4 and Juvenal *Satires* 6.387.

19. See C. G. Starr, "An Evening with the Flute-Girls," *Parola del Passato* 33 (1978): 401–10. For more recent discussion, see James Davidson, *Courtesans and Fish-cakes: The Consuming Passions of Classical Athens* (New York: St. Martin's Press, 1998), pp. 78–97.

20. Characterized as slave: Plautus *Aulularia* 451; Plautus *Pseudolus* 482; *CIL* 6.33970, the epitaph of Fulvia, *tibicina* and slave of Gaius. Characterized as concubine: Plautus *Mostellaria* 975; Plautus *Stichus* 560. Characterized as prostitute: Plautus *Poenulus* 1415; Plautus *Pseudolus* 528.

21. The *tibicina* and the pleasures of the wineshop: Plautus *Aulularia* 557–58; Horace *Epodes* 1.14.24–26; (drunken) Pliny the Elder *Natural History*, 34.63.1–2.

22. Fat *tibicina* rejected: Plautus *Aulularia* 332; *tibicina* praised for physical attributes: Plautus *Stichus* 380.

23. See, again, M. L. West, p. 89.

24. Cicero *Fragments of Philosophical Works* 10.3.1.4.

25. The duties of the (male) *tibicen*: Ovid *Fasti* 6.653; Livy 9.30; Valerius Maximus 2.5.4; Plutarch *Roman Questions* 55; Varro *Latin Language* 6.17; Festus (W. M. Lindsay, 1913), pp. 134–35; Censorinus *De die natali* 12.2.

26. Cicero *De haruspicum responso* 23.

27. The existence of the *collegium tibicinum Romanorum* demonstrates the antiquity and the importance of the occupation (for males). See *The Oxford Classical Dictionary*, s.v. "*collegium*."

28. See W. W. Buckland, *A Text-Book of Roman Law* (Cambridge: Cambridge University Press, 1921), pp. 92–93.

29. Ovid *Fasti* 6.650 ff. See also J. Delande, "Une Grève à Rome, il y a 2300 ans" ["A strike in Rome, 2300 Years Ago"], *Les Études classiques* 25 (1957): 432–37.

30. The *tibicina* as necessary participant in wedding ceremony: Terence *Adelphoe* 905. The *tibicina* as part of wedding preparations: Terence *Adelphoe* 907.

31. Plato *Symposium* 176e. The point here is that she is capable of actual professional entertainment.

32. Athenaeus *Deipnosophistai* 4.156.

33. See C. G. Starr (1978). In Plautus *Mostellaria* 975, a *tibicina* is manumitted for 3000 drachmas, roughly equivalent to twenty-five percent of the value of a villa in the same play. Another *tibicina* is manumitted for 2000 drachmas in Plautus *Pseudolus*.

34. For Themis and her daughter Dike, see T. Gantz, *Early Greek Myth*, vol. 1 (Baltimore: Johns Hopkins University Press, 1993), pp. 50–52.

35. Aratus *Phaenomina* 1.113.

36. Juvenal *Satires* 6.19; Juvenal's Astraea is a Latin variant for the Greek Dike.

37. Catullus, 68.153; Themis as personification of justice; Calpurnius Siculus 1.44.

38. *CIL* 4.5070, 5072.

39. See *Thesaurus Linguae Latinae* (Leipzig: Teubner, 1990) 3.201.30.

40. Hyginus *Fabulae* 165 (cithara upside down); Diodorus Siculus, 3.59.2–5 (singing while playing); Apuleius *Florida* 3 and 4.

41. Apuleius *Florida* 3 and 4.
42. See M. L. West, p. 368.
43. See W. Burkert, *Greek Religion*, trans. J. Raffan (Cambridge, Mass.: Harvard University Press, 1985), p. 224.
44. Hyginus *Fabulae* 165.5.
45. See, for example, Cicero *Pro archia* 24.3; Ovid *Metamorphosis* 12.163 and 12.608; Aulus Gellius *Attic Nights* 2.11.2.1.
46. See *Oxford Latin Dictionary*, s.v. "*claritas* 5"; *Thesaurus Linguae Latinae* 3.1269.5; Pliny *Natural History* 24.188 (plants) and 28.87 (animals).
47. Horace *Epodes* 2.1.195; Dio Cassius 43.23 and 62.10.3 ff.
48. Pliny *Natural History* 8.27: "from this accordingly [from its cowardly performance in the arena] it was seen that the giraffe was more conspicuous for its appearance than its ferocity, so it got hold of the name wild sheep" (translation mine).
49. See *Oxford Latin Dictionary*, s.v. "*medicina* 6"; Vergil *Eclogues* 10.60; Ovid *Tristia* 4.10.117; Propertius 3.17.4.
50. See *CIL* 6.802 and G. Capdeville, *Volcanus* (Rome: Ecole française de Rome, 1995) for an exhaustive treatment.
51. Varro *Latin Language* 6.20.
52. Lines 1–7 appear to be prose; lines 8–13 (excluding the final salute to Castrensis) are dactylic, with an error at the end of line 11. See also N. Kampen, "The Women of Pompeii," in *Women in the Classical World,* ed. E. Fantham et al. (Oxford: Oxford University Press, 1994), p. 337.
53. See J. Franklin, Jr., "Pantomimists at Pompeii: Actius Anicetus and His Troop," *American Journal of Philology* 108 (1987): 95–107.
54. Line 13 may show evidence of a second hand or, more likely, the same hand scratching the letters from an awkward lower position.
55. Ulpian *Digesta* 23.2.43, 3.2.4.4, 23.2.43.9; *Codex Theodosianus* 4.6.3, 9.7.1, 15.13.1; *Codex Iustinianus* 5.5.7.
56. *Copa*, 1.3 ff.
57. The cognomen Hedone is widely attested outside Pompeii. See H. Solin, *Die griechischen Personennamen in Rom*, 3 vols. (Berlin: De Gruyter, 1982), pp. 1238–40. In Pompeii the name is found in *CIL* 4.10233.
58. *CIL* 9.2689.
59. This is unlike *CIL* 4.7863, 7873, 7862, and 7866, which mention three bar girls who were available for sex.
60. Apuleius *Metamorphosis* 1.7 ff; the story is also picked up by Augustine *De civitate dei* 18.18.
61. Tacitus *Annals* 14.17. Tacitus lays the blame for the riot on the "illegal organizations," that is, the organized and passionately devoted fans.
62. *CIL* 4.7919.
63. *CIL* 4.8885, 8888a, 8888b, 8888c. Further salutation to Castrensis and Actius Anicetus: *CIL* 4.2413d.
64. On Pylades and the pantomime, see L. Friedländer, *Roman Life and Manners under the Early Empire*, 4 vols., 7th ed., trans. J. H. Freese and L. A. Magnus (London: Routledge, 1908–13), vol. 2, pp. 100–117, and R. C. Beacham, *The*

Roman Theater and Its Audience (Cambridge, Mass.: Harvard University Press, 1992), pp. 141–45.

65. See J. Franklin, Jr., *Pompeii: The Electoral Programmata, Campaigns, and Politics, AD 71–79* (Rome: American Academy in Rome, 1980), p. 102.
66. See R. Laurence, p. 85, and, more generally, pp. 70–88.
67. The prices mentioned are almost certainly inaccurate. Either they are artificially high because of the cachet that the association with Castrensis generates, or, conversely, they are low in order to entice the fans of Castrensis and Actius Anicetus.

TWO EXAMPLES OF WOMEN'S GRAFFITI

Corpus Inscriptionum Latinarum 4.8873:[1] *Tibicina*

Themis amat deos.[2] Vinca‹t›,[3] vinca‹t› pantorgana Tal[us]|

2   Cyt‹h›ar‹o›edus cantat Apol‹l›o. Tibicina n‹e›mpe ego.|
     Came‹l›opa‹r›dus ‹h›abet cor ut Acille‹s› ob clarit[atem].|
4   Sum rabid‹a›.[4] I‹a›m Vulcanus ‹e›m medicina est.|

---

[1] I use the following signs in the Latin text: [] denotes letters that are illegible or lost but restored by conjecture. < > denotes omitted letters that the composer intended to be present (orthographical errors, for example).| denotes the line end on the stone. { } denotes letters that should be removed from the text (orthographical errors). By convention, a sublinear dot marks a letter not clearly legible. Most of this graffito is not clearly legible, so I've chosen to forego sublinear dots entirely in an effort to produce a less forbidding text. The punctuation is mine. For further discussion of Latin epigraphy, see Lawrence Keppie, *Understanding Roman Inscriptions* (Baltimore: Johns Hopkins University Press, 1991); A. E. Gordon, *Illustrated Introduction to Latin Epigraphy* (Berkeley: University of California Press, 1983); Matteo Della Corte, *Notizie degli scavi di antichità* 5 (1927): 107; and Ernst Diehl, *Pompeianische Wandinschriften und Verwandtes* (Berlin: W. De Gruyter, 1930), no. 832.

[2] I am grateful to Charles Crowther at the Center for the Study of Ancient Documents, Oxford University, who kindly sent me a scan of the one extant photograph of this graffito. Della Corte (1927) and Diehl (1930) print *Homnes nego deos*. The text is my own, based largely on computer-generated imaging.

[3] The emendation to the third-person singular, present active subjunctive seems safe to me. There are numerous examples in Pompeian graffiti in which the final *t* is omitted. On this see V. Väänänen, *Le Latin vulgaire des inscriptions pompeiennes*, 2d ed. (Helsinki: Finnish Academy of Sciences, 1937), p. 70.

[4] This restoration seems safe to me. It is certainly more probable to think that a single letter (*-a*) was omitted than the two letters of the masculine ending (*-us*). In view of the first-person feminine construction in line 2, it follows logically.

Corpus Inscriptionum Latinarum **4.1679[5]**: **The Bar Girl**

Invicte Castres‹n›si‹s›[6]t‹u›|
2 habeas propiteos|
deos tu ‹C›astres‹n›si‹s› t‹u›|
4 e‹m› et qui leges|

calos ‹H›edone|
6 valeat qui legerit|
‹H›edone dicit|
8 assibus hic|
bibitur dipundium[7]|
10 si dederis meliora|
bibes qua{n}‹t›tus[8]|
12 si dederis vina {f}|
faler‹n›a bib<es>calos{c} Castre<n>si<s>t<u>. . . I<invicte>[9]

TRANSLATIONS BY ELIZABETH WOECKNER

The Flute Player

Themis loves the gods. Let Talus win, let him win the musical contest.
2 Apollo the citharode sings. Surely I am a *tibicina*.[1]
The giraffe has a heart like Achilles on account of its distinctiveness.
4 I am furious. Behold now, Volcanus is the cure.

---

[5]We should note that there is disagreement over whether this is a single text. See the following: C. Zangmeister, *CIL* 4.1679; G. Fiorelli, *Giornale degli scavi di Pompei* (1865): 4, 5, 7; Diehl (1930), no. 34; J. Franklin, Jr., "Pantomimists at Pompeii: Actius Anicetus and His Troup," *American Journal of Philology* 108 (1987): 100; *Carmina Latina Epigraphica*, ed. F. Buecheler and E. Lommatzsch (Stuttgart: Teubner, 1982), no. 931, lines 7–13; Matteo Della Corte, *Case ed abitanti di Pompei*, 3d ed. (Naples: Faustino Florentino, 1965), no. 335; Natalie Kampen, "The Women of Pompeii," in *Women in the Classical World*, Elaine Fantham et al. (Oxford: Oxford University Press, 1994), p. 337 (translation only); E. Courtney, *Musa Lapidaria* (Atlanta: Scholars Press, 1995), no. 72.

[6]The cognomen Castrensis is widely attested in Pompeii.

[7]This is a variant spelling of *dupondius*, attested in the Imperial period. See *The Oxford Latin Dictionary*, ed. P. G. W. Glare (Oxford: Clarendon Press, 1968–82), s.v. "*dupondius*."

[8]*Quattus* appears to be a variant of the relatively rare *quatrussis*, meaning "the sum of four asses." See *The Oxford Latin Dictionary*, s.vv. "*quattus*" and "*quatrussis*." Since the lowest price is a single *as* (line 8) and the prices increase in lines 9–11, it is reasonable that Falernian wine, a notable luxury, should sell for the most (four *asses*).

[9]This line is badly garbled and I offer this restoration based on the preceding lines.

[1]I am unaware of any recent discussion of the *tibicina*. See C. Daremberg and E. Saglio, *Dictionnaire des antiquités Grecques et Romaines* (Paris: Hachette, 1881–1919), s.v. "*tibia*."

The Bar Girl

    Undefeated Castrensis, you,
2   may you have the gods propitious, you Castrensis.
    Hey, also you who shall read this;

4/6 Way to go,[2] Hedone
    and may he prosper who has read this, says Hedone.
6/8 A person can drink
    here for an *as*; if you
10   give two *asses*, you
    will drink better wine;
12   if you give four *asses*,
    you will drink Falernian wine. Way to go, Castrensis, you
    undefeated . . .

BIBLIOGRAPHY

Primary Sources

Buecheler, F., and E. Lommatzsch, eds. *Carmina Latina Epigraphica*. 3 vols. Leipzig: 1895–1926.

Corpus Inscriptionum Latinarum: Inscriptiones Parietariae Pompeianae, Herculanenses, Stabianae, vol. 4, edited by C. Zangemeister (Berlin: Georg Reimer, 1871); *Supplementi Pars Posterior*, edited by A. Mau and C. Zangemeister (Berlin: Georg Reimer, 1909); *Supplementi Pars Tertia*, edited by M. Della Corte (Berlin: Georg Reimer, 1952); *Voluminis Quarti; Supplementi Pars Tertia*, edited by M. Della Corte (Berlin: Georg Reimer, 1970).

Della Corte, M. *Notizie degli scavi di antichità* 5 (1927): 107.

Courtney, E. *Musa Lapidaria: A Selection of Latin Verse Inscriptions*. Atlanta: Scholars Press, 1995.

Diehl, E. *Pompeianische Wandinschriften und Verwandtes*. Berlin: W. De Gruyter, 1930.

Fiorelli, G. *Giornale degli scavi di Pompei* (1865): 4, 5, 7.

Sogliano, A. *Notizie degli scavi di antichità* (1888): 519 n. 28.

Varone, A. *Erotica Pompeiana*. Rome: L'Erma di Bretschneider, 1994.

---

[2]I have translated *calos* as a salutation. There are two possibilities here: an adjective or a salutation. The word is clearly from the Greek adjective καλὸς or the adverbial form of the same, καλῶς. See *The Oxford Latin Dictionary*, s.v. "*calos*," which gives the adverbial salutation. It would be difficult to construe this as an adjective, as do Franklin (1987) and Kampen (1994), since there is no change of inflection between *Hedone* (feminine, line 4) and *Castrensis* (masculine, line 13). Even the most illiterate Greek would not fail to inflect this adjective properly. More to the point, *calos* is attested on the walls of Pompeii in graffiti that salute both male entertainers (*CIL* 4.652, 1256, 1294, 2150, 2179, 2180, 2253) and females (*CIL* 4.1283, 1309).

Secondary Works

Beacham, R. C. *The Roman Theater and Its Audience*. Cambridge, Mass: Harvard University Press, 1992.

Bernstein, F. S. *The Public Role of Pompeian Women*. Ph. D. diss., University of Maryland, 1989. Ann Arbor: UMI Dissertation Information Service.

Brennan, T. C. "The Poets Julia Balbilla and Damo at the Colossus of Memnon." *Classical World* 91 (1998): 215–34.

Buckland, W. W. *A Text-Book of Roman Law*. Cambridge: Cambridge University Press, 1921.

Burkert, W. *Greek Religion*. Translated by J. Raffan. Cambridge: Harvard University Press, 1985.

Capdeville, Gérard. *Volcanus: recherches comparatistes sur les origines du culte de Vulcain*. Rome: Ecole française de Rome, 1995.

Comotti, G. *Music in Greek and Roman Culture*. Translated by R. Munson. Baltimore: Johns Hopkins University Press, 1989.

Copley, F. O. "A Paraclausithyron from Pompeii: A Study of *CIL* IV Suppl. 5296." *American Journal of Philology* 60 (1939): 333–49.

Daremberg, C., and E. Saglio. *Dictionnaire des antiquités Grecques et Romaines*. Paris: Hachette, 1881–1919.

Davidson, J. *Courtesans and Fishcakes: The Consuming Passions of Classical Athens*. New York: St. Martin's, 1998.

Delande, J. "Une Grève à Rome, il y a 2300 ans" ["A Strike in Rome, 2300 Years Ago"]. *Les Études classiques* 25 (1957): 432–37.

Della Corte, M. *Loves and Lovers in Ancient Pompeii: A Pompeian Erotic Anthology*. Translated by A. W. Van Buren. Rome: Cava dei Tirreni, 1960.

———. *Case ed abitanti di Pompeii*, 3d ed. Naples: Faustino Fiorentino, 1965.

Eschebach, H. *Die stadtebauliche Entwicklung des antiken Pompeij*. Heidelberg: F. H. Kevle, 1970.

Fantham, E., et al., eds. *Women in the Classical World*. Oxford: Oxford University Press, 1994.

Franklin, J., Jr. "Pantomimists at Pompeii: Actius Anicetus and His Troupe." *American Journal of Philology* 108 (1987): 95–107.

———. *Pompeii: The Electoral Programmata, Campaigns and Politics, AD 71–79*. Rome: American Academy in Rome, 1980.

Friedländer, L. *Roman Life and Manners under the Early Empire*. 4 vols. 7th ed. Translated by J. H. Freese and L. A. Magnus. London: Routledge, 1908–13.

Gantz, T. *Early Greek Myth*. vol. 1. Baltimore: Johns Hopkins University Press, 1993.

Gordon, A. E. *Illustrated Introduction to Latin Epigraphy*. Berkeley: University of California Press, 1983.

Halporn, James W., et al. *The Meters of Greek and Latin Poetry*. London: Methuen, 1963.

Hawley, R., and B. Levick, eds. *Women in Antiquity: New Assessments*. London: Routledge, 1995.

Keppie, L. *Understanding Roman Inscriptions*. Baltimore: Johns Hopkins University Press, 1991.

Laurence, R. *Roman Pompeii: Space and Society*. London: Routledge, 1994.

Lowe, N. J. "Sulpicia's Syntax." *Classical Quarterly* 38 (1988): 193–205.

Palmer, L. R. *The Latin Language*. Norman: University of Oklahoma Press, 1954.

Raepsaet-Charlier, M.-Th. *Prosopographie des femmes de l'ordre sénatorial*. Lovanni: Aedibus Peeters, 1987.

Santirocco, M. S. "Sulpicia Reconsidered." *Classical Journal* 74 (1979): 229–39.

Solin, H. *Die Griechischen Personennamen in Rom*. 3 vols. Berlin: De Gruyter, 1982.

Starr, C. G. "An Evening with the Flute-Girls." *Parola del Passato* 33 (1978): 401–10.

Väänänen, V. *Le Latin vulgaire des inscriptions pompeiennes*. 2d ed. Helsinki: Finnish Academy of Sciences, 1937.

Wallace-Hadrill, A. *Houses and Society in Pompeii and Herculaneum*. Princeton, N.J.: Princeton University Press, 1994.

Ward-Perkins, John B., and Amanda Claridge. *Pompeii A.D. 79*. New York: Knopf, 1978.

West, M. L. *Ancient Greek Music*. Oxford: Clarendon Press, 1992.

The Fragment of Martial's Sulpicia

Judith P. Hallett

The Latin poet Marcus Valerius Martialis, whom English speakers generally refer to by the nickname Martial, came to Rome from the province of Spain in approximately 64 C.E. He attained literary prominence by winning the favor and patronage of the emperor Domitian, who reigned from 81 through 96 C.E. Martial has left us fourteen books of epigrams: short and witty poems in elegiac, hendecasyllabic, and other meters, often cynical in tone and risqué in topic. Many of his epigrams address or portray women with whom he was personally acquainted and call them by their actual names.[1]

In one such epigram, 7.69, Martial praises the fiancée of a fellow Spaniard and poet for writing poetry herself. He credits this woman, who has the Greek name Theophila, with employing an "Athenian" voice that would please the major Athenian philosophers. Characterizing her poetry as "not like a woman's poetry nor aimed at popular tastes," he even compares Theophila favorably to the sixth-century B.C.E. Greek poet Sappho. After asserting that "Sappho—a woman of erotic inclinations—used to praise someone composing poetry," he proceeds to judge Theophila more virtuous than Sappho, and to state that Sappho was not more learned (*doctior*) than Theophila. Nevertheless, as is so often the case with the Roman female poets mentioned by Roman male authors, none of this woman's poetry survives.

But a notable exception occurs with a woman Martial describes in two other epigrams, 10.35 and 10.38. The first praises her poetry:

Let all girls read Sulpicia who desire to please only one man;
let all husbands read Sulpicia who desire to please only one bride.
She does not claim as her subject the frenzy of Medea,

nor does she relate the banquets of dreadful Thyestes.
Nor does she believe that Scylla and Byblis have existed.
But she teaches virtuous and respectable passions, playful
erotic encounters, sensual pleasures, and witty remarks.
Anyone who has judged her poems fairly will say that no woman is
naughtier, that no woman is more honorable. Such, I believe,
were the playful jests of Egeria, under the dripping cave with Numa.
With Sulpicia as your fellow student, or with her as your teacher.
you, Sappho, would be more learned, and sexually well behaved;
but as soon as he had seen her alongside of you, hard-hearted Phaon
would have loved Sulpicia. And to no avail; for she would live
neither as the wife of Jupiter the Thunderer nor as the beloved
of Bacchus and Apollo, if Calenus were taken from her.

The second addresses Calenus, identifying him as Sulpicia's husband, and con-
soles him on her death, which has been dated to between 94 and 98 C.E.[2]

O the fifteen years of marriage with your Sulpicia, pleasurable
to you, Calenus, which the god has generously allowed and
accomplished! O every night and every hour, marked by the
precious pebbles of India's shore! O what battles, what struggles
on both sides the happy little bed and lantern did witness,
drunk with clouds of Nicerotian scent! You [have] lived,
Calenus, five years times three: this is the entire
accounting of your life and you count only your days as
a husband. If the fate Atropos were to give you back even one,
long-requested, day, you would prefer it to four times the old
age of Nestor.

Later Latin authors also refer to the poetry of this Sulpicia, who is obviously
a different Sulpicia from the Augustan elegist anthologized in the third book of
Tibullus. Two of these authors—the fifth-century C.E. writers Sidonius Apollinaris, at *Ad felicem* 9.261, and Fulgentius *Mythologiae* 1. pp. 4, 12–13—represent
this poetry as sexually playful. Sidonius speaks of it as *iocus*, "jest"; Fulgentius as
procacitas, "erotically charged self-assertiveness." On p. 218 of his *Cento nuptialis*, however, the fourth-century C.E. Ausonius is less complimentary, characterizing Sulpicia's writing as coarse and offensively bawdy. For he claims *prurire
opusculum Sulpiciae, frontem caperare*, "Sulpicia's petite effort itches with lust,
her brow wrinkles as a goat's."[3]

It merits emphasis that at some point in the late fourth or early fifth century
C.E., shortly before Sidonius and Fulgentius began writing, someone even composed a verse satire, the *Sulpiciae conquestio*, in seventy hexameter lines under

this Sulpicia's name. These two authors may, therefore, be assessing this satire, not the poetry praised by Martial. And although this satirical text is patently by a much later, and perhaps male, imitator, it does indirectly provide us with further information about the poetry written by "Martial's Sulpicia." For example, it suggests that references to Sulpicia's husband Calenus and the legendary Roman nymph Egeria (both of whom Martial also mentions in his first poem about Sulpicia) were, in the words of Amy Richlin, "trademarks of her work." This text also furnishes evidence for Richlin's claim that Sulpicia wrote "consciously as a woman to a female audience."[4]

Finally, a thousand years after this satire was written, an Italian scholar named Giorgio Valla, in his edition of the satires by Sulpicia's contemporary Juvenal, quoted two lines, in iambic trimeters, of this Sulpicia's actual writing. Valla's source on Sulpicia—which has somehow been lost during the past five hundred years—is a manuscript attributed to one Probus, a commentator of the late fourth century C.E. When commenting on Juvenal's use of a rare word, *cadurcum*, Valla reported that Probus sought to elucidate this word's meaning by invoking Sulpicia:

[By *cadurcum*] the female genital (says Probus) is understood, since it is the covering of the female genital. Or as others claim, it is a strip on which a bed is stretched. Whence Sulpicia says, "If, after the bindings of my bed frame (*cadurcum*) have been put back in place, [it]would bring me forth, nude, lying down with Calenus."

A century after Valla, the reference to Calenus prompted Pierre Pithou of Troyes, author of a 1585 edition of Juvenal (and owner of the ninth-century Montpellier manuscript of Juvenal known as P in honor of Pithou), to identify the author as the Sulpicia mentioned by Martial in 10.35 and 10.38. The identification has been widely accepted since. Accordingly, several standard reference books cite these two lines as our only authentic fragment of Sulpicia's actual writing.[5]

How are we to judge these two lines in the context of what other ancient sources say about Sulpicia, and in a larger Roman literary context? Sulpicia's expression of her desire to lie down, nude, on her bed, with her husband may not have struck sophisticated Roman audiences in her day as coarse and offensively bawdy. Still, these details certainly support the characterization of her poetry as sexually playful. Why, however, does Martial not only claim that no woman writes naughtier poetry but also maintain that no woman is more honorable than Sulpicia? That Sulpicia teaches virtuous and respectable passions? That with Sulpicia as a fellow student or teacher the Greek poet Sappho would have been better behaved sexually? Presumably Martial is willing to call Sulpicia "honorable" and "sexually well behaved" because she restricts her sexual playfulness, her naughtiness, to her relations with his own friend, Sulpicia's husband Calenus.

It warrants attention that in both of his epigrams about Sulpicia, Martial echoes earlier love poetry by both Catullus and Propertius, poetry celebrating extramarital liaisons. As Richlin points out, the opening lines of 10.35 are modeled closely on Catullus 45.21–24. Poem 45 portrays the mutual love of Acme, whose name identifies her as a Greek courtesan, and a Roman named Septimius:

> It is Acme alone whom poor little Septimius loves more than
> the lands of Syria and Britannia; for Septimius alone faithful
> Acme provides pleasures and sensual delights.[6]

Furthermore, Martial's comparison between Sulpicia and Sappho in 10.35 calls to mind Catullus's associations between his lover and the earlier Greek female poet. First and foremost is Catullus's use of the pseudonym "Lesbia"—which alludes to Sappho and her native island—for his beloved, whom the second-century C.E. Apuleius tells us at *Apology* 10 was actually named Clodia. These associations also include Catullus's poems about this woman in the Sapphic meter that evoke, and at times translate, Sappho's lyrics. They include as well his reference in poem 35 to the poetically appreciative inamorata of his friend as "more learned than the Sapphic muse."

Epigram 10.38 abounds in echoes of Propertius 2.15, an elegy commemorating a night that Propertius claims he and his beloved, whom he calls Cynthia, spent in bed making love. As we have seen, Martial 10.38 opens with three phrases beginning with "O!" The opening couplet of Propertius 2.15 similarly contains three phrases, each beginning with the same word: "O fortunate me! O night bright for me! O you little bed, made blessed by my delight!" Both the unusual, diminutive word for the bed that Propertius addresses here, *lectulus*, and the word for lamp, *lucerna*, that Propertius employs in the following line are found in line 7 of Martial's poem. Propertius's characterization of his and Cynthia's erotic activity as physical struggle—with the words *rixa*, "brawl," and *luctata est*, "she wrestled"—is recalled by Martial's representation of the lovemaking between Calenus and Sulpicia in 10.38.6 as *proelia*, "struggles," and *pugnas*, "battles."[7]

To be sure, the two surviving lines of Sulpicia's own poetry appear to evoke Propertius 2.15 as well. Sulpicia expresses the wish that she be brought forth nude, *nudam*, lying down, *concubantem*, with Calenus. Propertius emphasizes both his and Cynthia's nudity. Indeed, he employs the adjective *nudus* three times in the space of four lines when likening their lovemaking to that of the mythic figures Helen, Endymion, and Diana. Her use here—in the present active participial form *concubantem*—of an otherwise unattested verb *concubare* also recalls Propertius's use of the perfect active infinitive *concubuisse*, from the related *concumbo*, when describing erotic nudity in the same passage: *ipsa Paris nuda fertur periisse Laecaena, / cum Menelao surgeret e thalamo; / nudus et Endymion*

Phoebi cepisse sororem / dicitur et nudae concubuisse deae, "Paris is said to have perished of love at the sight of Helen of Sparta naked, when she rose from the bedchamber of Menelaus; naked Endymion is said to have captured the sister of Apollo, and to have lain with the naked goddess" (13–16).

Yet in 10.35 and 10.38 Martial is not merely alluding to the Propertian elegy that would seem to be echoed by Sulpicia's own poetic efforts. Rather, he summons to mind—and implicitly validates—a wider array of Latin love poems by Propertius and Catullus, notwithstanding the illicit liaisons that both authors portray. Again, Martial seems to have done so because Sulpicia and her husband Calenus enjoy the erotic pleasures extolled by these earlier poems in their roles as husband and wife, rather than as extramarital partners.

Two details from this fragment of Sulpicia's poetry may suggest that she was also familiar with, and seeking to echo, the love poems of the Augustan female elegist who shared her name. One is her use of the participial form *concubantem*. Like Propertius, the Augustan Sulpicia also employs the perfect active infinitive *concubuisse*, in 3.9, when describing how she would like to bed down with her beloved when he goes out hunting.

It is unclear who or what is the subject of the third person singular present subjunctive verb *proferat*, "would bring me forth," in the fragment quoted by Giorgio Valla. But it may well be the goddess Venus, on the analogy of what her namesake proclaims in 3.13. There the earlier Sulpicia claims that Venus has brought her lover to her, *attulit* (from *affero*, a compound of *fero*, "to bring," which also gives us *proferat*) and placed him in her embrace, *deposuit*. Consequently Martial's Sulpicia might also, and somewhat ironically, be evoking the earlier Sulpicia's portrayals of extramarital passion in writing about her marital relationship with her own husband.[8]

We are, regrettably, limited to mere speculation in trying to determine whether, and how, this Sulpicia's writing was indebted to other literary works. Martial's poems about Sulpicia abound in Greek literary allusions. He praises her chaste and properly amatory subject matter in 10.35 after listing two Greek mythological topics and two Greek mythological figures that are not treated in her poetry. All four Greek myths are associated with dreadful and immoral behavior. The madness displayed by the woman of Colchis, Medea, culminated in the murder of her own children. At a banquet prepared by the brother he had cuckolded, Thyestes unknowingly devoured the bodies of his own sons. Scylla betrayed her father and his city to the invading king Minos. Byblis consummated her incestuous passion for her own brother.

As we have seen, however, in this same poem Martial compares Sulpicia favorably to the Greek poet Sappho. Martial proceeds to contend that—had Sulpicia and Sappho been fellow students or teacher and student—Sulpicia would have improved Sappho's poetry and character. He also asserts that Phaon, the young ferryman whose rejection of Sappho legendarily drove Sappho to suicide, would have loved Sulpicia. The poem claims that Calenus would prize one day with his wife more than four times the years that the long-lived Greek mythic warrior Nestor spent on earth.

But did Sulpicia herself utilize Greek allusions or elaborate upon themes immortalized in earlier Greek writing or look to Greek poetry for her literary models? If she herself had also emphasized that she wrote as a woman to a female audience, she may have wished to evoke earlier Greek female poets—such as Sappho and Corinna—who drew attention to both their own gender and that of those whom they addressed. For example, Sulpicia's preoccupation with her con-jugal bed, and its physical restoration, may seek to recall Homer's *Odyssey* 23.171 ff. There, Penelope, wife of Odysseus, exploits his knowledge of the unusual features of their marriage bed to trick him into revealing an ultimate proof of his true identity.

Sulpicia may, moreover, resemble the Augustan elegist Sulpicia in evoking and responding to Vergil's portrayal of the Carthaginian queen Dido. Vergil describes Dido at *Aeneid* 4.496 ff. as preoccupied with the marriage bed, *lectus iugalis*, that she shared with Aeneas. Indeed, Dido replicates this object as her own funeral pyre. Unlike Dido, however, Sulpicia rejoices in life rather than embracing death in talking about the bed on which she lay with Calenus.

Whether or not Sulpicia sought to evoke earlier Greek literature, or Vergil's epic, it may also be significant that the Greek mythic characters whom Martial cites as absent from Sulpicia's own poetry are all remembered for heinous treat-ment of their blood relations. Indeed, Medea's victims included her brother and father as well as her sons, and Thyestes is reported to have fathered a son by his own daughter. Proper treatment of blood kin was expected from respectable Roman women. By observing that Sulpicia's poetry did not even countenance fic-tional violations of blood ties by mythic Greek figures in her poetry, Martial rein-forces her claims to conventional virtue.

NOTES

1. See the article on Martial by M. Citroni in *The Oxford Classical Dictionary*, 3d ed., ed. Simon Hornblower and Antony Spawforth (Oxford: Oxford University Press, 1996).
2. See the article on Sulpicia (2) by M. Citroni in *The Oxford Classical Dictionary*, 3d, ed.
3. See Holt Parker, "Other Remarks on the Other Sulpicia"; Judith P. Hallett, "Mar-tial's Sulpicia and Propertius' Cynthia"; and Amy Richlin, "Sulpicia the Satirist"; in *Classical World* 86.2 (November–December 1992): 89–95; 99–123; 125–40.
4. Richlin, p. 134.
5. Hallett, pp. 104–5. As Richlin observes on 131 ff., other sources describe the *cadurcum* not as a bed frame, but bedding linen.
6. Richlin, p. 129.

7. Hallett, pp. 110–11.
8. On *proferat*, see Richlin, pp. 131–32.

FRAGMENT BY MARTIAL'S SULPICIA

[Unde ait Sulpicia]
Si me cadurci restitutis fasciis
nudam Calendo concubantem proferat.

TRANSLATION BY JUDITH HALLETT

"If, after the bindings of my bed frame have been put back in place
[it] would bring me forth, nude, lying down with Calenus."

BIBLIOGRAPHY

Citroni, Mario. "Martial" and "Sulpicia (2)." In *The Oxford Classical Dictionary*, edited by Simon Hornblower and Anthony Spaworth. Oxford: Oxford University Press, 1996.
Hallett, Judith P. "Martial's Sulpicia and Propertius' Cynthia." *Classical World* 86.1 (1992): 99–123.
Parker, Holt. "Other Remarks on the Other Sulpicia." *Classical World* 86.1 (1992): 89–95.
Richlin, Amy. "Sulpicia the Satirist." *Classical World* 86.2 (1992): 125–40.

The Vindolanda Letters from Claudia Severa

Judith P. Hallett

Prior to the mid-1980s, the list of extant Latin writings by women of the classical era would have ended with the two-line fragment by Martial's Sulpicia. In consequence this list would have been limited to women residing in the capital city of Rome itself. It would, moreover, have been restricted to women who came from what are known to have been leading families and literary circles (and, in the case of Cornelia, mother of the Gracchi, and the elegist Sulpicia, both).

During the past fifteen years, however, excavations at the Roman fort of Vindolanda in northern England have unearthed some other ancient Latin texts by women. All are dated to approximately 100 C.E. The two that have been made accessible to a wider audience, in a 1994 volume by Alan K. Bowman, are letters. They were written to Sulpicia Lepidina, wife of Flavius Cerealis, prefect of the military cohort, by Claudia Severa, wife of another military officer named C. Aelius Brocchus. Cerealis hailed from Batavia, in lower Germany. Brocchus may have come from the eastern part of the Roman Empire, and apparently went on to hold the command of a cavalry unit in Pannonia, south and west of the Danube River. Both husbands belonged to Rome's equestrian—second highest—social class, and regularly corresponded with one another as well.[1]

As Bowman notes in his discussion of these two letters: "The correspondence between Lepidina and Severa was not an isolated phenomenon in the equestrian officer class. Lepidina also received a letter from a woman whose name was probably Paterna. Another letter, perhaps written by a woman named Valatta to Cerealis, refers to some concession made to her through the influence of Lepidina (*per auctoritatem Lepidinae*), doubly interesting for the implication that Cerealis's wife participated in his business even if it was merely social. Thus, the regular inclusion of women in greetings may be somewhat formulaic but need not be considered meaningless: *Pacatam saluta verbis meis* ("Greet Pacata in my words") may refer to another wife of an officer."[2]

These letters provide unmistakable evidence for the presence in these military posts of officers' wives (and, as Severa also mentions her little son, children). A speech attributed to a Roman senator named Caecina Severus by the early first-century C.E. historian Tacitus at *Annales* 3.33, while clearly fictional, is of particular relevance to these texts. For this speech implies that even wives of provincial governors and generals did not begin accompanying their husbands on tours of duty until the reign of Tiberius, approximately seventy-five years before the date of this letter (and only did so amid great resistance and protest).[3]

Two different scribes seem to have written the two letters from Claudia Severa to Sulpicia Lepidina. One of these letters, however, concludes with three lines in Severa's own hand—and is thus said to be the earliest known example of writing in Latin by a woman.[4] And even though these letters were not written for a wide audience in accordance with stylistic precepts governing poetic composition or rhetorical expression, they nonetheless have many features that should be regarded as literary.

Bowman refers to the words of the first letter that are written in Severa's own hand as "the most striking of all" in the Vindolanda documents, and as "elaborate and elegant." He suggests, moreover, that "the elegance of the Latin may well be due to Severa herself," observing that her other letter, though penned by an amanuensis, "is also very good." By way of contrast, Bowman finds the Latinity of a man called Karus, one of Cerealis's correspondents, substandard. Still, he does commend a draft letter from Cerealis himself as "exceptional for the quality of the Latin which has a literary flavour and some elegance—manifestly the work of an elegant stylist." Presumably Severa was aware that Lepidina's husband wrote in a literary and elegant fashion and applied high standards to her own mode of expression.[5]

These two letters also share several features, thematic as well as stylistic, with the other surviving writings in Latin by women of the classical era. For they, too, evoke earlier Latin as well as Greek literature; emphasize family, and in particular blood family, ties; and represent women as occupied in ritual celebration, in this case of the letter writer's birthday. But before examining these similarities, we should first focus upon a major difference: that not only is the writer of these two texts a woman, but so also is her addressee. The elegist Sulpicia may address elegies (and portions of elegies) to female goddesses such as Juno and voice a hope that those of either sex without romantic experiences of their own will read her poems as a surrogate. Yet she does not expressly write for a female audience. Later authors seem to imply that Martial's Sulpicia wrote as a woman for women readers (and Martial pointedly encourages women to read this Sulpicia's work). Yet the surviving two lines of this Sulpicia's poetry do not indicate a specific addressee, much less her or his gender.

Claudia Severa, however, not only writes to Sulpicia Lepidina, but also does so in affectionate, even erotically tinged, language. Most obviously, she calls her "sister" three times in the first letter and twice in the second (even though the two women's very different names would suggest that no blood relationship existed between them: Roman sisters ordinarily shared the female form of their father's name). Severa claims in the first letter that her presence would make the day they spend together more pleasurable (and using a word for "pleasurable," *iucundus*, that connotes strong, sensual delight).[6] She refers to Lepidina as "my most precious soul" (*anima . . . karissima*) in the first letter, and as "most precious and adored soul" (*karissima et anima desideratissima*) in the second. By bidding Lepidina "farewell . . . and hail" (*vale . . . et have*) in the first letter, she may well allude to the emotionally charged phrase "hail and farewell" (*ave atque vale*)— from Catullus 101, his celebrated elegy on the death of his beloved brother.

Such woman-centered writing, of course, immediately calls to mind the poetry of the sixth-century B.C.E. Greek poet Sappho. To be sure, Severa is writing prose. So, too, there is no indication that these two women were physically or romantically involved with one another (whereas Sappho's poems imply, and sources on Sappho's life assert, that she loved other women with a powerful, perhaps physically expressed, passion). Severa conveys greetings to Sulpicia's husband and extends greetings from her husband and son. As we shall see shortly, her affectionate language resembles that which biological sisters are portrayed as using with one another in earlier Latin poetry.

But the sentence inviting Sulpicia "to come, and make the day more pleasurable for me by your arriving, if you come" uses forms of the Latin word *venire*, "to come," three times in succession (*venias, interventu*, and apparently *venies*) and two forms of the Latin word meaning "make" (*facias, factura*). In so doing Severa employs a figure of speech known as the *figura etymologica*, one common in early Latin poetry (and also employed by the elegist Sulpicia in such poems as 3.13). Furthermore, Severa's invitation may recall Sappho's request, in her first poem, to the goddess Aphrodite—that "she come and . . . accomplish what her heart desires to be done."

Yet another, Latin, literary model for this letter appears to be the fourth book of the *Aeneid*, in which Dido and her sister Anna converse. At *Aeneid* 4.8 Vergil refers to Anna as Dido's *unanimam sororem*, "sister sharing a soul," and has Anna call Dido "cherished more than life" (*luce magis dilecta sorori*) at 4.31. We know nothing about the educational or even the social backgrounds of Claudia Severa and Sulpicia Lepidina and should not automatically assume that they—like Cornelia, the Augustan Sulpicia, or Martial's Sulpicia—would have been familiar with earlier, Greek or Latin, literary texts. Yet the likelihood that Severa's sentiments and language were influenced by Vergil's epic is suggested by another letter in the same Vindolanda archive.

Written by a man who addresses another man as "dearest brother" (*karissime frater*) much as Severa calls Sulpicia "dearest" (*karissima*) and "sister" (*soror*), it directly quotes a line from the ninth book of the *Aeneid*, 473.[7] Curiously, the subject of this line is *fama*, the personification of Rumor that figures in the story of Dido and also plays a key role in a poem by the elegist Sulpicia. This line, moreover, is from a passage depicting an emotionally wrenching situation: here *fama* is said to bring a Trojan woman in Aeneas's entourage the tragic news that her son and his male lover have died bravely in battle against their Italian foes.

Both Claudia Severa's use of *soror* as a term of endearment for a woman not her biological sister and the appearance of *frater* as a term of endearment among men who may not have been blood relations testify to the importance of blood family ties generally among Romans of the classical period, or at the very least among those Romans stationed far from Rome on the edges of empire. After all, these words, which technically refer to blood family members of one's own generation, are here utilized for other, nonkindred, individuals clearly accorded emotional value. Sulpicia Lepidina and the unnamed male addressee are referred to in other affectionate words. The unnamed male is addressed on a tablet that quotes a line from a poetic passage portraying a mother's emotional pain at the loss of her son. Severa's reference to her own little son bespeaks the importance of the mother-child blood tie to her too. Both women owe their presence at Vindolanda to their officer husbands; Sulpicia Lepidina is officially identified at the end of the letter as wife of Cerealis. Thus one might expect Severa to mention both Aelius and Cerealis—but not necessarily her son.

The Latin word that Claudia Severa employs for her birthday celebration, *sollemnis*, warrants special attention. It means "ceremonial, solemn, performed in accordance with the forms of religion."[8] It therefore suggests that the event to which Severa invites Sulpicia Lepidina is to her an important annual religious occasion. Such, of course, is also the implication of the Augustan elegist Sulpicia's poem, 3.12, about her own birthday party, which addresses Juno in her capacity as birthday goddess, and which refers to offerings of incense, cake, and wine. What is more, we should note that Sulpicia describes her own mother's presence at her birthday celebration (3.12.15) and that Claudia Severa says nothing about including either her own husband or Sulpicia Lepidina's husband in her invitation. It may well have been that Roman women's birthday celebrations—or at least some portion of the day's events—were all-female events, perhaps even restricted to the celebrant and her close female kin. Should that have been the case, and considering that Severa's own female relations were likely to have been far away from the frontier outpost of Vindolanda, Severa may have employed the term *soror* for a nonkindred woman, Sulpicia Lepidina, precisely because she expected Sulpicia Lepidina to substitute for the female members of her own family on this ritual occasion.

NOTES

1. Alan Bowman, *Life and Letters on the Roman Frontier* (London: British Museum Press, 1994), pp. 17, 25–27, 54–57.
2. Bowman, p. 57.
3. Bowman, pp. 56–57.
4. Bowman, p. 88.
5. Bowman, p. 93.
6. See *The Oxford Latin Dictionary*, ed. P. G. W. Glare (Oxford: Oxford University Press, 1982), s.v. "*iucundus.*"
7. See Alan J. Bowman and J. David Thomas, "New Texts from Vindolanda," *Britannia* 18 (1987): 130–31; Bowman, pp. 18 (on *Tab. Vindol.* 2.118–21) and 91–92.
8. See *Oxford Latin Dictionary*, s.v. "*sollemnis.*"

CLAUDIA SEVERA'S VINDOLANDA LETTERS

Claudia Severa to Sulpicia Lepidina (*Tab. Vindol.* 2.291)[1]

i

Cl(audia). Severa Lepidinae [suae
       [sa]l[u]tem
iii Idus Septembr[e]s soror ad diem
   sollemnem natalem meum rogo
   libenter facias ut venias
   ad nos iucundiorem mihi

ii

[diem] interventu tuo factura si
    s
Cerial[em t]uum saluta Aelius meus.
et filiolus salutant
    sperabo te soror
[By a second hand]
    vale soror anima
    mea ita valeam
    karissima et have
[Back, by the first hand]
  Sulpiciae Lepidinae
  Cerialis
  a S[e]vera

---

[1]Bowman, p. 127. I follow the layout in the volume.

Claudia Severa to Sulpicia Lepidina (*Tab. Vindol.* 2.292)[2]

i
salutem
ego soror sicut tecum locuta fueram et promiseram
ut peterem a Broccho et venirem at te peti
et res[po]ndit mihi ‹i›ta corde semp[er li]citum una
ii
quomodocumque possim
at te pervenire sunt enim
necessaria quaedam qua[e]
iii
rem meum epistulas meas
accipies quibus scies quid
sim actura haec nobis
v

. . . .
ra eram et Brigae mansura
Cerialem tuum a me saluta
[Back, by a second hand]
[val]e m soror
karissima et anima
ma desideratissima
[Back, by the first hand]
Sulpiciae Lepidi
nae Ceria[li]s
a Severa Brocchi

TRANSLATIONS BY JUDITH P. HALLETT

Claudia Severa to Sulpicia Lepidina (*Tab. Vindol.* 2.291)

Claudia Severa sends greetings to her Lepidina.
On the third day before the Ides of September, sister, I warmly invite you
for the day of the celebration of my birthday, to make sure that you come
to us, in order to make the day more pleasurable for me by your arrival, if
you come.
Send my greetings to your Cerealis. My Aelius and my little son send their
greetings.

---

[2]Bowman, pp. 127–28.

[By a second hand, presumably that of Claudia Severa]
I shall hope to see you, sister. Farewell, sister, my most precious soul, thus
may you fare well, and hail.
[Back of the letter, by the first hand]
To Sulpicia Lepidina, (wife) of Flavius Cerealis, from Severa

Claudia Severa to Sulpicia Lepidina (*Tab. Vindol.* 2.292)

Greeting. Sister, just as I had spoken with you and had pledged that I
would ask Brocchus and come to you, I did ask him and he told me in
response that it was always sincerely granted to me, along with . . . to go
to visit you in whatever way I can. There are indeed certain necessary
matters which . . . you will receive my letters by which you will know what
I am about to do . . . I was and am about to stay at Briga. Send greetings
from me to your Cerealis.
[Back of the letter, by a second hand]
Farewell, sister, most precious and adored soul.
[Back of the letter, by the first hand]
To Sulpicia Lepidina, wife of Cerealis, from Severa . . . wife of Brocchus

BIBLIOGRAPHY

Bowman, Alan. *Life and Letters on the Roman Frontier*. London: British Museum Press,
1994.
Bowman, Alan, and J. David Thomas. "New Texts from Vindolanda." *Britannia* 18 (1987:
130–31).
Glare, P. G. W., ed. *The Oxford Latin Dictionary*. Oxford: Oxford University Press, 1982.

Late Antiquity and the Early Christian Era

Vibia Perpetua: Mystic and Martyr

Judith Lynn Sebesta

On the morning of March 7, 203 C.E., Carthaginian spectators took their seats in the amphitheater with greater anticipation than usual, for in addition to the usual beast hunts and gladiator combats celebrating the thirteenth birthday of Geta Caesar, younger son of the emperor Septimius Severus, five Christians were scheduled for execution. Among these five were two women, Vibia Perpetua, who had recently stopped nursing her young son, and her slave-woman, Felicity, who had given birth the day before. Immobilized in nets, the two women were charged and tossed by a maddened cow. Though bruised, Perpetua calmly picked herself up, rearranged her torn dress, and helped the stunned Felicity. Having faced her punishment, Perpetua could now expect to be dispatched quickly out of sight of the crowd. Instead, she was made to stand in the middle of the arena, where the young gladiator-in-training was so unnerved that when he drew his sword, he only sliced into her bones without killing her. Perpetua screamed, but then took his hand, guided the sword across her throat, and died.

During the months the Christians had spent in prison, Perpetua had already shown herself as a leader, even though she was only twenty-two, extremely anxious for the baby she was nursing, and still a recent catechumen. During her imprisonment, she kept a diary in Latin that forms the major portion of the *Passio Sanctarum Perpetuae et Felicitatis*.[1]

Perpetua begins her account with her arrest but gives no explanation why she and her fellow Christians were singled out. The government's motivation, however, for beginning a persecution is easily explained. Though the government willingly tolerated other religions and even, on occasions, formally instituted the worship of a foreign deity, it did insist that its subjects engage, at least outwardly, in religious ceremonies that formed the cult of the emperors.[2] Participation in this cult provided a focus of allegiance for all the diverse populations living in the empire. Just as family members offered prayers and sacrifices for the continued well-being of their "father of the family" (*pater familias*), so the members of the empire offered their prayers and sacrifices for the "father of the country" (*pater patriae*), a title held by every emperor since Augustus. Because they refused to participate in this cult of the emperor, Christians were regarded as traitors who would not engage in religious ceremonies to ensure the prosperity of their fellow citizens. As a successor to the cruel and debauched Commodus and survivor of several campaigns against rivals for the throne, Septimius was suspicious of any apparent source of disaffection. He issued an edict in late 201 or early 202 C.E. forbidding conversion to Christianity and announced severe penalties for those who did convert or persevered in their conversion.

Perpetua's assumption of leadership within her group exemplifies one of the aspects of Christianity that particularly attracted women. Traditionally in the Mediterranean cultures that formed the Roman Empire, women were expected to confine themselves to the maintenance of their home and family life and engage very little in public life—and then only in clearly defined and limited ways. In the itinerant ministry of Jesus, however, and in the early church, women played prominent roles. They helped spread the gospel, formed and presided over house churches, and prophesied. In some towns women comprised the whole Christian community.[3] Early Christian communities, moreover, not only valued women generally as leaders in the church, but also esteemed their expression of ideas whether in oral or written form. As God was believed to speak to both sexes, both men and women could, and did, prophesy in church. That Christians of North Africa particularly valued prophecy by women is suggested by the spread of Montanism within North African Christian communities in 200–207 C.E. Among her fellow prisoners, Perpetua seems to have been acknowledged as a prophetic leader, for one of her Christian brothers encouraged her to ask for her first vision (4.1).

Perpetua received four visions: that of the ladder to heaven; of her deceased younger brother Dinocrates in torment; another of Dinocrates, now released from torment; and of her victory over the devil in the guise of an Egyptian in the amphitheater. These visions confirm her resolve during her final days of spiritual conflict with the world and help her understand more clearly the real dimensions of this conflict. According to Elizabeth Petroff, the placement of these visions in her narrative reveals

> a very conscious structuring of the relationships between vision and reality, between human confrontation and divine resolution. The four visions of Perpetua are balanced by four confrontations with secular authority ... each vision is carefully placed in a personal and historical context. The nonvisionary episodes are dramatic presentations of confrontations with the non-Christian world, where words and gestures count heavily in the total picture provided for us.[4]

Two scenes that show how Perpetua reacts to the conflict posed by her family ties precede her first vision. She begins her narrative while she and the others are still under a form of house arrest. When her father tries to persuade her to recant, she confutes him with a single question. Frustrated and angry, he flies at her as though to do her injury, but stops and departs, as Perpetua says, with his Devil-inspired arguments. Within a few days the Christians are imprisoned in a dark cell, and; worried for her son's health, she gives the baby to her mother. Through longing for her child, Perpetua's health declines, and having petitioned the prison official, she is reunited with her baby and regains soundness of body and mind.

Upon being urged by her brother in faith, Perpetua asks for a vision to learn whether she will be martyred or be dismissed to rejoin her family. To her, the ensuing vision of the ladder to heaven is not only an answer to this request, but also a charismatic gift in response to her prayer a few days earlier after her baptism, when, upon being urged by the Spirit, she prayed for nothing but endurance of the body.

Since she grew up in a city shaped by Phoenician, Greek, and Roman cultures, it is not surprising that Perpetua mixes pagan symbols from these cultures with Christian ones in this vision. The ladder in her vision parallels the ladders in Egyptian and Mithraic thought and in Jewish wisdom literature.[5] The narrowness of her ladder may be inspired by Jesus' comment that the gate to eternal life is narrow.[6] The instruments of torture and death that ring the ladder are clearly those that await martyrs in the prison, court, and arena. The serpent (*draco*) guarding the ladder combines both Jewish and Christian symbolism. In the Old Testament, a serpent, Leviathan, or other water monster is understood as a "created being that acts as an evil force to keep humanity from relying upon God, thereby taking to itself divine prerogative."[7] In Christian apocalyptic writings such as Revelation, Satan is represented as a serpent.[8] Equally important for this vision, the serpent in the Old Testament personifies a state or the leader of a state and here in Perpetua's vision represents the emperor, whom Christians viewed as Satan's agent. When she steps on the serpent's head in order to climb the ladder, Perpetua performs a symbolic gesture of victory, widespread in Mediterranean cultures.[9] Having climbed the ladder, she meets an aged shepherd, who recalls both the image of Yahweh as the Ancient of Days and the Shepherd of His People and as the image of Jesus as the Good Shepherd. From this vision, Perpetua understands that she will be martyred. In thinking that she will enter into Paradise immediately after her death, she reflects a belief common in her time, that the righteous dead will dwell in Paradise immediately after their deaths. As Perpetua had been a catechumen for only a few months before her arrest, the Old Testament and Christian elements in this vision give us an idea of what her instruction had included.[10]

In addition to the "public" Christian symbolism, this vision also connects to her family life. The father she rejected and who leaped at her as though to do her harm is paralleled by the divine father figure who calls her "child," and who has, in the spiritual sense, given her birth. Her biological father, who opposes her martyrdom, is also latent in the monstrous serpent that tries to keep her from Paradise.

The second and third visions follow Perpetua's confrontation with the pro-consul Hilarianus in court. When she is condemned to death, Perpetua's father refuses to give her son back to her. Her heavenly father also makes final, as she thinks, the separation from her child (and hence from her family) by causing her milk to dry up immediately. But within a few days God reconnects Perpetua to one member of her family through two visions of her deceased younger brother, Dinocrates. From the very fact that she is given sudden remembrance of Dinocrates, Perpetua understands herself to be in a state of grace, an understanding that helps strengthen her in prison. As with the first vision, these visions of Dinocrates in the afterlife contain pagan and Christian elements. To pagans, Hades was a dark, murky place, where the dead might suffer, at least for a short while. Similarly, Dinocrates appears out of a dark hole, pale, dirty, feverish, thirsty. Pagans thought, moreover, that the dead retained all scars and wounds they suffered on earth, and Perpetua sees on Dinocrates' face the ulcer that caused his death. Pagans also believed that the living can affect the status of the dead and ameliorate, if not end, their suffering and that the dead may forget their past by drinking from the Water of Oblivion. In Perpetua's vision, this water is conflated with the Christian image of the spring of the Water of Life found in Revelation 21:6. Perpetua gazes at Dinocrates across a great gulf that recalls the great gulf between heaven and hell in Jesus' parable of Lazarus and the rich man.[11] Lastly, another element of this vision, that children remain children and are gathered in a special place, is found in Vergil's description of the underworld and in the Apocalypse of Peter.[12] Notwithstanding the pagan images that infuse the first vision of Dinocrates, the second vision is informed with Christian belief in the grace of God. Though Perpetua prayed for her brother, it is God who, in this vision, effects the amelioration of his state by lowering the fountain for Dinocrates.[13]

The last confrontation with "authority" is the final visit of her father, if any authority can be said to reside in this despairing man who mourns before his daughter as he will before her dead body. Though she pities him, Perpetua otherwise remains distant from him, preserving her resolution to die unwaveringly in her faith. Soon after, she receives her fourth and final vision, one that, unlike the other three, has only Christian imagery. In this vision, she is summoned forth to the arena by Pomponius, one of the deacons who have been helping the prisoners. Pomponius acts as messenger of Jesus, who had promised his spirit would be close to his believers, especially in captivity.[14] The hilly, rough country they walk through echoes Jesus' description of the way to heaven as a difficult path.[15] After arriving at the amphitheater, Perpetua is forced to fight against an Egyptian gladiator; the dark color of the Egyptians was equated by early Christians with Satan, the Prince of Darkness.[16] As was customary, assistants undress her, and she discovers that she has now been changed into a man. Perpetua's astonishing transformation of gender may be explained by Paul's statement that in Christ there is no male or female, but is more likely due to Gnostic thought such as that expressed in the *Gospel of Thomas*. When, in *Logeion* 114, Peter tells Mary to leave because women are not worthy of life, Jesus replies, "I myself will lead her in order to make her male, so that she too may become a living spirit resembling you males. For every woman who will make herself male will enter the Kingdom of Heaven."[17] Perpetua is next anointed with oil, as was customary in such games, though here her anointing may be understood as being anointed as the Lord's elect, as was David.[18] The Egyptian, however, rolls in the dust, echoing, first, the prophecy in Genesis that the serpent will eat dust all its days and, second, the prophetic account in the *Shepherd of Hermas*, in which Hermas meets a monstrous serpent stirring up dust.[19] Lastly, the immense trainer in Perpetua's vision obviously is to be identified with Christ, and his gift to the victorious Perpetua of the green branch with golden apples again echoes the *Shepherd of Hermas*, in which a tall angel cuts and hands out branches from a willow tree. The angel then asks that each branch be returned. Some people return branches that are rotted or damaged by insects, but those who return green branches bearing fruit are given a seal, shining white clothing, and a crown. Then they are allowed to enter the walled city of Paradise. In Perpetua's dream, the award of the green, golden-fruited branch identifies her as a genuine, faithful Christian.[20]

Patricia Wilson-Kastner suggests that Perpetua's diary is evidence that early Christianity gave women an opportunity to exercise their "voice":

> While one can debate various positions about Christianity's effect on the social standing of women in the Roman Empire, unquestionably it released previously untapped well-springs of energy among women to whom the Gospel was preached. Of the writings which we possess or even know about from women in the Roman Empire after the days of Augustus, only some of the poetry of Sulpicia is extant; all the other works are by Christian women.[21]

Well educated even for an elite woman—her refutation of her father (3.2) suggests she was familiar with Platonic argument—Perpetua seems to have selected and arranged the episodes of her narrative so that there is "dramatic symmetry between the visions in prison and the realistic, dramatic confrontations with the uncomprehending secular world."[22] Perpetua writes, however, with seemingly unconscious simplicity, even banality: she mentions that her breasts did not become inflamed, that the restoration of her baby made the prison a palace to her. Unlike earlier martyrs, who speak verbosely in their accounts, Perpetua speaks concisely and precisely to her father and to the judge, Hilarianus. Her simple, homely style is far different from that of the author of the introductory chapter, who begins with a rhetorical question and continues with complicated sentences flowing on with many subordinate clauses that are intended to intensify the strength of his argument. Perpetua, however, lets the content of her words conjure up scenes of intense emotion.

Following Perpetua's death, the *Passio* was translated almost immediately into Greek, and an abridged Latin version was made for reading in church services. Presumably it was at this time that an anonymous editor made several additions to Perpetua's narrative. In the two introductory paragraphs, and in the concluding exhortation, the editor argues that the power of God's spirit was still active in the world and continued to speak through new prophecies such as Perpetua's. His words indicate that Perpetua's diary was almost immediately recognized as an important text for the faithful. Both Perpetua and Felicity were included in the official Constantinian calendar of martyrdoms, and several inscriptions naming the women have been found at Carthage. After the games were banned in the sixth century C.E. a chapel marking the spot of the women's martyrdom was constructed in the amphitheater. Images of Perpetua were included in various collections of saints' portraits adorning church buildings in the western empire, such as the Archepiscopal Chapel in Ravenna. In short, the existence of the *Passio* made Perpetua and her slave Felicity prominent among martyrs.

Although the *Passio* provides a vivid account of the arrest and martyrdom of several Christian women and men at the beginning of the third century C.E., it is also an account of protest not only against the repression of the Roman government and Roman patriarchal society, but against any repression of thought and action by a hierarchy. Nevertheless, despite the prominent role women had in the early church and the value placed upon their religious experiences and expressions, the church of the fourth and fifth centuries C.E. reformed itself into a male hierarchical structure that proved just as restrictive to women as had Roman pagan society. Still extant, for example, are the three sermons given by St. Augustine, bishop of Carthage (354–430 C.E.), on the anniversaries of Perpetua and Felicity's martyrdom. These sermons reveal the difficulty the male ecclesiastical hierarchy had with the *Passio*, for he is disquieted by the fact that two women are the central characters in the narrative and that four visions are given to a woman and only one to a man, Saturus—and even in that vision Perpetua is equally important as Saturus. Despite such misgivings on the part of the male hierarchy, Perpetua's prison diary continued to be copied and read through the centuries.

NOTES

1. The text of the *Passio* as it has come down to us includes more than just Perpetua's account. It includes an introduction that explains why "contemporary" prophecies should be read as well as those contained in Scripture; Saturus's relation of his own vision during imprisonment; an account of the last days of Perpetua and her companions and the manner of their death in the arena; and a final argument for the importance of "contemporary" prophecy. In the interests of brevity, I have omitted from the Latin text sections 9 and 11. I include, however, summaries of these sections in my translation. My Latin text is based on the texts *La Passio SS Perpetuae et Felicitatis* by Pio Franchi De'Cavalieri (Rome:

Herder'shen Verlagshandlung, 1896) and *The Acts of the Martyrdom of Perpetua and Felicity* by James Rendel Harris (London: C.J. Clay and Sons, 1890).

2. For example, in 202 B.C.E. the Senate imported the image of Cybele from Asia Minor in response to a Sibylline prophecy that her worship would bring defeat to Hannibal.
3. Renate Bridenthal, Claudia Koonz, and Susan Stuard, *Becoming Visible: Women in European History*, 2d ed. (Boston: Houghton Mifflin, 1998), pp. 86–87.
4. Elizabeth A. Petroff, *Medieval Women's Visionary Literature* (Oxford: Oxford University Press, 1986), pp. 45–46.
5. Cecil M. Roebuck, Jr., *Prophecy in Carthage: Perpetua, Tertullian, and Cyprian* (Cleveland, Ohio: Pilgrim Press, 1992), pp. 28–29.
6. Matthew 7:14.
7. Roebuck, *Prophecy in Carthage*, p. 25.
8. Revelation 20:2. Nebuchadnezzar as serpent, Jeremiah 51:34. Leviathan, Job 40:25 and Isaiah 27:1. Pharaoh as serpent, Ezekiel 29:3, 32:2.
9. Roebuck, *Prophecy in Carthage*, pp. 30, 33. For the crushing of the serpent's head, see Genesis 3:14–15.
10. Roebuck, *Prophecy in Carthage*, p. 39.
11. Parable of Lazarus and the rich man, Luke 16:19–31.
12. Roebuck, *Prophecy in Carthage*, p. 50.
13. Eugenio Corsini, "Proposte per una lettura della 'Passio Perpetuae,'" in *Forma Futuri: Studi in Onore del Cardinale Michele Pellegrino* (Turin: Erasmo, 1975), p. 503, quoted in Roebuck, *Prophecy in Carthage*, p. 54.
14. Roebuck, *Prophecy in Carthage*, pp. 61–62.
15. Matthew 7:14.
16. Roebuck, *Prophecy in Carthage*, p. 62.
17. Thomas O. Lambdin, "Gospel of Thomas," in *The Nag Hammadi Library*, ed. James Robinson (San Francisco: Harper & Row, 1981), p. 130, quoted in Roebuck, *Prophecy in Carthage*, p. 65.
18. 1 Samuel 16:1; 2 Samuel 2:4.
19. Roebuck, *Prophecy in Carthage*, p. 63.
20. Roebuck, *Prophecy in Carthage*, p. 67.
21. Patricia Wilson-Kastner, preface to *A Lost Tradition: Women Writers of the Early Church*, by Patricia Wilson-Kastner et al. (Lanham, Md.: University Press of America, 1981), p. viii.
22. Petroff, *Medieval Women's Visionary Literature*, p. 29.

THE MARTYRDOM OF SAINTS PERPETUA AND FELICITY[1]

1. 1. Si vetera fidei exempla, et Dei gratiam testificantia et aedificationem hominis operantia, propterea in litteris sunt digesta ut lectione eorum quasi

---

[1]The Latin text is based the texts *La Passio SS Perpetuae et Felicitatis* by Pio Franchi De'Cavalieri (Rome: Herder'shen Verlagshandlung, 1896) and *The Acts of the Martyrdom of Perpetua and Felicity* by James Rendel Harris (London: C.J. Clay and Sons, 1890).

repraesentatione rerum et Deus honoretur et homo confortetur, cur non et nova documenta aeque utrique causae convenientia et digerantur? 2. Vel quia proinde et haec vetera futura quandoque sunt et necessaria posteris, si in praesenti suo tempore minori deputantur auctoritati, propter praesumptam venerationem antiquitatis. 3. Sed viderint qui unam virtutem Spiritus unius Sancti pro aetatibus iudicent temporum, cum maiora reputanda sunt novitiora quaeque, ut novissimiora, secundum exuperationem gratiae in ultima saeculi spatia decretam. 4. In novissimis enim diebus, dicit Dominus, effundam de Spiritu meo super omnem carnem, et prophetabunt filii filiaeque eorum; et super servos et ancillas meas de meo Spiritu effundam: et iuvenes visiones videbunt, et senes somnia somniabunt. 5. Itaque et nos, qui sicut prophetias ita et visiones novas pariter repromissas et agnoscimus et honoramus, ceterasque virtutes Spiritus Sancti ad instrumentum Ecclesiae deputamus (cui et missus est idem omnia donativa administraturus in omnibus, prout unicuique distribuit Dominus) necessario et digerimus et ad gloriam Dei lectione celebramus, ut ne qua aut inbecillitas aut desperatio fidei apud veteres tantum aestimet gratiam divinitatis conversatam, sive in martyrum sive in revelationem dignatione, cum semper Deus operetur quae repromisit, non credentibus in testimonium, credentibus in beneficium. 6. Et nos itaque quod audivimus et contrectavimus, annuntiamus et vobis, fratres et filioli, uti et vos qui interfuistis rememoremini gloriae Domini, et qui nunc cognoscitis per auditum communionem habeatis cum sanctis martyribus, et per illos cum Domino nostro Iesu Christo, cui est claritas et honor in saecula saeculorum. Amen.

2. 1. Apprehensi sunt adolescentes catechumeni: Revocatus et Felicitas, conserva eius, Saturninus et Secundulus; inter hos et Vibia Perpetua, honeste nata, liberaliter instituta, matronaliter nupta, 2. habens patrem et matrem et fratres duos, alterum aeque catechumenum, et filium infantem ad ubera. 3. Erat autem ipsa circiter annorum viginti duo. Haec ordinem totum martyrii sui iam hinc ipsa narravit, sicut conscriptum manu sua et suo sensu reliquit.

3. 1. "Cum adhuc," inquit, "cum prosecutoribus essemus, et me pater verbis evertere cupiret et deicere pro sua affectione perseveraret, "Pater," inquam, "vides verbi gratia vas hoc iacens, urceolum sive aliud?" Et dixit, "Video." 2. Et ego dixi ei, "Numquid alio nomine vocari potest quam quod est?" Et ait, "Non." "Sic et ego aliud me dicere non possum nisi quod sum, Christiana." 3. Tunc pater motus hoc verbo mittit se in me, ut oculos mihi erueret, sed vexavit tantum, et profectus est victus cum argumentis diaboli. 4. Tunc paucis diebus quod caruissem patre, Domino gratias egi et refrigeravi absentia illius. 5. In ipso spatio paucorum dierum baptizati sumus, et mihi Spiritus dictavit non aliud petendum ab aqua nisi sufferentiam carnis. Post paucos dies recipimur in carcerem, et expavi, quia numquam experta eram tales tenebras. 6. O diem asperum! Aestus validus turbarum beneficio, concussurae militum. Novissime macerabar sollicitudine infantis ibi. 7. Tunc Tertius et Pomponius, benedicti diaconi qui nobis ministrabant, constituerunt praemio uti paucis horis emissi in meliorem locum carceris refriger-

aremus. 8. Tunc exeuntes de carcare universi sibi vacabant: ego infantem lactabam iam inedia defectum; sollicita pro eo adloquebar matrem et confortabam fratrem, commendabam filium; tabescebam ideo quod illos tabescere videram mei beneficio. 9. Tales sollicitudines multis diebus passa sum; et usurpavi ut mecum infans in carcere maneret; et statim convalui et relevata sum a labore et sollicitudine infantis, et factus est mihi carcer subito praetorium, ut ibi mallem esse quam alicubi.

4. 1. Tunc dixit mihi frater meus, "Domina soror, iam in magna dignatione es, tanta ut postules visionem et ostendatur tibi an passio sit an commeatus." 2. Et ego quae me sciebam fabulari cum Domino, cuius beneficia tanta experta eram, fidenter repromisi ei dicens, "Crastina die tibi renuntiabo." Et postulavi, et ostensum est mihi hoc: 3. Video scalam aeream mirae magnitudinis, pertingentem usque ad caelum et angustam per quam nonnisi singuli ascendere possent, et in lateribus scalae omne genus ferramentorum infixum. Erant ibi gladii, lanceae, hami, machaerae, verruta, ut si quis neglegenter aut non sursum adtendens ascenderet, laniaretur et carnes eius inhaererent ferramentis. 4. Et erat sub ipsa scala draco cubans mirae magnitudinis, qui ascendentibus insidias praestabat et exterrebat ne ascenderent. 5. Ascendit autem Saturus prior, qui postea se propter nos ultro tradiderat (quia ipse nos aedificaverat), et tunc cum adducti sumus, praesens non fuerat. 6. Et pervenit in caput scalae, et convertit se et dixit mihi, "Perpetua, sustineo te; sed vide ne te mordeat draco ille." Et dixi ego, "Non me nocebit in nomine Iesu Christi." 7. Et desub ipsa scala, quasi timens me, lente eiecit caput; et quasi primum gradum calcarem, calcavi illi caput et ascendi. 8. Et vidi spatium immensum horti et in medio sedentem hominem canum in habitu pastoris, grandem, oves mulgentem, et circumstantes candidati milia multa. 9. Et levavit caput et aspexit me et dixit mihi, "Bene venisti, tegnon." Et clamavit me et de caseo quod mulgebat dedit mihi quasi buccellam; et ego accepi iunctis manibus et manducavi; et universi circumstantes dixerunt: "Amen." 10. Et ad sonum vocis experrecta sum, commanducans adhuc dulce nescio quid. Et retuli statim fratri meo, et intelleximus passionem esse futuram, et coepimus nullam iam spem in saeculo habere.

5. 1. Post paucos dies rumor cucurrit ut audiremur. Supervenit autem et de civitate pater meus, consumptus taedio, et ascendit ad me ut me deiceret dicens, 2. "Miserere, filia, canis meis, miserere patri, si dignus sum a te pater vocari, si his te manibus ad hunc florem aetatis provexi, si te praeposui omnibus fratribus tuis: ne me dederis in dedecus hominum. 3. Aspice fratres tuos, aspice matrem tuam et materteram, aspice filium tuum, qui post te vivere non poterit. 4. Depone animos, ne universos nos extermines; nemo enim nostrum libere loquetur si tu aliquid fueris passa." 5. Haec dicebat quasi pater pro sua pietate, basians mihi manus et se ad pedes meos iactans et lacrimans me iam non filiam nominabat sed dominam. 6. Et ego dolebam casum patris mei quod solus de passione mea gravisurus non esset de toto genere meo et confortavi eum dicens, "Hoc fiet in illa catasta quod

Deus voluerit; scito enim nos non in nostra esse potestate constitutos, sed in Dei."
Et recessit a me contristatus.

6. 1. Alio die cum pranderemus, subito rapti sumus ut audiremur. Et pervenimus ad forum. Rumor statim per vicinas fori partes cucurrit, et factus est populus immensus. 2. Ascendimus in catastam. Interrogati ceteri confessi sunt. Ventum est et ad me. Et apparuit pater ilico cum filio meo, et extraxit me de gradu dicens, "Supplica; miserere infanti." 3. Et Hilarianus procurator, qui tunc loco proconsulis Minuci Timiniani defuncti ius gladii acceperat: "Parce," inquit, "canis patris tui, parce infantiae pueri. Fac sacrum pro salute imperatorum." 4. Et ego respondi, "Non facio." Hilarianus: "Christiana es?" inquit. Et ego respondi, "Christiana sum." 5. Et cum staret pater ad me deiciendam, iussus est ab Hilariano proici, et virga percussus est. Et doluit mihi casus patris mei, quasi ego fuissem percussa: sic dolui pro senecta eius misera. 6. Tunc nos universos pronuntiat et damnat ad bestias; et hilares descendimus ad carcerem. 7. Tunc quia consueverat a me infans mammas accipere et mecum in carcere manere, statim mitto ad patrem Pomponium diaconum, postulans infantem. 8. Sed pater dare noluit. Et quomodo Deus voluit, neque ille amplius mammas desideravit neque mihi fervorem fecerunt, ne sollicitudine infantis et dolore mammarum macerarer.

7. 1. Post dies paucos, dum universi oramus, subito media oratione profecta est mihi vox et nominavi Dinocraten. Et obstipui quod numquam mihi in mentem venisset nisi tunc, et dolui commemorata casus eius. 2. Et cognovi me statim dignam esse et pro eo petere debere. Et coepi de ipso orationem facere multum et ingemescere ad Dominum. 3. Continuo ipsa nocte ostensum est mihi hoc: 4. Video Dinocraten exeuntem de loco tenebroso, ubi et conplures erant, aestuantem valde et sitientem, sordido vultu; et colore pallido; et vulnus in facie eius, quod cum moreretur habuit. 5. Hic Dinocrates fuerat frater meus carnalis, annorum septem, qui per infirmitatem facie cancerata male obiit, ita ut mors eius odio fuerit omnibus hominibus. 6. Pro hoc ergo orationem feceram; et inter me et illum grande erat diastema, ita ut uterque ad invicem accedere non possemus. 7. Erat deinde in illo loco, ubi Dinocrates erat piscina plena aqua, altiorem marginem habens quam erat statura pueri; et extendebat se Dinocrates quasi bibiturus. 8. Ego dolebam, quod et piscina illa aquam habebat, et tamen propter altitudinem marginis bibiturus non esset. 9. Et experrecta sum et cognovi fratrem meum laborare, sed fidebam me profuturam labori eius. Et orabam pro eo omnibus diebus quousque transivimus in carcerem castrensem; munere enim castrensi eramus pugnaturi: natale tunc Getae Caesaris. 10. Et feci pro illo orationem die et nocte gemens et lacrimans ut mihi donaretur.

8. 1. Die quo in nervo mansimus, ostensum est mihi hoc: video locum illum quem retro videram, et Dinocraten mundo corpore, bene vestitum, refrigerantem, et ubi erat vulnus, video cicatricem: 2. et piscinam illam, quam retro videram, summisso margine usque ad umbilicum pueri, et aquam de ea trahebat sine cessatione; 3. et; super marginem fiala aurea plena aqua. Et accessit Dinocrates et de ea bibere coepit, quae fiala non deficiebat. 4. Et satiatus accessit de aqua ludere

more infantium gaudens. Et experrecta sum. Tunc intellexi translatum eum esse de poena.

. . . .

10. 1. Pridie quam pugnaremus, video in horomate hoc: venisse Pomponium diaconum ad ostium carceris et pulsare vehementer. 2. Et exivi ad eum et aperui ei; qui erat vestitus discincta candida, habens multiplices galliculas. 3. Et dixit mihi, "Perpetua, te expectamus. Veni." Et tenuit mihi manum, et coepimus ire per aspera loca et flexuosa. 4. Vix tandem pervenimus anhelantes ad amphitheatrum, et induxit me in media arena et dixit mihi, "Noli pavere: hic sum tecum et conlaboro tecum." Et abiit. 5. Et aspicio populum ingentem adtonitum, et quia sciebam me ad bestias damnatam esse, mirabar quod non mitterentur mihi bestiae. 6. Et exivit quidam contra me Aegyptius foedus specie cum adiutoribus suis, pugnaturus mecum. Veniunt et ad me adolescentes decori, adiutores et fautores mei. 7. Et expoliata sum, et facta sum masculus. Et coeperunt me favisores mei oleo defricare quodmodo solent in agonem; et illum contra Aegyptium video in afa volutantem. 8. Et exivit vir quidam mirae magnitudinis, ut etiam excederet fastigium amphitheatri, discinctatus, purpuram inter duos clavos per medium pectus habens, et galliculas multiformes ex auro et argento factas, et ferens virgam quasi lanista, et ramum viridem in quo erant mala aurea. 9. Et petiit silentium et dixit, "Hic Aegyptius, si hanc vicerit, occidet illam gladio; haec, si hunc vicerit, accipiet ramum istum." Et recessit. 10. Et accessimus ad invicem et coepimus mittere pugnos; ille mihi pedes adprehendere volebat; ego autem illi calcibus faciem caedebam. 11. Et sublata sum in aere, et coepi eum sic caedere quasi terram non calcans. At ubi vidi moram fieri, iunxi manus, ut digitos in digitos mitterem, et apprehendi illi caput et cecidit in faciem et calcavi illi caput. 12. Et coepit populus clamare et favisores mei psallere. Et accessi ad lanistam et accepi ramum. 13. Et osculatus est me et dixit mihi, "Filia, pax tecum." Et coepi ire cum gloria ad portam Sanavivariam. 14. Et experrecta sum. Et intellexi me non ad bestias, sed contra diabolum esse pugnaturam; sed sciebam mihi esse victoriam. 15. Hoc usque in pridie muneris egi; ipsius autem muneris actum, si quis voluerit, scribat.

. . . .

12. 1. Et venimus prope locum cuius loci parietes tales erant quasi de luce aedificati; et ante ostium loci illius angeli quattuor stabant, qui introeuntes vestierunt stolas candidas. 2. Et introivimus et audivimus vocem unitam dicentem, "Agios, agios, agios," sine cessatione. 3. Et vidimus in eodem loco sedentem quasi hominem canum, niveos habentem capillos et vultu iuvenili, cuius pedes non vidimus. 4. Et in dextera et in sinistra seniores quattuor, et post illos ceteri seniores conplures stabant. 5. Et introeuntes cum admiratione stetimus ante

thronum, et quattuor angeli sublevaverunt nos, et osculati sumus illum, et de manu sua traiecit nobis in faciem. 6. Et ceteri seniores dixerunt nobis, "Stemus," et stetimus et pacem fecimus. Et dixerunt nobis seniores, "Ite et ludite." 7. Et dixi Perpetuae, "Habes quod vis." Et dixit mihi, "Deo gratias, ut, quomodo in carne hilaris fui, hilarior sim et hic modo."

13. 1. Et exivimus et vidimus ante fores Optatum episcopum ad dexteram et Aspasium presbyterum doctorem ad sinistram, separatos et tristes. 2. Et miserunt se ad pedes nobis et dixerunt, "Componite inter nos, quia existis, et sic nos reliquistis." 3. Et diximus illis, "Non tu es papa noster, et tu presbyter? Ut vos ad pedes nobis mittatis?" Et moti sumus et conplexi illos sumus. 4. Et coepit Perpetua Graece cum illis loqui, et segregavimus eos in viridiarium sub arbore rosae. 5. Et dum loquimur cum eis, dixerunt illis angeli, "Sinite illos refrigerent, et si quas habetis inter vos dissensiones, dimittite vobis invicem." 6. Et conturbaverunt eos, et dixerunt Optato, "Corrige plebem tuam, quia sic ad te conveniunt quasi de circo redeuntes et de factionibus certantes." 7. Et sic nobis visum est quasi vellent claudere portas. 8. Et coepimus illic multos fratres cognoscere, sed et martyras. Universi odore inenarrabili alebamur, qui nos satiabat. Tunc gaudens experrectus sum."

14. 1. Hae visiones insigniores ipsorum martyrum beatissimorum Saturi et Perpetuae, quas ipsi conscripserunt. 2. Secundulum vero Deus maturiore exitu de saeculo adhuc in carcere evocavit, non sine gratia, ut bestias lucraretur. 3. Gladium tamen etsi non anima, certe caro eius agnovit.

15. 1. Circa Felicitatem vero, et illi gratia Domini eiusmodi contigit: 2. Cum octo iam mensium ventrem haberet (nam praegnans fuerat adprehensa), instante spectaculi die in magno erat luctu, ne propter ventrem differetur (quia non licet praegnantes poenae repraesentari) et ne inter alios postea sceleratos sanctum et innocentem sanguinem funderet. 3. Sed et conmartyres graviter contristabantur, ne tam bonam sociam quasi comitem solam in via eiusdem spei relinquerent. 4. Coniuncto itaque unito gemitu ad Dominum orationem fuderent ante tertium diem muneris. 5. Statim post orationem dolores invaserunt. Et cum pro naturali difficultate octavi mensis in partu laborans doleret, ait illi quidam ex ministris cataractariorum, "Quae sic modo doles, quid facies obiecta bestiis, quas contempsisti cum sacrificare noluisti?" 6. Et illa respondit, "Modo patior quod patior; illic autem alius erit in me qui patietur pro me, quia et ego pro illo passura sum." 7. Ita enixa est puellam, quam sibi quaedam soror in filiam educavit.

16. 1. Quoniam ergo permisit et permittendo voluit Spiritus Sanctus ordinem ipsius muneris conscribi, etsi indigni ad supplementum tantae gloriae describendae, tamen quasi mandatum sanctissimae Perpetuae, immo fideicommissum eius exequimur, unum adicientes documentum de ipsius constantia et animi sublimitate. 2. Cum tribunus castigatius eos castigaret, quia ex admonitionibus hominum vanissimorum verebatur ne subtraherentur de carcere incantationibus aliquibus magicis, in faciem ei Perpetua respondit, 3. "Quid utique non

permittis nobis refrigerare noxiis nobilissimis, Caesaris scilicet, et natali eiusdem pugnaturis? Aut non tua gloria est, si pinguiores illo producamur?" 4. Horruit et erubuit tribunus, et ita iussit illos humanius haberi, ut fratribus eius et ceteris facultas fuerit introeundi et refrigerandi cum eis, iam et ipso optione carceris credente.

17. 1. Pridie quoque cum illam cenam ultimam quam liberam vocant, quantum in ipsis erat, non cenam liberam sed agapem cenarent, eadem constantia ad populum verba iactabant, comminantes iudicium Dei, contestantes passionis suae felicitatem, inridentes concurrentium curiositatem, dicente Saturo: 2. "Crastinus satis vobis non est? Quid libenter videtis quod odistis? Hodie amici, cras inimici. Notate tamen vobis facies nostras diligenter, ut recognoscatis nos in die illo." 3. Ita omnes inde adtoniti discedebant, ex quibus multi crediderunt.

18. 1. Illuxit dies victoriae illorum, et processerunt de carcere in amphitheatrum, quasi in caelum, hilares, vultu decori, si forte gaudio paventes non timore. 2. Sequebatur Perpetua lucido vultu et placido incessu, ut matrona Christi, ut Dei delicata, vigore oculorum deiciens omnium conspectum. 3. Item Felicitas, salvam se peperisse gaudens ut ad bestias pugnaret, a sanguine ad sanguinem, ab obstetrice ad retiarium, lotura post partum baptismo secundo. 4. Et cum ducti essent in portam et cogerentur habitum induere, viri quidem sacerdotum Saturni, feminae vero sacratarum Cereris generosa illa in finem usque constantia repugnavit. 5. Dicebat enim, "Ideo ad hoc sponte pervenimus, ne libertas nostra obduceretur; ideo animam nostram addiximus, ne tale aliquid faceremus; hoc vobiscum pacti sumus." 6. Agnovit iniustitia iustitiam: concessit tribunus, quomodo erant, simpliciter inducerentur. 7. Perpetua psallebat, caput iam Aegyptii calcans; Revocatus et Saturninus et Saturus populo spectanti comminabantur. 8. Dehinc ut sub conspectu Hilariani pervenerunt, gestu et nutu coeperunt Hilariano dicere, "Tu nos," inquiunt, "te autem Deus." 9. Ad hoc populus exasperatus flagellis eos vexari per ordinem venatorum postulavit; et utique gratulati sunt quod aliquid et de dominicis passionibus essent consecuti.

19. 1. Sed qui dixerat, "Petite et accipietis," petentibus dederat eum exitum quem quis desideraverat. 2. Nam, si quando inter se de martyrii sui voto sermoncinabantur, Saturninus quidem omnibus bestiis velle se obici profitebatur, ut scilicet gloriosiorem gestaret coronam. 3. Itaque in commissione spectaculi ipse et Revocatus leopardum experti etiam super pulpitum ab urso vexati sunt. 4. Saturus autem nihil magis quam ursum abominabatur; sed uno morsu leopardi confici se iam praesumebat. 5. Itaque cum apro subministraretur, venator potius qui illum apro subligaverat, subfossus ab eadem bestia post dies muneris obiit; Saturus solummodo tractus est. 6. Et cum ad ursum substrictus esset in ponte, ursus de cavea prodire noluit. Itaque secundo Saturus inlaesus revocatur.

20. 1. Puellis autem ferocissimam vaccam, ideoque praeter consuetudinem conparatam, diabolus praeparavit, sexui earum etiam de bestia aemulatus. 2. Itaque

dispoliatae et reticulis indutae producebantur. Horruit populus alteram respiciens puellam delicatam, alteram a partu recentem stillantibus mammis. 3. Ita revocatae et discinctis indutae. Prior Perpetua iactata est, et concidit in lumbos. 4. Et ubi sedit, tunicam a latere discissam ad velamentum femoris reduxit, pudoris potius memor quam doloris. 5. Dehinc, acu requisita, et dispersos capillos infibulavit; non enim decebat martyram sparsis capillis pati, ne in sua gloria plangere videretur. 6. Ita surrexit, et elisam Felicitatem cum vidisset, accessit et manum ei tradidit et suscitavit illam. 7. Et ambae pariter steterunt. Et populi duritia devicta, revocatae sunt in portam Sanavivariam. 8. Illic Perpetua a quodam tunc catechumeno, Rustico nomine, qui ei adhaerebat, suscepta et quasi a somno expergita (adeo in spiritu et in extasi fuerat) circumspicere coepit, et stupentibus omnibus ait, "Quando," inquit, "producimur ad vaccam illam nescio quam?" 9. Et cum audisset quod iam evenerat, non prius credidit nisi quasdam notas vexationis in corpore et habitu suo recognovisset. 10. Exinde accersitum fratrem suum, et illum catechumenum, adlocuta est dicens, "In fide state et invicem omnes diligite, et passionibus nostris ne scandalizemini."

21. 1. Item Saturus in alia porta Pudentem militem exhortabatur dicens, "Ad summam," inquit, "certe, sicut praesumpsi et praedixi, nullam usque adhuc bestiam sensi. Et nunc de toto corde credas: ecce prodeo illo, et ab uno morsu leopardi consummor." 2. Et statim in fine spectaculi leopardo obiectus de uno morsu tanto perfusus est sanguine, ut populus reverti illi secundi baptismatis testimonium reclamaverit, "Salvum lotum, salvum lotum." 3. Plane utique salvus erat qui hoc modo laverat. 4. Tunc Pudenti militi, "Vale," inquit, "et memento fidei et mei; et haec te non conturbent, sed confirment." 5. Simulque ansulam de digito eius petiit, et vulneri suo mersam reddidit ei hereditatem, pignus reliquens illi et memoriam sanguinis. 6. Exinde iam exanimis prosternitur cum ceteris ad iugulationem solito loco. 7. Et cum populus illos in medio postularet, ut gladio penetranti in eorum corpore oculos suos comites homicidii adiungerent, ultro surrexerunt et se quo volebat populus transtulerunt, ante iam osculati invicem ut martyrium per sollemnia pacis consummarent. 8. Ceteri quidem inmobiles et cum silentio ferrum receperunt; multo magis Saturus, qui et prior ascenderat, prior reddidit spiritum; nam et Perpetuam sustinebat. 9. Perpetua autem, ut aliquid doloris gustaret, inter ossa conpuncta exululavit, et errantem dexteram tirunculi gladiatoris ipsa in iugulum suum transtulit. 10. Fortasse tanta femina aliter non potuisset occidi, quae ab inmundo spiritu timebatur, nisi ipsa voluisset. 11. O fortissimi ac beatissimi martyres! O vere vocati et electi in gloriam Domini nostri Iesu Christi! Quam qui magnificat et honorificat et adorat, utique et haec non minora veteribus exempla in aedificationem Ecclesiae legere debet, ut novae quoque virtutes unum et eundem semper Spiritum Sanctum usque adhuc operari testificentur, et omnipotentem Deum Patrem et Filium eius Iesum Christum Dominum nostrum, cui est claritas et inmensa potestas in saecula saeculorum. Amen.

TRANSLATION BY JUDITH LYNN SEBESTA

1. 1. If the ancient deeds[1] of faith, that both testify to the grace of God and fortify the spiritual resolve of men, were particularly made known through writing so that through their being read[2] as though presenting a picture of the events both God should be honored and mankind strengthened, why should not new examples also be written to contribute equally to both these ends? 2. For indeed, in like manner, these new examples will sometime become ancient and indispensable for posterity, even if in their own time they are thought to have lesser influence because antiquity is given greater respect. 3. But let those who adjudge the one power of the one Holy Spirit to be affected by the different ages of time consider this: since events that are more recent should be considered to be more important because they are the most recent of all, as a consequence of the abundance of grace promised us in the last days of the world.[3] 4. For "God says, in the very last days, I will pour out from my Spirit over all flesh, and their sons and daughters will prophesy; and I will pour out from my Spirit over slave men and women; and the young men will see visions and the old men will dream dreams."[4] 5. And so we, too, who both recognize and honor both recent prophecies and the visions[5] equally just as they have been promised to us and who consider the other powers of the Holy Spirit intended for the use of the church (for which that Spirit was sent to give likewise all gifts to all men as the Lord allotted to each one), by necessity publish these visions and prophecies, and through reading them we honor the glory of God, so that no weakness or failing of faith should judge that the divine grace was bestowed only upon the ancients, whether they were worthy of martyrdom or of revelation, since God always accomplishes what He promises as a testimony for those who do not believe and as blessing for those who do believe. 6. And also what we have heard and examined we announce to you, brothers and little children,[6] so that you too who were present[7] may remember the glory of God, and you who now know through hearing of these deeds may have communion with the holy martyrs, and through them with our Lord Jesus Christ, to whom be glory and honor for ever and ever.[8] Amen.

---

[1]These ancient deeds include those found in the Old and New Testaments, such as the visions of Ezekiel and Abraham in Acts and in Revelation.

[2]The author of the preface means not only personal reading, but also particularly public reading of such accounts to those assembled for worship. The *Passio* of Perpetua and Felicity, for example, was read to the Christian congregations each year in Carthage on the date of their martyrdoms.

[3]The belief that the second coming of Christ was imminent was very strong among Christians of this period, and particularly among the Montanists.

[4]This quotation is from Acts 2:17, which is a quotation from Joel 3:1–5.

[5]That is, visions and accounts such as the *Passio* of Perpetua and Felicity.

[6]The author may here be distinguishing between those who have been baptized and the catechumens, or perhaps between those who were present at the martyrdom and those who only hear of it through this account.

[7]That is, at the martyrdom of Perpetua and Felicity.

[8]The writer is quoting from 1 John 1:1–4.

2. 1. Some young catechumens were arrested; Revocatus and Felicity, his fellow slave, Saturninus and Secundulus; among them were also Vibia Perpetua, of good family and recently married, well educated,[9] who had a father, mother, two brothers—one also a catechumen—and an infant son at her breast. 2. Moreover, she was about twenty-two years old. From this point on this is her entire story of her martyrdom just as she wrote it with her own hand and in her own phrasing.

3. 1. "When we were still," she says," with the arresting officers,[10] and my father both wanted to drive out and overturn[11] my resolve with argument and was persevering out of love for me, I said, "Father, do you see this vase called a waterpot?" And he said, "I see it." 2. And I said to him, "Can it be called by any other name than its own?" And he said, "No." "Just so, I am not able to call myself by any other term than what I am, a Christian." 3. Then my father, angered by my argument, flew at me as though he would pluck out my eyes, but he only shook me, and, vanquished, went away with his devil-inspired arguments. 4. Then because for a few days I was left unvisited by my father, I thanked God and I was strengthened through his absence. 5. During this space of a few days we were baptized, and the Spirit told me not to pray for anything after the water except my body's endurance.[12] After a few days we were taken into prison, and I was very afraid because I had never experienced such darkness.[13] 6. O what a harsh day! The heat was great[14] because of the crowd of people, and there were the beatings by the soldiers. Above all I was worried with anxiety for my baby there. 7. Then Tertius and Pomponius, those blessed deacons who were taking care of us,[15]

---

[9]The Latin words indicate that Perpetua belonged to a notable provincial family. The name Vibius was born by numerous Roman aristocrats, some of whom lived in the imperial entourage. Most young women of rank studied music and literature and probably, as did Perpetua, learned the Greek language. The Latin words *matronaliter nupta* appear on an epitaph (*CIL* 8.870.3): *Pescennia . . . bonis natalibus nata matronaliter nupta*. These three Latin phrases describing Perpetua are in the style of an epitaph, and, in a sense, serve as her epitaph.

[10]At this point Perpetua and her companions were not in the city prison, but in custody under the guard of the officers.

[11]The verb *deicere*, which is frequently used by Perpetua, had a military connotation and was used by Tertullian and Cyprian to express the efforts of the devil to weaken the resolve of Christians.

[12]As the early Christians viewed baptism as truly giving one a new birth and a state of pure innocence, the first prayers of the newly baptized were thought to have particular potency.

[13]Roman prisons were often of two levels, the lower one being particularly dark. To the Christians the darkness was a favorite place for the devil, resembling in its darkness hell. Tertullian *Ad martyras* 1.4: "The prison is the house of the devil in which he maintains all his family."

[14]Because the lower level of prisons generally had no windows and was a fairly small room, the heat generated by the bodies of the prisoners, the heat of the climate, and the lack of air circulation presented a very real danger of suffocation. It is mentioned in several other accounts of martyrs.

[15]Deacons were ordained persons (male and female) who performed many functions in the early church, including the distribution of alms, administration of church moneys, and visiting imprisoned Christians to bring them what help they could.

arranged for a price that we could be released for a few hours into a better room of the prison so we could refresh ourselves. 8. Then we all went out of the prison and were left to ourselves, I nursing my baby, who was weak due to lack of milk; worried for him, I spoke to my mother and encouraged my brother, I entrusted my son to them; I grieved because I saw them grieving on my behalf. 9. Such cares I endured for many days, and I got permission for my baby to stay in jail with me; and I immediately became stronger and recovered from my care and concern over the child, and suddenly the prison became like a palace to me so that I preferred to be there rather than any other place.

4. 1. Then my brother[16] said to me, "Lady sister,[17] you are now in great grace, so much so that you could ask for a vision and it could be shown to you whether you will be martyred or discharged."[18] 2. And I who knew that I talked with the Lord, whose great grace I had already experienced, responded to him with faith, saying, "I will tell you tomorrow." And I asked and this was revealed to me:[19] 3. I saw a ladder of wonderful length, made of bronze, stretching right up to heaven, and narrow, along which only one person at a time could ascend, and on the edges of the ladder every kind of weapon was attached. There were swords, lances, hooks, swords, spikes, so that if anyone was climbing carelessly or inattentively, he would be sliced and his flesh would adhere to the weapons.[20] 4. And there was reclining under this ladder a serpent[21] of wonderful size, which would attack those climbing up and scare them so that they would not ascend. 5. Saturus, however, climbed up first, who had given himself up after us (because he had built up our faith), and then, when we were arrested, had been absent. 6. And he went to the top of the ladder, and turned around and said to me, "Perpetua, I am awaiting you, but see that that serpent does not bite you." And I said to him, "He will not harm me, in the name of Jesus Christ." 7. And underneath that ladder, as if afraid of me, the serpent slowly stretched out its head; and as if I were stepping on the first rung, I stepped on his head[22] and climbed up. 8. And I saw an immense

---

[16]It is unclear whether Perpetua means her blood brother who was a catechumen or whether she means a brother in faith, e.g. Saturus, who plays a role in her vision.

[17]The word *domina* gives recognition to social rank of Perpetua's family and her rank as *matrona*.

[18]As is noted above, the Christians used words or phrases that had a military connotations and reflected their self-conception of "soldiers of Christ."

[19]To ask for visions or revelatory dreams was a common practice among both pagans and Christians. Spells for ensuring true dreams are found in some papyri, and at some oracular sites one would pray for a dream and then go to sleep on the site.

[20]On the symbolism of the ladder, see the introduction. That Perpetua's ladder has iron instruments of war indicates clearly her death by martyrdom. This prophetic dream "comes true" in 21.8, in which a soldier slashes her neck with a sword.

[21]The serpent recalls the serpent of Genesis 3:15 and that of Revelation 20:2 and that described in the *Shepherd of Hermas* 4.1:5–16.

[22]Perpetua's words recall the prophecy in Genesis 3:15, where God predicts that the woman shall bruise the serpent with her heel.

space, a garden, and a white-haired man sitting in its midst, dressed like a shepherd, a very tall man, milking his sheep, and many thousands of people dressed in shining white standing around him.[23] 9. And he lifted up his head and looked at me and said, "You are welcome, child." And he called me over and gave me some of the cheese he had milked, a mouthful of it; and I took it in my clasped hands and I ate it, and everyone standing around said, "Amen." 10. And at the sound of their voices I woke up, still chewing, as it were, on something that was sweet.[24] And I immediately went to my brother, and we knew that it would be martyrdom, and we began to have no further hope in this world.

5. 1. After a few days a rumor came that we were to be tried. My father, moreover, came from the town, worn down with grief, and climbed up the hill[25] to me so that he could overturn my resolve, saying, 2. "Take pity, daughter, on my white hair, take pity on your father, if I am worthy to be called father by you, if with these hands I raised you to this prime of your life, if I preferred you before all your brothers; do not shame me before everyone. Look at your brothers, look at your mother and your aunt her sister, look at your son, who will not be able to live after your death. Put aside your pride, do not ruin us all; for not one of us will speak freely if you suffer any harm." 5. He said these things as if he were speaking as a loving father, kissing my hands and throwing himself at my feet and crying,[26] he called me not daughter but Lady.[27] 6. And I was sorry for my father's situation because he was the only one of my whole family who would not rejoice at my martyrdom and I comforted him saying, "What will happen on the platform[28] will be what God wishes; for you should know that we are not in our own power, but in God's." And he went away from me grief-stricken indeed.

6. 1. On another day when we were eating at midday, we were suddenly taken to be tried. And we came to the forum. The news immediately ran every-

---

[23]Revelation 6:11 describes the Son of Man as white-haired; he is likewise described as the Ancient of Days in Daniel 7:9. In calling Perpetua "child," the white-haired man takes on a paternal aspect and thus recalls her earthly father, whom she describes as white-haired and aged. Christ is frequently represented in contemporary catacomb paintings in Africa and elsewhere as a shepherd. In Revelation 6:11 and 7:13, elderly men clothed in white surround Christ.

[24]It was the custom for the neophytes to drink milk and honey immediately after their baptism: the milk symbolizing their rebirth, the honey the sweetness of God's word. Perpetua had been baptized only a few days before this vision. The cheese also recalls the celebration of communion, which helped prepare martyrs for their death.

[25]The prison was on the acropolis called the Bursa.

[26]These actions were the customary ones of supplication.

[27]Amat notes (*Passion* 209 s.v. "*dominam*") that epitaphs often give the title *domina*, or "lady," to the deceased and speculates that Perpetua's father may regard his daughter as already dead if she does not abandon her faith.

[28]Perpetua presumably means the platform on which the procurator will interrogate the prisoners (6.2).

where through the forum, and a huge crowd gathered. 2. We climbed up onto the platform. The others were questioned and confessed their faith. It was my turn. And my father appeared there with my son and drew me off of the steps saying, "Beg, take pity on your baby." 3. And Hilarianus the procurator,[29] who then had received the power of capital punishment in place of the deceased proconsul Minucius Timinianus,[30] said, "Spare your father's white hair, spare your child's infancy. Sacrifice on behalf of the health and safety of the emperors." 4. And I responded, "I will not." Hilarianus said, "Are you a Christian?" And I responded, "I am a Christian." 5. And since my father was still trying to persuade me, Hilarianus ordered him to be thrown to the ground and he was beaten with a rod.[31] And I was sorry for my father's situation, as if I had been the one beaten: so I grieved because of his unhappy old age. 6. Then Hilarianus gave judgment on all of us and condemned us to the beasts, and we went happily back to the prison. 7. Then because my baby had been accustomed to nurse my breasts and to stay with me in prison, I immediately sent Pomponius the deacon to my father, asking for my baby. 8. But my father did not wish to give him over. And as God wished, neither did my baby want my breasts anymore nor did they grow feverish so that I would not be worn down with concern for my baby or by pain in my breasts.

7. 1. A few days afterward, when we were all praying, suddenly in the middle of my prayer a voice came from me[32] and the name Dinocrates came to my lips. And I was amazed because he had never before come into my mind except then, and remembering his fate I grieved. 2. And I knew immediately I was worthy in grace to pray for him and ought to do so. And I began to pray at length for him and to mourn over him before the Lord. 3. Immediately that very night this vision was shown to me: 4. I saw Dinocrates coming out of a very dark place (where there were also several others) very hot and thirsty, with dirty face and body and pale in color, and with that sore on his face that he had when he died.[33] 5. This Dinocrates was my brother of the flesh, seven years old, who had died weak and in great pain because of the sore on his face so that everyone was horrified by his death. 6. On his behalf, therefore, I prayed; and there was between me

---

[29]As the *procurator Augusti* Hilarianus was in charge of the financial affairs of the province, but also had some other administrative duties. Tertullian (*Ad scapulam* 3.1) states that Hilarianus was a fierce opponent of Christians.

[30]The proconsul was the chief administrative officer of a province. Timinianus is not known from inscriptions or other sources.

[31]Normally, beating was a punishment reserved for slaves and children. This punishment is part of the shame her father feared (5.2).

[32]The expression indicates that God inspired the voice.

[33]The darkness indicates hell (see note 13). Dinocrates was still suffering from the fever caused by the sore still visible on his face. His dirty clothing may indicate his unsaved state, for those who were baptized and saved would be wearing shining white garments (as in 4.8).

and him a great distance so that neither of us could get to the other.[34] 7. There was then in that place where Dinocrates was a basin full of water, the lip of which was higher than he was; and Dinocrates stretched up toward it as if he would drink. 8. And I grieved because that basin had water and still, because of its height, he could not drink.[35] 9. And I woke up and I knew my brother was suffering, but I was full of faith that I could help his suffering. And I prayed for him[36] all the days that we passed in the military prison;[37] for we were to fight at the military games: on the birthday of Geta Caesar. 10. And I prayed for Dinocrates day and night, moaning and weeping that he might be given to me.

8. 1. On the day on which we were chained up, this vision was shown to me: I saw that place that I had seen earlier, and Dinocrates, now clean in body, well clothed, restored to health, and where his cancer had been, I saw a scar:[38] 2. and that basin that I had seen earlier now had its lip lowered and reached up to the boy's waist, and he kept on drinking water from it. 3. And above the lip of the basin was a golden bowl full of water. And Dinocrates approached the golden bowl and began to drink from it, and the bowl never became empty. 4. And when he had enough to drink, he came away from the water happy to play, as children like to do. And I woke up. Then I knew that he had been released from punishment.

[9. *During the next few days the prison warden Pudens, recognizing the spiritual powers of the Christians, gave others free access to the prisoners to enable each group to strengthen their spirits. Perpetua's father also came, tearing out the hairs of his beard in grief and prostrating himself on the floor. Though Perpetua was sorry for him, she remained resolute in her faith.*]

10. 1. On the day before we were to fight, I saw this in a vision: Pomponius the deacon came to the door of the prison and knocked on it hard. 2. And I went to the door and opened it for him who was dressed in a shining white, unbelted garment,[39] with elaborate small Gallic shoes.[40] 3. And he said to me, "Perpetua, we are waiting for you. Come." And he took me by my hand, and we began to go

---

[34]As in the vision of Lazarus and the rich man in Luke 16:19–31.

[35]The basin seems to represent the Waters of Life offered by Christ (Revelation 21:6), which an unbaptized person could not obtain.

[36]So, too, Tertullian (*De monogamia* 10.4) urges Christians to pray for the dead so that they may be helped.

[37]At first Perpetua and her companions seem to have been kept in the city prison, guarded by the city's public slaves. Apparently, after their trial, they were removed to the military prison under the control of the military tribune; the garrison seems likely to have been a detachment of the *Legio III Augusta*, stationed at Lambesis.

[38]The "healing" of his sore is another indication of his "healed" or "saved" soul.

[39]An unbelted garment was worn by angels (see, for example, *Passio Mariani* 7.3) and by the *orantes* (figures of people praying in Paradise) painted on the walls of Christian catacombs.

[40]The Latin word *multiplices* ("elaborate") suggests that the shoes were made of many thin leather straps, similar perhaps to modern huaraches. The significance of these shoes is not understood.

through rough, winding places.[41] 4. Finally we managed to arrive at the amphitheater gasping for breath, and he led me into the middle of the arena and said to me, "Do not be afraid: here I am with you and I am helping you."[42] And he went away. 5. And I saw a huge crowd, all amazed at me, and because I knew I was condemned to the beasts, I wondered why they did not send in the beasts to me. 6. And there came out against me a certain Egyptian, horrible to look at, with his assistants, ready to fight me. There came to my side handsome young men, my helpers and encouragers.[43] 7. And I was undressed and found myself to be a man.[44] And my helpers began to anoint me with oil as they do in gladiatorial fights,[45] and I saw that Egyptian opposite me rolling around in the sand. 8. And there came out a certain man of wondrous height so that he even rose above the amphitheater wearing an unbelted purple tunic,[46] with two stripes, one on either side of his chest and wearing elaborate Gallic shoes made from gold and silver, and carrying a rod as a referee does and a green branch on which were golden apples.[47] 9. And he asked for silence and said, "This Egyptian, if he defeats this woman, will kill her with his sword. This woman, if she defeats him, will receive

---

[41]These details symbolize martyrdom as a difficult passage and may echo Matthew 7:14, "It is . . . a hard road that leads to Life. . . ."

[42]At this point Pomponius seems to merge with the figure of Christ who, martyrs thought, was present with them in the arena. His admonition occurs more than once in theophanies in the Old Testament, e.g., Isaiah 43:1.

[43]In early Christian literature and art, the Devil was represented as an Egyptian, in part due to the imagery in Ezekiel 29:3, where God says, "I am set against you, Pharaoh, king of Egypt, you huge serpent, who lie in the middle of your rivers." His assistants probably represent attendant devils, just as Perpetua's handsome young men are to be understood as angels.

[44]Athletes frequently contested in the nude, and Perpetua's transformation is perhaps a natural consequence of her configuration as an athlete. Paul, however, points out that "in Christ there is no male nor female," and her transformation may be understood as reinforcing the concept of the equality of the sexes in Christianity. The idea that both sexes possessed equal spirituality, moreover, is an important tenet among the Montanists.

[45]Though such anointing with oil was customary before athletic contests, here it bears also the Christian symbolism of being anointed with oil ("unction") customarily performed before and after baptism. Unction was thought to give protection and strength against the devil. The term *agonem* here translated as "gladiatorial fights" was used by Christians to denote spiritual combat.

[46]The trainer apparently represents Christ. Deities appearing in prophetic dreams, both Christian and pagan, often possessed great size. All purple garments were restricted by law to the emperors; here the purple tunic represents Christ's majesty.

[47]The rod not only symbolizes the referee's authority to direct the combat, but also metaphorically stands for the rod used to chastise fools and children (Proverbs 10:13 and 22:15) and the iron scepter with which God shatters the nations of the earth (Psalms 2:9). It may also allude to the staves of Aaron (Exodus 7:9 passim) and of Moses (Exodus 14:16), which marked them out as leaders chosen by God. The green branch, customarily of the laurel tree, was the traditional award for the victorious combatant. The golden apples recall the golden fruits in the garden of the Hesperides and perhaps also the golden fruits of the Tree of Life in Eden (I Enoch 25).

this branch." And he withdrew. 10. And we came together and we began to fight. He wanted to catch me by my feet; I, however, kept hitting him on his face with my heels. 11. And I was lifted up in the air,[48] and I began to strike him thus as though I was not walking on the ground. And when I saw a lull in the fight, I joined my hands linking my fingers together, and I approached his head and fell on his face and he fell on his face and I kicked his head. 12. And the crowd began to shout and my helpers began to sing psalms. And I went up to the trainer and I took the branch. 13. And he kissed me and said to me, "Daughter, peace be with you." And I began to go in glory to the Sanavivaria Gate.[49] 14. And I woke up. And I knew I would fight not against the beasts, but against the devil, but I knew victory would be mine. 15. I wrote this on the day before the games; let him who wishes write what happened at the games themselves."

[*11. At this point Perpetua's narrative ends. Saturus recounts his vision: Immediately after he and Perpetua have died in the arena, four angels carry them eastward and upward. As they approach a huge light, he tells Perpetua that they have received God's promise. When their angelic escorts put them down in a garden, four more angels greet them. They then begin to walk along a road and meet some Christians martyred a short while before. The angels then invite Saturus and Perpetua to greet the Lord.*]

12. 1. And we came near a place which had walls that seemed made of light; and before the door of this place stood four angels who dressed those entering with shining white garments.[50] 2. And we entered and heard voices in unison saying unceasingly, "Holy, holy, holy."[51] 3. And we saw in that same place someone who looked like an old man with snow-white hair and young face, whose feet we did not see.[52] 4. And on his right and left were four older men and behind them several other older men stood. 5. And entering with amazement we stood before the throne, and the four angels lifted us up, and we kissed him, and he caressed our faces with his hand. 6. And the other older men said to us, "Let us rise," and we stood and exchanged kisses of peace. And the older men said to us, "Go and rejoice." 7. And I said to Perpetua, "You have what you want." And she said to me, "Thanks be to God, as happy as I was in life, I am even happier here thus."

13. 1. And we went out and we saw before the doors the bishop Optatus on the right and the teacher and presbyter Aspasius on the left, far apart from each

---

[48]Her levitation is a sign of her spiritual power.

[49]This is the gate the victorious gladiators exited (its name means "Gate of Health and Life"). Dead gladiators were carried out of the Porta Libitinensis ("Gate of Burials").

[50]Revelation 4:6 describes the floor before the throne of God as a sea of glass like crystal. The garments are shining white because they "have been washed white in the blood of the Lamb" (Revelation 7:14).

[51]An echo of Revelation 4:8 in which the four living beings by the throne of God sing unceasingly, "Holy."

[52]This image of Christ is very like that of Perpetua's first vision, and reflects that in Revelation 1:13–14. The invisible feet presumably are symbolic of Christ's divinity.

other and sad.[53] And they knelt at our feet and said, "Settle our quarrel, because you went away and left us thus in disagreement." 3. And we said to them, "Are you not our father and you our presbyter? Why then should you kneel to us?" And we were moved and embraced them. 4. And Perpetua began to speak Greek with them, and we led them apart into the garden under a rose tree. 5. And while we spoke with them, the angels said to them, "Let them refresh themselves, and if you have any quarrel amongst yourselves, forgive each other in turn." 6. And the angels shamed them, and they said to Optatus, "Chasten your flock, because they have thus come to you as if returning from the chariot races and arguing about the teams."[54] 7. And it seemed to us as if they wished to close the gates.[55] 8. And we began to recognize many of our brethren there, but also the martyrs. We all were nourished by a perfume that cannot be described, which satisfied us.[56] Then I woke up rejoicing.

14. 1. These were the extraordinary visions of the blessed martyrs themselves, Saturus and Perpetua, which they themselves wrote. 2. But God called Secundulus out of the world still earlier, while he was in prison, not without grace, so he would avoid the beasts. 3. Nevertheless, though his soul did not know the sword, his flesh certainly did.[57]

15. 1. As for Felicity, the grace of God befell her too. 2. Though she was eight months pregnant (for she was pregnant when she was arrested), as the day of the spectacle neared she suffered in labor so that her punishment would not be postponed (for it is not permitted to send pregnant women to their punishment)[58] and so that she would not pour out her innocent blood later along with wicked criminals. 3. But her fellow martyrs were also very sad, fearing they would leave

---

[53]Optatus was bishop of Carthage and was responsible for administrating the congregations in his bishopric. A presbyter was the leader of a congregation of Christians. The title teacher indicates that Aspasius expounded doctrine to the congregation and catechumens. Their physical distance from one another reflects the distance between their theological positions. While the reasons for their disagreement are not known, this passage may be making a veiled reference to the third-century conflict in Carthage over what to do about Christians who fled persecution or lapsed into paganism in the face of persecution, matters that both Tertullian and Cyprian, respectively, dealt with in their writings. I thank Dr. Stephen Perry, Religious Studies, University of South Dakota, for these suggestions.

[54]Chariot racing was a far more popular pastime than gladiatorial combats. Competition between the fans of the four teams was fierce, and arguments over the wins and losses of teams could result in public brawls and riots.

[55]It is unclear what is intended by this phrase. Optatus and Aspasius, however, are alive, and so perhaps the angels are closing the gates of Paradise to them.

[56]In Revelation 7:16, the blessed know neither hunger nor thirst. In pagan literature, a wonderful odor is one sign of the presence of divinity, and Christians thought the bodies of martyrs gave off a wonderful perfume. As the soul is noncorporeal, it should be sustained by a noncorporeal food, such as a perfume.

[57]While it is clear that Secundulus died in prison, it is not clear whether he died from violence at the hands of the guards or whether he was executed, as a non-Christian Roman citizen would have been.

[58]Roman law prohibited the execution of a pregnant women until she had given birth.

behind not only a good friend but also a companion alone on the road to the same hope. 4. And so joined together in one lamentation they poured forth prayer to God two days before the games. 5. Immediately after their prayer, labor pains invaded her. And when she was suffering in labor because of the natural difficulty of an eight months' birth, a certain one of the prison wardens said to her, "You are suffering now, but what will you do when thrown to the beasts which you thought of no account when you refused to sacrifice?" 6. And she responded, "I am only suffering now what I suffer; there in the arena, however, another will be in me who will suffer for me, because even now I am about to suffer for him." 7. Thus she gave birth to a girl whom a certain sister[59] brought up as her own daughter.

16. 1. Since therefore the Holy Spirit permitted, and by permitting showed its will that this account of the games be written down, although by one unworthy of describing glories so great as a supplement to the accounts, still as if commanded by the most holy Perpetua, we will assuredly carry out her bequest,[60] adding one example of her constancy of faith and loftiness of soul. 2. When the tribune[61] was treating them very severely, because he was afraid, due to the suggestions of very stupid people, that they would be removed from prison by some sort of magical spells,[62] Perpetua said right to his face, 3. "Why do you not allow us to refresh ourselves, the 'most noble of the criminals,' the property of Caesar, who are about to fight on his birthday: Will it not be to your credit if we are brought forth healthier in body?" 4. The tribune was disturbed and grew red in face, and ordered that her brothers and others be allowed to enter and eat with them, and indeed at this point the prison warden was also a Christian.[63]

17. 1. Also, on the day before the games, when they were eating their last meal (which is usually called the "free meal") not as at a "free meal" but a "love feast,"[64] they responded to the crowd with that same constancy of purpose, threatening them with the judgment of God, arguing for the happiness present in their suffering, and mocking the curiosity of those crowding in to see them, with Saturus saying: 2 "Won't tomorrow satisfy you? Why do you willingly come to see what you hate? Today we are friends, tomorrow enemies. Still, take careful note of our faces so that you can recognize us tomorrow." 3. And everyone went away from there astonished, and many of them came to believe in Christ.

---

[59]Presumably a fellow Christian, and not Felicity's biological sister.

[60]The author of this section alludes to Perpetua's words in 10.15.

[61]The tribune was the chief officer in charge of the prison.

[62]Compare the apostles' escape from prison in Acts 5:19 and the conversion of the jailer in Acts 16:29–34.

[63]Hence, Saturus gives the prison warden, Pudens, a memento of his martyrdom in 21.5 and speaks to strengthen his newfound faith.

[64]The "free meal" was the banquet given to gladiators the day before the combats and was known for its indulgence in food, luxury, and sex. The Christians' "love feasts" were modest meals open to all, including the poor and beggars.

18. 1. Their day of victory dawned, and they proceeded from the prison into the amphitheater as though going into heaven, cheerful, with composed faces, as if quivering with joy not fear. 2. Perpetua followed along with shining face and calm step, like a wife of Christ, like a darling of God, turning aside the gaze of all with the intensity shining from her eyes. 3. Likewise Felicity, rejoicing that she had safely given birth so that she could contend with the beasts, proceeded going from bloodbath to bloodbath, from the midwife to the net-gladiator,[65] about to wash herself after childbirth in a second baptism.[66] 4. And when they were brought to the gate and were being forced to put on costume, the men that of the priests of Saturn, the women that of the priestesses of Ceres,[67] that noble-hearted woman resisted with constancy of purpose. 5. For she kept saying, "We came here of our own free will so that freedom should not be taken from us; we dedicated our lives[68] so that we would do no such thing as this; we agreed on this with you." 6. Injustice recognized justice: the tribune gave way, and they were brought into the arena dressed just as they were. 7. Perpetua began to sing psalms as though she were already "kicking the head of the Egyptian" as she did in her last vision. Revocatus and Saturninus and Saturus began to warn the crowd watching them. 8. Then when they came within the sight of Hilarianus, they began to say to him by their gesturing and motioning,[69] "You are punishing us, but God will punish you." 9. At this the crowd lost patience and demanded that they be punished with whips before the line of beast-gladiators; however, they were happy because they had gained something of the sufferings of the Lord.[70]

19. 1. But he who had said, "Ask and you will receive,"[71] had given to those who prayed that death which each had desired. 2. For, whenever they were discussing among themselves about the martyrdom each wanted, Saturninus especially proposed that he should be offered to all the beasts so that he would

---

[65]The net-gladiator entangled his opponent with a net and killed him with his trident. The author may here be anticipating what actually happened to Felicity and Perpetua in the amphitheater: at first they were wrapped in a net for a cow to gore (20.2).

[66]Of blood, rather than of water. Women were considered unclean after childbirth until they had ritually purified themselves.

[67]The worship of Saturn and Ceres was widespread in the province of Africa. If the Christians were to dress themselves in these garments, they would, in a sense, be acting as priests and priestesses as well as sacrificial victims to the pagan gods, on behalf of the emperor's health and safety.

[68]The Latin phrase *animam addiximus* is used by gladiators in handing themselves over to their trainer.

[69]Hilarianus was sitting in an elevated seat, and this, along with the roars and shouts of the crowd, would make it hard for him to hear anything said by the Christians.

[70]The gladiators who fought the beasts carried whips to force the beasts and their human prey into the arena. The Christians allude to the flagellation of Christ before his crucifixion (Matthew 27:26 and Mark 15:15).

[71]Christ's words in John 16:24.

definitely win a more glorious crown.[72] 3. And also in the beginning of the games he and Revocatus were first matched with a leopard and then, bound to a platform,[73] were attacked by a bear. 4. Saturus, however, feared nothing more than a bear; but thought he would be killed with one bite of a leopard. 5. And when he was offered to a wild boar, the beast-gladiator who had tied him to the boar was gored from below by that same beast and died some days after the games; Saturus was only dragged by the beast. 6. And when he was bound in the stocks for the bear, the bear refused to come out of its cage. And so Saturus was called back again unharmed.

20. 1. For the young women, however, the devil prepared an extremely fierce cow, an unusual matching, but he wanted to match their sex with the beast.[74] 2. And so, stripped of their clothing and bound with nets, they were led out. The crowd was horrified upon seeing the one a delicate young girl and the other just having given birth, with her breasts dripping milk. 3. And so they were called back and reclothed with unbelted tunics. Perpetua was the first to be tossed by the cow, and she fell on her loins. 4. And when she sat up, she pulled down her tunic, that had been ripped along its side, to cover her thighs, being more mindful of modesty than of pain. 5. Then she asked for a hairpin and rebound her untidy hair; for it was not fitting that she should be martyred with her hair loose and free, in fear that she might seem to be mourning in the moment of her glory.[75] 6. And thus she stood up, and when she saw that Felicity had been knocked to the ground, she went to her and gave her her hand and raised her up. 7. And both stood side by side. And having appeased the hard-hearted crowd, they were recalled to the Gate of Life. 8. There Perpetua was held up by a certain catechumen named Rusticus, who had kept close to her, and, as if woken up from sleep (for she had been in the Spirit and in ecstasy), she began to look around and said to her amazed companions, "When will we be taken out to that cow or whatever?" 9. And when she heard that her punishment had already happened, she did not believe it until she saw the definite marks of her tossing on her body and dress. 10. And then she summoned and spoke to her brother and that catechumen, saying, "Stand in the faith and love each other, and do not be disheartened by our sufferings."[76]

---

[72]Crowns made of various kinds of leafy branches and emblems corresponded to today's medals of honor and were given to soldiers who had performed various deeds of courage and accomplishment. As "soldiers of Christ" martyrs were thought to be awarded a crown in heaven and are frequently depicted in early Christian art as wearing or holding their crowns.

[73]Such platforms are depicted in some Roman mosaics as being on wheels for easy movement and having a pole to which the victim was bound.

[74]Normally such victims were matched with a bull.

[75]It was an important sign of modesty and chastity for Roman married women to have their hair bound up. A married woman, however, would unbind her hair as a ritual gesture of mourning.

[76]This exhortation echoes 1 Corinthians 16:13.

21. 1. Likewise Saturus at another gate was encouraging the soldier Pudens,[77] saying, "I have thus exactly foretold and predicted this, and up till now I have suffered through no beast. And now you may believe with your whole heart: look, I am going in and I will be killed with one bite of a leopard." 2. And immediately, at the end of the spectacle, he was thrown to a leopard and lost so much blood after a single bite that the crowd shouted a proof of his second baptism[78] to him as he returned, "Well washed, well washed." 3. Clearly he was well washed who had washed in this manner. 4. Then he said to the soldier Pudens, "Good-bye, and remember the faith and me; and these things will not upset you, but will strengthen you." 5. And at the same time he asked for a ring from Puden's finger, and having dipped it in his blood, he returned it to him as an inheritance, leaving it as a pledge to him and memorial of his blood.[79] 6. And soon after he was thrown down, already fainting, along with the others in the place used for cutting the throats.[80] 7. And when the crowd demanded that they be brought out into the middle of the arena, so that they might, as participants in the slaughter of the martyrs, fasten their eyes on the sword as it penetrated their bodies, the martyrs all got up together and went to where the crowd wanted them, first kissing each other in turn so that they might complete their martyrdom through the kiss of peace.[81] The others bore the sword blow unmoving and in silence, particularly Saturus, who, as he had climbed the ladder first, gave up his spirit first, for even then he was awaiting Perpetua.[82] 9. Perpetua, however, in order to taste some pain,[83] screamed when her bones were cut with the sword and bore the wavering hand of the gladiatorial recruit across her throat herself.[84] 10. Perhaps so great a woman, who was feared by the unclean spirit, could not be killed in any other manner except in the way she herself wished to die. 11. O most brave and blessed martyrs! O you who are truly called into and selected for the glory of our Lord Jesus Christ! Anyone who exalts and honors and worships this glory ought assuredly read these examples that are no less splendid than the old examples for the edification of the Church, so that new examples of virtue should also testify that the one and the same Holy Spirit is always and still active down to our day,

---

[77]Pudens is the prison guard who had shown sympathy to the Christians (9.1) and then had himself converted (16.4).

[78]The second baptism is that of the blood of martyrdom.

[79]By this gesture, Saturus makes Pudens, in a sense, his spiritual heir. Saturus could expect that the ring would become an object of veneration by Pudens and other Christians.

[80]This place in the amphitheater, called the *spoliarium*, was where dead gladiators were stripped of their clothing and armor and where any victims still living would finally be dispatched.

[81]This ritual kiss usually closed any Christian ceremony.

[82]As he did in her first vision.

[83]She had been unconscious of pain when tossed by the cow.

[84]The task of killing unarmed victims was given to such recruits to accustom them to killing. In courageously directing his hand, Perpetua assumes yet another masculine characteristic.

together with God, omnipotent, the Father and his Son Jesus Christ our Lord, to whom is glory and immense power forever and ever. Amen.

BIBLIOGRAPHY

Primary Sources

Amat, Jacqueline. *Passion de Perpétue et de Félicité*. Paris: Les Éditions du Cerf, 1996.

De'Cavalieri, Pio Franchi. *La Passio SS. Perpetuae et Felicitatis*. Rome: Herder'schen Verlagshandlung, 1896.

Harris, James Rendel. *The Martyrdom of Perpetua and Felicitas*. London: C.J. Clay and Sons, 1890.

Musurillo, Herbert. *The Acts of the Christian Martyrs*. Oxford: Clarendon Press, 1972.

Van Beek, C. I. M. I. *Passio Sanctarum Perpetuae et Felicitatis*, vol. 1. Nijmegen: Dekkerand Van de Vogt, 1936.

Secondary Works

Bridenthal, Renate, Claudia Koonz, and Susan Stuard, eds. *Becoming Visible: Women in European History*, 2d ed. Boston: Houghton Mifflin, 1998.

Dronke, Peter. *Women Writers of the Middle Ages: A Critical Study of Texts from Perpetua (†203) to Marguerite Porete (†1310)*. Cambridge: Cambridge University Press, 1984.

Petroff, Elizabeth. *Medieval Women's Visionary Literature*. Oxford: Oxford University Press, 1986.

Roebuck, Cecil M., Jr. *Prophecy in Carthage: Perpetua, Tertullian, and Cyprian*. Cleveland, Ohio: Pilgrim Press, 1992.

Salisbury, Joyce E. *Perpetua's Passion: The Death and Memory of a Young Roman Woman*. New York: Routledge, 1997.

Von Franz, Marie-Louise. *The Passion of Perpetua*. Irving, Tex.: Spring Publications, 1980.

Wilson-Kastner, Patricia, G. Ronald Kastner, Ann Millen, Rosemary Rader, and Jeremiah Reedy, eds. *A Lost Tradition: Women Writers of the Early Church*. Lanham, Md.: University Press of America, 1981.

Faltonia Betitia Proba: A Virgilian Cento in Praise of Christ

Bernice M. Kaczynski

The Roman aristocrat Faltonia Betitia Proba, a convert to Christianity, composed her *Cento Virgilianus de laudibus Christi* in about 360 C.E.[1] It is a remarkable work, a retelling of episodes from the Bible in language taken directly from Virgil—from the *Aeneid*, mostly, but also from the *Eclogues* and the *Georgics*. The *Cento* is an epic poem of 694 hexameters. Its subject is scripture: the Genesis account of the creation of the world and other early events in biblical history, and, in greater detail, scenes from the life of Christ. In form it is a patchwork, made up almost entirely of lines and half lines borrowed from Virgil and rearranged so as to express a new meaning. At first encounter, such compositions may seem bizarre to modern readers. But centos, as works in the genre are known, were very popular in Late Antiquity, especially in the educated aristocratic circles to which Proba and her family belonged. Both pagans and Christians wrote them. Ausonius wrote the best-known pagan cento, the *Cento nuptialis*, and Proba the most successful Christian one.[2] It was a species of literary composition that required learning and leisure, and—in Proba's case, at least—a commitment to Christian education. In her own time, Proba's *Cento* won high praise: *Maro mutatus in melius* (Virgil changed for the better), wrote an admirer as he prepared to dedicate a copy of the *Cento* to the emperor Arcadius.[3]

Not a great deal is known about Proba's life. She names herself in the invocation to her poem: *uatis Proba* (I, Proba, prophetess).[4] In the past, scholars disputed her identity, but now most would agree that the Proba of the poem was Faltonia Betitia, born ca. 322 and died ca. 370, a member of a distinguished senatorial family, the Petronii.[5] Her position in society enabled her to acquire a fine education—one put fully on display in the *Cento*, with its virtuoso command of the writings of Virgil. Before writing the *Cento*, she wrote another epic poem, now lost, on the uprising of Magnentius against Constantius II, an event that occurred in 353. Proba was probably still a pagan at the time of its composition, for in the *Cento* she remarks that its subject was war and that now she wishes to turn away from battles and slayings in order to write of holy things.[6]

Faltonia Betitia was a wife and mother. Her husband, Clodius Celsinus Adelphius, who was prefect of Rome in 351, was then a pagan and later became a Christian, perhaps at the urging of his wife. This would not have been an unusual pattern. Many senatorial families remained pagan down to the end of the fourth century, and wives often converted first, followed by their husbands. In the last verses of her poem, Proba addresses Adelphius as her *dulcis coniunx* (sweet husband).[7] And when Faltonia Proba died, Adelphius placed an inscription on her tomb: *uxori inconparabili* (to an incomparable wife).[8] She was mother of two sons (Clodius Hermogenianus Olybrius and Faltonius Probus Alypius) and stepmother of a third (Clodius Hermogenianus Caesarius), all of whom attained offices and honors in the imperial administration. Faltonia Betitia's family was powerful and wealthy and remained so for generations. Her Christian descendants included notable women: her granddaughter Faltonia Anicia Proba, a Roman matron who corresponded with Augustine, and her great-great-granddaughter Demetrias, whose adolescent vow of perpetual virginity won her a letter of congratulation from Jerome.

Indeed, it is through the actions of members of her family that we are able to reconstruct most of what we know about Proba's life.[9] The *Cento* itself reveals little in the way of personal detail. The elevated Virgilian diction, the limitations of the poetic genre, even, perhaps, the aristocratic reticence of the author—all of these combine to create a work that is very formal in its presentation.[10] Yet scholars have seen traces of Proba's own character in her emphasis on the beauty of the natural world, readily apparent in her account of the creation. Proba's description of the Garden of Eden is joyous and exuberant, making use of the words that Virgil found for the Golden Age.[11] The *Cento* also suggests her regard for domestic matters, for marriage and the family, for marital devotion and filial piety, as well as her lack of interest in asceticism. Virginity and poverty are not recurring themes. Among the most interesting narratives in the poem are the Gospel stories enjoining Christians to the renunciation of wealth. As Proba tells them, the message of renunciation is quite muted, and Christians are encouraged merely to share their possessions with their families.[12] Proba's attitudes are characteristic of her time and place and reflect the social expectations of her class, for she was living during a period of transition in the history of the early church, after the age of martyrs and before the age of ascetics. A decade or two after Proba wrote her poem, many women from aristocratic families would begin to turn to asceticism, and some would even go to Palestine, to settle in monastic communities there. She did not. And, according to Elizabeth Clark, "because Proba opted for home and family, when those about her were on the verge of casting them off . . . later generations were left something exceedingly rare: a piece of early Christian literature written not by a theologian, a priest, or a monk, but by a female layperson."[13]

Proba was one of a number of Christian poets in the fourth, fifth, and sixth centuries who set about retelling biblical narratives in long hexameter poems.[14] She was the first who did not merely paraphrase scripture, but who selected episodes and fashioned them into stories: the creation, the fall of Adam and Eve, Cain and Abel, the flood, the birth of Jesus and the slaughter of the innocents, the baptism and temptation of Christ, the sermon on the mount, the encounter with the rich young man, the stilling of the storm, Jesus' entry into Jerusalem, the last supper, the crucifixion, resurrection, and ascension. She was the first, too, to adapt a particular poetic genre, the Virgilian cento, to this end. The habit of piecing together poems using quotations from classical authors was an old one in the Mediterranean world. The Greeks had turned to Homer, the Romans to Virgil. It was an understandable impulse in societies whose literary culture was saturated by particular texts: the *Iliad*, the *Odyssey*, and the *Aeneid*. To construct a poem from bits and pieces of the *Aeneid* was not so different, perhaps, from constructing a mosaic from bits and pieces of stone—another favorite enterprise for artists in Late Antiquity. Proba chose the most prestigious of literary styles and deployed it on behalf of her new religion.[15] She would write a Christian epic: *Uergilium cecinisse loquar pia munera Christi* (That Virgil put to verse Christ's sacred duties / Let me tell).[16]

Of course, it was an impossible task. There was a fundamental dissonance between the epic diction of Virgil and the *sermo humilis* of the early Fathers, between the pagan hero Aeneas and the Jesus of the Gospels, and between the gentle teachings of the New Testament and the imperial cadences now being used to express them. The *Cento* met with predictable opposition. It began in about 395, when Jerome wrote a letter to Paulinus of Nola condemning the writers of centos: "Garrulous old women, men in their dotage, verbose windbags," all think of themselves as experts in scripture. Centos are "puerile nonsense, like the play of charlatans," he writes, and illustrates his point with examples from Proba's verse. Nor does he let the topic rest; in another letter he remarks, "What has Horace to do with the Psalter, Virgil with the Gospels, Cicero with Paul?"[17] Jerome was the first, and possibly the most damaging, of Proba's critics. There have been many over the years—some objecting to her gender, some to her theology, and some who simply do not like the cento form. The genre, says Harald Hagendahl, is "preposterous."[18]

More recently, however, scholars have looked upon the *Cento* with renewed interest. "An extraordinary fascination with language for its own sake is needed to engage in this kind of writing," comments one.[19] They draw attention to the originality of Proba's enterprise and to the technical literary skill with which she conducted it. She sought in her writing to unify classical and Christian culture, and in her appropriation of Virgilian diction these scholars see a creative act.

Consider some of the practical difficulties. An immediate problem for anyone constructing a narrative is to establish the cast of characters. Yet a centoist who is relying on the *Aeneid* for words to use in telling Bible stories has no suitable proper names: no Adam, no Eve, no Jesus, no Mary. Proba finds names for

God the Father quite readily in Virgil's descriptions of Jupiter (*pater, summus pater, pater caeli cui sidera parent, pater omnipotens, deus, praesens deus, genitor*, and so on). Names for Jesus, however, present a greater challenge, and are drawn from the epithets of a wide variety of persons—Aeneas, of course, but also Heracles, Apollo, Cupid, the personification of Sleep, Musaeus, Camilla, Hector, and others (*deus, dominus potens, rex, aeterna potestas, sacra effigies, heros, caelestis origo, divinae stirpis origo, infans, puer, fortunatus puer*, and so on).[20] Even then, the principal characters are not always clear, and Proba finds herself relying on passive constructions and circumlocutions. As a result, the narrative flow of this 694-line poem is not really very smooth, and sometimes transitions are so abrupt as to be incomprehensible.

Another difficulty imposed by the cento form has to do with dialogue. Exchanges between gods and goddesses, or Aeneas and Dido, or indeed, any two Virgilian personages, do not at first glance seem promising sources for the words that Proba's biblical characters might be expected to utter. Yet Proba can be quite skillful in her adaptation of Virgilian speech. This is particularly evident in scenes from the Old Testament. For instance, in the excerpt on the Creation printed below, God, Adam, Eve, and the Serpent converse quite plausibly in Virgilian hexameters. Proba faces a more difficult task in her rendering of New Testament dialogue. To modern readers, more likely to know the Gospels than the *Aeneid*, the very notion of Jesus as a classical hero may be unsettling. In scenes where Jesus speaks at length, for instance, in the sermon on the mount—the sense of epic diction is quite pronounced and quite foreign to our ears. More than the tone is changed, however, when Proba recasts the words of Matthew, Mark, Luke, and John. Her account of the crucifixion is truly startling. She shows us an angry Jesus, who, even as he is dying on the cross, vows vengeance on his enemies:

> Ille autem inpauidus "quo uincula nectitis?" inquit.
> "tantane uos generis tenuit fiducia uestri?
> post mihi non simili poena commissa luetis."

> Yet he, undaunted, said, "What makes you tie
> These bonds? Has overweening racial pride possessed you?
> Some day, for wrongs committed, you will pay
> With punishment unlike this one to me."
>   (*Cento* 621–23)[21]

Proba's *Cento Virgilianus de laudibus Christi* belongs to the earliest period of Christian Latin poetry. It was written during a time when many aristocratic Christians were recent converts, still uncertain about the proper relationship between their new faith and the classical literary tradition in which they had been educated. Even Jerome, despite his professions of scorn, felt deeply attracted to the Latin classics, and so, famously, did Augustine. Proba did not seem to see a conflict. She embarked upon a remarkable poetic experiment, one possible only for a person with her knowledge of Virgil and her commitment to Christianity. Her *Cento* is the "earliest complete and extant work in Christian history that we are sure was written by a woman."[22] Despite Jerome, and despite a papal decree relegating it to the Apocrypha, many people took a lively interest in it, and only in the nineteenth century did Proba's *Cento* cease to give them pleasure.[23]

NOTES

1. The *Cento* is edited by Carolus Schenkl, *Poetae Christiani Minores,* Corpus Scriptorum Ecclesiasticorum Latinorum 16.1 (Vienna: F. Tempsky, 1888; repr. New York and London: Johnson 1972), pp. 511–609. The most complete English translation is by Elizabeth A. Clark and Diane F. Hatch, in *The Golden Bough, the Oaken Cross: The Virgilian Cento of Faltonia Betitia Proba,* American Academy of Religion Texts and Translations Series 5 (Chico, Calif.: Scholars Press, 1981).

2. In the *Cento nuptialis*, probably written soon after Proba's work, Ausonius uses Virgilian diction to describe the goings-on of a newly married couple. It is, in fact, quite lewd. For text and commentary, see R. P. H. Green, *The Works of Ausonius* (Oxford: Clarendon Press, 1991), pp. 132–39, 518–26. For a rendering of the Latin into English using lines and half lines from Shakespeare, see *Ausonius: Three Amusements,* trans. David R. Slavitt (Philadelphia: University of Pennsylvania Press, 1998). Schenkl's *CSEL* volume contains editions of several other Christian centos by various poets. For a general introduction to the Latin literature of the period, see Michael Roberts, "The Latin Literature of Late Antiquity," in *Medieval Latin Studies: An Introduction and Bibliographical Guide,* ed. F. A. C. Mantello and A. G. Rigg (Washington, D.C.: Catholic University Press of America, 1996), pp. 537–46.

3. The dedication to Arcadius is printed by Schenkl, *Cento Probae,* p. 568.

4. *Cento* 12. Translated by Clark and Hatch, *The Golden Bough,* p. 15.

5. For these details, see Clark and Hatch, *The Golden Bough,* pp. 97–108; Reinhart Herzog, "Faltonia Betitia Proba," in *Restauration und Erneuerung: Die lateinische Literatur von 284 bis 374 n. Chr.,* ed. Reinhart Herzog et al., *Handbuch der lateinischen Literatur der Antike,* vol. 5 (Munich: C.H. Beck, 1989), pp. 337–38; Anne Jensen, "Proba," in *Metzler Lexikon antiker Autoren,* ed. Oliver Schütze (Stuttgart and Weimar: J.B. Metzler, 1997), pp. 579–81; Mario Spinelli, "Proba Petronia," in *Enciclopedia Virgiliana,* vol. 4, ed. Francesco della Corte (Rome: Istituto della Enciclopedia Italiana, 1988), cols. 283–85. For a vigorous statement of an alternative position, see Danuta Shanzer, "The Anonymous *Carmen contra paganos* and the Date and Identity of the Centonist Proba," *Revue des Études Augustiniennes* 32 (1986): 232–48. For historical background on Proba's world, see Gillian Clark, *Women in Late Antiquity: Pagan and Christian Life-Styles* (Oxford: Oxford University Press, 1993).

6. *Cento* 1–28.

7. *Cento* 693.

8. Clark and Hatch, *The Golden Bough*, p. 98.
9. See Elizabeth A. Clark, "Faltonia Betitia Proba and Her Virgilian Poem: The Christian Matron as Artist," in *Ascetic Piety and Women's Faith: Essays on Late Ancient Christianity*, ed. Elizabeth A. Clark, Studies in Women and Religion 20 (Lewiston, N.Y. : Edwin Mellen, 1986), p. 128.
10. The apparent lack of autobiographical detail led Peter Dronke, who admired the poem (calling it "ingenious and spirited"), to exclude Proba from consideration in his *Women Writers of the Middle Ages* (Cambridge: Cambridge University Press, 1984). Dronke's interest was in women writers whose works reflected specific, individual experience, not those whose texts appeared to be paradigmatic, intended to edify and instruct. The tone of the *Cento*, Dronke observes, is "too august to reveal anything concretely about Proba herself" (p. 286).
11. *Cento* 144–47; see excerpt printed below.
12. Clark, "Faltonia Betitia Proba and Her Virgilian Poem," pp. 139–40.
13. Clark, "Faltonia Betitia Proba and Her Virgilian Poem," p. 147. A similar point is made by Jensen, "Proba," p. 580: "Eine positive Einstellung zu Liebe und Sexualität, zu Ehe und Familie wie überhaupt zur Diesseitigkeit des Lebens findet auch in ihrem Gedicht seinen deutlichen Ausdruck, und das muss hervorgehoben werden, da im 4. christlichen Jahrhundert im allgemeinen die Asketen die theologisch-literarische Szene beherrschten."
14. On the genre of biblical epic, see Reinhart Herzog, *Die Bibelepik der lateinischen Spätantike: Formgeschichte einer erbaulichen Gattung* (Munich: Wilhelm Fink Verlag, 1975), and Daniel J. Nodes, *Doctrine and Exegesis in Biblical Latin Poetry*, ARCA Classical and Medieval Texts, Papers and Monographs 31 (Leeds: Francis Cairns, 1993).
15. On this point see Michael Roberts, *Biblical Epic and Rhetorical Paraphrase in Late Antiquity*, ARCA Classical and Medieval Texts, Papers and Monographs 16 (Liverpool: Francis Cairns, 1985), p. 107.
16. *Cento* 23. Translated by Clark and Hatch, *The Golden Bough*, p. 17.
17. Jerome, *Epistula* 53.7 and *Epistula* 22.29.6, translated by R. A. Markus, "Paganism, Christianity and the Latin Classics in the Fourth Century," in *Latin Literature of the Fourth Century*, ed. J. W. Binns (London and Boston: Routledge and Kegan Paul, Ltd., 1974), 6. Jerome's response was complicated by several factors; see Wolfgang Kirsch, *Die lateinische Versepik des 4. Jahrhunderts*, Schriften zur Geschichte und Kultur der Antike 28 (Berlin: Akademie Verlag, 1989): 140–50; and Carl P. E. Springer, "Jerome and the *Cento* of Proba," *Studia Patristica* 28 (1993): 96–105. Indeed, Jerome himself wrote centos; see Clark and Hatch, *The Golden Bough*, p. 104.
18. *Latin Fathers and the Classics: A Study on the Apologists, Jerome, and Other Christian Writers* (Göteborg: Acta Universitatis Gothoburgensis, 1958), p. 189.
19. See Zoja Pavlovskis, "Proba and the Semiotics of the Narrative Virgilian Cento," *Vergilius* 35 (1989): 75–76. For another highly favorable assessment of Proba's strategy of composition, see Joseph Pucci, "Proba," in *Medieval Latin*, 2d ed., ed. K. P. Harrington, rev. Joseph Pucci (Chicago and London: University of Chicago Press, 1997), p. 112. More generally, Nodes remarks that "in their use of classical

epic diction to paraphrase and comment on this perceived truth, biblical epic poets gave new meanings to the words and phrases they appropriated, transforming the language of Roman epic into the language of Christian anticipation" (*Doctrine and Exegesis,* p. 6).

20. See Ilona Opelt, "Der zürnende Christus im Cento der Proba," *Jahrbuch für Antike und Christentum* 7 (1964): 109–10. See also Elizabeth A. Clark and Diane F. Hatch, "Jesus as Hero in the Virgilian *Cento* of Faltonia Betitia Proba," in *Ascetic Piety and Women's Faith,* ed. Clark, pp. 153–71.

21. *Cento* 621–23. Translated by Clark and Hatch, *The Golden Bough,* p. 85. For a more detailed analysis of both the sermon on the mount (*Cento* 463–496) and the crucifixion (*Cento* 607–37), see Opelt, "Der zürnende Christus."

22. Clark and Hatch, *The Golden Bough,* p. 6.

23. In 496 a decree attributed to Pope Gelasius I declared it apocryphal; see Herzog, "Faltonia Betitia Proba," p. 340. For an analysis of the later history of the poem, see Pavlovskis, "Proba and the Semiotics of the Narrative Virgilian Cento." Proba was sometimes seen as an exemplar for women writers. The sixteenth-century Dutch writer Anna Bijns was described by her seventeenth-century editor Aubertus Le Mire as "another ... PROBA FALCONIA in her battle ... [writing to defend her faith] ..." For the text, see Hermina Joldersma, "Anna Bijns," in *Women Writing in Dutch,* ed. Kristiaan Aercke, Women Writers of the World 1 (New York: Garland, 1994), p. 120.

CENTO PROBAE[1]

Felicemque trahit limum fingitque premendo
pingue solum primis extemplo a mensibus anni.
iamque inprouiso tantae pietatis imago
procedit noua forma uiri pulcherrima primum,
120   os umerosque deo similis, cui mentem animumque
maior agit deus atque opera ad maiora remittit.
quaeritur huic alius; nec quisquam ex agmine tanto
audet adire uirum sociusque in regna uocari.
haut mora continuo placidam per membra quietem
125   dat iuueni et dulci declinat lumina somno.
atque illi medio in spatio iam noctis opacae
omnipotens genitor costas et uiscera nudat.

---

[1]The Latin text is reproduced from the critical edition by Carolus Schenkl, *Poetae Christiani Minores,* Corpus Scriptorum Ecclesiasticorum Latinorum 16.1 (Vienna: F. Tempsky, 1888; repr. New York and London, 1972), pp. 511–609 (here: pp. 576–585). Schenkl's edition also gives line-by-line references to Proba's Virgilian sources (the *Aeneid, Eclogues,* and the *Georgics*), and to the corresponding passages in Scripture (in this excerpt, all are from Genesis). These references, which are quite detailed, have been omitted from the text printed here.

harum unam iuueni laterum conpagibus artis
eripuit subitoque oritur mirabile donum—
130   argumentum ingens—claraque in luce refulsit
insignis facie et pulchro pectore uirgo,
iam matura uiro, iam plenis nubilis annis.
olli somnum ingens rumpit pauor: ossaque et artus
coniugium uocat ac stupefactus numine pressit
135   excepitque manu dextramque amplexus inhaesit.
    His demum exactis torquet qui sidera mundi
infit: eo dicente premit placida aequora pontus
et tremefacta solo tellus, silet arduus aether:
"uiuite felices interque nitentia culta
140   fortunatorum nemorum sedesque beatas.
haec domus, haec patria est, requies ea certa laborum.
his ego nec metas rerum nec tempora pono:
imperium sine fine dedi, multosque per annos
non rastros patietur humus, non uinea falcem.
145   at genus inmortale manet, nec tarda senectus
debilitat uires animi mutatque uigorem.
uos contra quae dicam animis aduertite uestris.
est in conspectu ramis felicibus arbos,
quam neque fas igni cuiquam nec sternere ferro,
150   religione sacra numquam concessa moueri.
hac quicumque sacros decerpserit arbore fetus,
morte luet merita: nec me sententia uertit.
nec tibi tam prudens quisquam persuadeat auctor
conmaculare manus—liceat te uoce moneri—,
155   femina, nec te ullius uiolentia uincat,
si te digna manet diuini gloria ruris."
postquam cuncta pater, caeli cui sidera parent,
conposuit, legesque dedit camposque nitentis
desuper ostentat, tantarum gloria rerum.
160   ecce autem primi sub limina solis et ortus
deuenere locos, ubi mollis amaracus illos
floribus et dulci adspirans conplectitur umbra.
hic uer purpureum atque alienis mensibus aestas,
hic liquidi fontes, hic caeli tempore certo
165   dulcia mella premunt, hic candida populus antro
inminet et lentae texunt umbracula uites.
inuitant croceis halantes floribus horti
inter odoratum lauri nemus ipsaque tellus
omnia liberius nullo poscente ferebat.

170   fortunati ambo, si mens non laeua fuisset
       coniugis infandae: docuit post exitus ingens.
           Iamque dies infanda aderat: per florea rura
       ecce inimicus atrox inmensis orbibus anguis
       septem ingens gyros, septena uolumina uersans
175   nec uisu facilis nec dictu affabilis ulli
       obliqua inuidia ramo frondente pependit,
       uiperam spirans animam, cui tristia bella
       iraeque insidiaeque et crimina noxia cordi.
       odit et ipse pater: tot sese uertit in ora
180   arrectisque horret squamis, et, ne quid inausum
       aut intemptatum scelerisue doliue relinquat,
       sic prior adgreditur dictis seque obtulit ultro:
       "dic" ait, "o uirgo—lucis habitamus opacis
       riparumque toros et prata recentia riuis
185   incolimus—, quae tanta animis ignauia uenit?
       strata iacent passim sua quaeque sub arbore poma,
       pocula sunt fontes liquidi: caelestia dona
       adtractare nefas: id rebus defuit unum.
       quid prohibet causas penitus temptare latentes?
190   uana superstitio. rerum pars altera adempta est.
       quo uitam dedit aeternam? cur mortis adempta est
       condicio? mea si non inrita dicta putaris,
       auctor ego audendi sacrata resoluere iura.
       tu coniunx, tibi fas animum temptare precando.
195   dux ego uester ero: tua si mihi certa uoluntas,
       extruimusque toros dapibusque epulamur opimis."
       sic ait, et dicto citius, quod lege tenetur,
       subiciunt epulis olim uenerabile lignum
       instituuntque dapes contactuque omnia foedant.
200   praecipue infelix pesti deuota futurae
       mirataque nouas frondes et non sua poma,
       causa mali tanti, summo tenus attigit ore.
       maius adorta nefas maioremque orsa furorem
       heu misero coniunx aliena ex arbore germen
205   obicit atque animum subita dulcedine mouit.
       continuo noua lux oculis effulsit; at illi
       terrentur uisu subito nec plura morati
       corpora sub ramis obtentu frondis inumbrant:
       consertum tegumen: nec spes opis ulla dabatur.
210   at non haec nullis hominum rerumque repertor
       obseruans oculis caedes et facta tyranni

praesensit: notumque furens quid femina posset.
continuo inuadit: "procul, o procul este profani"
conclamat, caelum ac terras qui numine firmat.
215 atque illi longe gradientem ac dira frementem
ut uidere, metu uersi retroque ruentes
diffugiunt siluasque et sicubi concaua furtim
saxa petunt. piget incepti lucisque, neque auras
dispiciunt: taedet caeli conuexa tueri.
220   Nec longum in medio tempus, cum creber ad aures
uisus adesse pedum sonitus genitorque per auras
hunc, ubi uix multa maestum cognouit in umbra,
talibus adloquitur dictis atque increpat ultro:
"infelix, quae tanta animum dementia cepit?
225 quis furor iste nouus? quo nunc, quo tenditis" inquit
"regnorum inmemores, quae mentem insania mutat?
dicite, quae lucis miseris tam dira cupido?
maturate fugam totoque absistite luco:
nec reuocare gradum, si quando aduersa uocarint,
230 est licitum; flammis ambit torrentibus amnis
per medium stridens torquetque sonantia saxa
attollitque globos flammarum et sidera lambit."
ille sub haec: "tua me, genitor, tua tristis imago
. . . .
his posuere locis: merui nec deprecor," inquit
235 "omnipotens, sonitumque pedum uocemque tremesco
conscius audacis facti: monitisque sinistris
femina fert tristis sucos tardumque saporem.
illa dolos dirumque nefas sub pectore uersans
insontem infando indicio, moritura puella
240 dum furit, incautum crudeli morte peremit;
suasit enim, scis ipse, neque est te fallere cuiquam.
ut uidi, ut perii, ut me malus abstulit error,
contigimusque manu quod non sua seminat arbor."
tum pater omnipotens solio sic infit ab alto:
245 "accipite ergo animis atque haec mea figite dicta:
tuque prior, scelere ante alios inmanior omnis,
quem nec longa dies pietas nec mitigat ulla,
hortator scelerum, coluber, mala gramina pastus
desidia latamque trahens inglorius aluum
250 cede locis, nullis hominum cogentibus, ipse,
tenuis ubi argilla et dumosis calculus aruis."
"at tibi pro scelere" exclamat, "pro talibus ausis
omne aeuum ferro teritur, primusque per artem,

heu miserande puer, terram insectabere rastris
255 et sonitu terrebis aues: horrebit in aruis
carduus et spinis surget paliurus acutis
lappaeque tribolique et fallax herba ueneni.
at si triticeam in messem robustaque farra
exercebis humum, frustra spectabis aceruum
260 concussaque famen in siluis solabere quercu.
insuper his subeunt morbi tristisque senectus
et labor et durae rapit inclementia mortis.
haec tibi semper erunt, tuque, o saeuissima coniunx,
non ignara mali, caput horum et causa malorum,
265 magna lues commissa tibi: heu perdita nescis
nec quae te circum stent deinde pericula cernis.
nunc morere, ut merita es, tota quod mente petisti:
nec mea iam mutata loco sententia cedit."

TRANSLATION

Translated by Elizabeth A. Clark and Diane F. Hatch, in *The Golden Bough, the Oaken Cross: The Virgilian Cento of Faltonia Betitia Proba*, American Academy of Religion Texts and Translations Series 5 (Chico, Calif.: Scholars Press, 1981), pp. 11–95 (here: 27, 29, 31, 33, 35, 37, 39, 41, 43, 45.) Reprinted by permission of the publisher. Clark and Hatch have added subtitles to clarify the narrative, and these are reproduced here. The lines of the English translation are more numerous than those of the Latin text; I have added line numbers to serve as approximate guides. I have also added notes to the translation.

The Creation of Adam and Eve

He pulled plump clay and gave it shape[1]
By kneading on the spot the fertile ground,
Its soil quickened from the year's first months.
And now—so suddenly—the image of
Such holiness![2] Man's new shape went forth,
Handsome at first beyond comparison,
120 Resembling God in countenance and shoulders—
Man, whose mind and intellect a greater God
Influences, and so sends forth to greater tasks.
For man a match is sought; but from so large

[1]Genesis 2:7.
[2]Genesis 1:27.

A throng none dared approach the Man; none dared
Be named helpmeet to his new realm.[3]
Without delay, at once God gave untroubled
125   Rest throughout the young man's limbs,[4]
And made his eyes close in pleasant sleep.
And now in the middle course of shady night,
The Almighty Sire laid the ribs and entrails bare.
One of these ribs he plucked apart from
The well-knit joints of youthful Adam's side,
And suddenly arose a wondrous gift—
130   Imposing proof—and shone in brilliant light:
Woman, a virgin she, unparalleled
In figure and in comely breasts, now ready
For a husband, ready now for wedlock.
For him, a boundless quaking breaks his sleep;
He calls his bones and limbs his wedded wife.[5]
Dazed by the Will divine he took and clasped
135   Her hand in his, folded his arms around her.[6]

God Instructs Adam and Eve

This done, at length he puzzled who
Created heaven's stars, and as he queried,
Ocean smoothed her surface calm, and earth's
Foundation quaked; high heaven grew still:
"Live happily among the planted fields[7]
140   And blissful seats of prospering wooded glades.[8]
This is your home, this is your native land,[9]

---

[3]Genesis 2:20. None of the animals is suitable as a partner for Adam.
[4]Genesis 2:21.
[5]Genesis 2:23.
[6]Genesis 2:24. Adam's taking of Eve's hand in his is a gesture without precedent in Latin literature. Husband and wife joined hands in the Roman marriage ceremony, and Proba seems to be presenting their relationship as a marriage. Many scholars have commented on the tenderness implicit in the scene; see, especially, Jensen, who remarks that it conveys all the gentle charm of a love story ("Proba", p. 580).
[7]Genesis 1:28.
[8]Genesis 2:15. God gives Adam and Eve the Garden of Eden as their home.
[9]These lines were probably startling to readers familiar with Virgil's works, for they include some of the most famous passages in the *Aeneid*: *Aeneid* 7.122, 3.393, and, especially, 1.278–79, in which Jupiter foretells the destiny of the Romans: *His ego nec metas rerum nec tempora pono; imperium sine fine dedi* ("For these I set neither bounds nor periods of empire; dominion without end have I bestowed").

A guaranteed repose from honest toil.
On this I put no end, nor hour of destiny:
Dominion without end have I bestowed.

Eden a "Golden Age"

The ground will not endure the iron hoe[10]
As many a year wheels by, nor vineyard the hook.
145   Your race abides untouched by death, and slow
Old age will not abate the keenness of
Your intellect, nor alter hearty energy.
But do you both in turn now take my words to heart.[11]

The Forbidden Tree

There is, in view, a tree with fruitful boughs;
To topple it with flame or blade is sacrilege.
150   On sacred principle it does not suffer
Interference. Whoever robs this tree
Of hallowed fruit will pay with death deserved:
No sentiment has swayed me. Let no
Counselor, however wise, persuade *you* to
Pollute your hands. I grant that you be warned
155   With Woman—that one word—and let no creature's
Passion get the best of you, if glory
From the godly fields, befitting you, awaits."
After the Father, whom heaven's stars obey,
Assigned each thing its place, he gave out laws,
And from above displayed the shining plains,
The Father, glory of so great a world.
160   When, see! Just at the sun's first wakening,
They reached a place where tender, fragrant marjoram
Wrapped them about with blooms and pleasant shade.
Here is rosy spring, and summer out
Of season; flowing fountains;[12] here at heaven's
Determined time sweet honey swells; here
165   White poplar overhangs the cave,

---

[10]In these lines Proba describes the Garden of Eden using the words Virgil found for the Golden Age: *Eclogue* 4.40; *Georgics* 4.208, *Aeneid* 9.610–11.
[11]Genesis 2:16.
[12]Genesis 2:6, 2:10.

And pliant vines plait full the shady nooks.
Breathing with golden blooms, the gardens lure
Amid a pungent grove of bay, and earth
Herself keeps bringing forth all things
In rich profusion and without request.
170 O blissful pair, had not the mind of wife
—the impious wife—been misdirected; afterward
The grievous exodus instructed them.

The Serpent Visits Eve

And now the day drew near, unfit to name:[13]
Through flower-laden fields, behold! a snake,
A baneful thing with endless coils, ill-willed,
With seven spirals vast, snaking about
175 With seven twists; not easily discerned,
Not courteous to anyone in speech,
It hung with hate disguised from greening branch,
Breathing a viper's breath, and in its heart
Lurked bitter wars, ill temper, plots
And guilty crimes. Even God himself despised it.
It took upon itself so many miens,
180 It bristled with its scales puffed out, and—
That it not leave a mite of sin or craft
Undared, untried—it first approached with speech,
Displayed itself, and voluntarily,

The Serpent Tempts Eve

"Tell me," it said, "O maid—my home is in
The dim-lit woods; on slopes of river banks
I dwell, and meadows freshened by streams—
185 What cowardice has come upon your daring?
Strewn everywhere lie fruits, each beneath its tree.
Your cups are flowing streams; yet it's sacrilege
To touch the sacred gifts; that right alone
Is lacking to your state. But what prevents
Your testing out the reasons deeply hid?
Futile religious awe! You've been deprived

---

[13]Genesis 3:1.

190   Of the second part of your estate.
        Then to what end gave He eternal life?
        Why have the terms of death been canceled?
        If you suppose my words to be of use,
        I, daring's author, dare to cancel the sacred
        Laws. You are his wife; it's right for you
        To test his will by pleading. I shall be
195   Your guide. If your good will towards me is sure,
        Then we shall pile the couches high
        And dine on sumptuous feasts." It spoke this way,
        And quicker than its word, the two of them,
        The snake and Eve, subjected to their feast
        What was prohibited by law—the tree,
        Once hallowed—and began the meal, defiling

Eve Tempts Adam

200   Everything with the contagion. She in particular,
        The hapless Eve, vowed to future ruin,[14]
        Admired the brand-new leaves; the fruit (not hers),
        The cause of such great sin, she brought
        To her mouth; she touched it with her lips.
        Having dared this greater sinful deed,
        She rose to greater madness; wife, alas,
205   She thrust in wretched Adam's way the fruit
        From the forbidden tree, and moved
        His mind with unexpected charm. New light
        Of understanding straightway dazed their eyes;
        Yet quickly, frightened by their sudden sightedness,
        They veiled their bodies under branching clothes of leaves.[15]

God Has Foreseen This Fall

        No hope of aid was given. Yet with watchful
210   Eyes mankind's and world's Creator, while
        Observing these events, foresaw destruction
        And the tyrant's[16] deeds, perceived ahead of time

---

[14]Genesis 3:6.

[15]Genesis 3:7.

[16]The tyrant is the serpent, or the devil.

What woman, giving in to frenzy's grip, could do.
Then he rebuked: "Away, be far away,
O impious outsiders," he proclaimed,
Who strengthens heaven and earth with majesty.
215   And they, when they observed him stalking from
Afar and shouting threats, turned tail,
Routed by fear, and running where they came,
They fled and sought out woods and hollow rocks,
If anywhere, in stealth. They dreaded dawn's
New light, nor marked the freshening air; they did not
Have the heart to look on heaven's vault.

God Rebukes Adam

220   Nor was it long before their ears picked up the sound—
And close—of footsteps seeming to draw near.[17]
The Father spoke to Adam[18] on the wind
(Barely God knew him skulking in the gloom)
With words like these, and freely chastised him:
"What madness, wretch, has overcome your mind?
225   What new frenzy is this? Where aim you now?
O where," he said, "unmindful of your realm?
What madness changed your mind? The two of you,
Speak out: what longing, so disastrous, for enlightenment

The Expulsion from Eden

Have you, poor humankind? Hasten your flight, and
This whole garden leave; to set your foot
In it again, though adverse circumstances
Visit you, is strictly forbidden.
230   A river straitens it with scorching flames,
Goes hissing through the midst of it, and twists
The thundering rocks along the way; it heaves up
Balls of flame, and licks the stars."
His subject, Adam, said:[19] "Your image, Father,
            Your sad image[20]

. . . .

---

[17]Genesis 3:8.
[18]Genesis 3:9.
[19]Genesis 3:12.
[20]There is a lacuna, or missing part, in the Latin text.

Have put me in these realms. And I deserve it;
235   I have no alibi," he said. "Almighty,
I cringe before your footfalls and your voice,
Guilty of a defiant deed; with perverse
Prompting, woman brought the bitter sap and
Lingering taste. Beneath her breast she pondered
Guile and disastrous sin; a girl who, as
She raged, was doomed by damning evidence,
240   She wholly ruined me with cruel death,
Though I was innocent and all unwary.
For it persuaded her, as you well know,
For nothing can deceive you. As I beheld,
How I was lost! How sinful the mistake
That did beguile me![21] And we grasped it with
Our hands, that fruit, no product of its parent tree."

God Sentences the Serpent

Then God almighty said from his high throne:[22]
245   "Take well to heart and firmly fix my words:
You first, whose sin looms large beyond the rest,
Whom not long days, nor any social conscience
Make mild; O sin-inciter, serpent, feeding
On harmful herbs, trailing your belly broad
With sloth; unhonored, get you from this place,
250   Without mankind's constraint, to a place where clay is scant
And pebbles are in the brambled fields. But for

God Sentences Adam: The End of the Golden Age

Your sin," he cried, "for such audacity,[23]
Is all your life worn thin with iron tools.
Alas, poor youth, for you will be the first
With practiced hand to harass the earth with rakes
255   And frighten birds with speech; and in the fields
The thistle will sprout rough, the thorn spring up
Sharp-spined; burrs too, and caltrops;

---

[21]The Latin text reads: *ut me malus abstulit error*, and Proba may be punning with the Latin word *malus* (apple tree).
[22]Genesis 3:14–15.
[23]Genesis 3:17–19.

Treacherous with drugs, likewise the herb.
But you, if you persist in training up the soil
Into the wheaten crop and hardy spelt,
Will look, to no avail, on stores piled high,
And will assuage your hunger in the woods,
260   Shaking the oak tree for your sustenance.
And in addition sad old age, disease,
Hard work as well, will come upon you, and
Unkind, unmitigated death will take you off.

Eve's Condemnation

Always these evils will be yours. And you, O
Most remorseless wife,[24] not unaware of wrong,
Of all these ills the origin and cause,
265   You shall atone for your egregious sins.
Alas, lost one, you do not know, do not perceive
What dangers stand about you from now on.
Now die, deserving death—you sought it wittingly.
My purpose does not yield, nor now is altered."

BIBLIOGRAPHY

Primary Sources

Proba. *Cento.* In *Poetae Christiani Minores*, edited by Carolus Schenkl. Corpus Scriptorum Ecclesiasticorum Latinorum 16.1, pp. 511–609. Vienna: F. Tempsky, 1888; repr.
New York and London, 1972.

Translations

Cariddi, Caterina. *Il centone di Proba Petronia (nobildonna del IV secolo della letteratura
cristiana).* Naples: Luigi Loffredo, 1971.
Clark, Elizabeth A., and Diane F. Hatch. *The Golden Bough, the Oaken Cross: The Vir-
gilian Cento of Faltonia Betitia Proba.* American Academy of Religion Texts and
Translations Series 5. Chico, Calif.: Scholars Press, 1981.
Reedy, Jeremiah. "Proba's Cento." In *A Lost Tradition: Women Writers of the Early
Church*, edited by Patricia Wilson-Kastner, G. Ronald Kastner, Ann Millin, Rosemary
Rader, and Jeremiah Reedy, pp. 45–69. Washington, D.C.: University Press of America,
1981.

---

[24]Genesis 3:16.

Secondary Works

Clark, Elizabeth A. "Faltonia Betitia Proba and Her Virgilian Poem: The Christian Matron as Artist." In *Ascetic Piety and Women's Faith: Essays on Late Ancient Christianity*, Studies in Women and Religion 20. edited by Elizabeth A. Clark, pp. 124–52. Lewiston, N.Y.: Edwin Mellen, 1986.

————, and Diane F. Hatch. "Jesus as Hero in the Virgilian *Cento* of Faltonia Betitia Proba." In *Ascetic Piety and Women's Faith: Essays on Late Ancient Christianity*, Studies in Women and Religion 20 edited by Elizabeth A. Clark, pp. 153–71. Lewiston, N.Y.: Edwin Mellen, 1986.

Clark, Gillian. *Women in Late Antiquity: Pagan and Christian Life-Styles.* Oxford: Oxford University Press, 1993.

Dronke, Peter. *Women Writers of the Middle Ages.* Cambridge: Cambridge University Press, 1984.

Hagendahl, Harald. *Latin Fathers and the Classics: A Study on the Apologists, Jerome, and Other Christian Writers.* Göteborg: Acta Universitatis Gothoburgensis, 1958.

Harrington, K. P., ed. *Medieval Latin*, 2d ed., revised by Joseph Pucci. Chicago and London: University of Chicago Press, 1997.

Herzog, Reinhart. *Die Bibelepik der lateinischen Spätantike: Formgeschichte einer erbaulichen Gattung.* Munich: Wilhelm Fink Verlag, 1975.

————. "Faltonia Betitia Proba." In *Restauration und Erneuerung: Die lateinische Literatur von 284 bis 374 n. Chr.*, edited by Reinhart Herzog et al., pp. 337–40. *Handbuch der lateinischen Literatur der Antike*, vol. 5. Munich: C. H. Beck, 1989.

Jensen, Anne. "Proba." In *Metzler Lexikon antiker Autoren*, edited by Oliver Schütze, pp. 579–81. Stuttgart and Weimar: J. B. Metzler, 1997.

Kirsch, Wolfgang. *Die lateinische Versepik des 4. Jahrhunderts.* Schriften zur Geschichte und Kultur der Antike 28. Berlin: Akademie Verlag, 1989.

Markus, R. A. "Paganism, Christianity and the Latin Classics in the Fourth Century." In *Latin Literature of the Fourth Century*, edited by J. W. Binns, pp. 1–21. London and Boston: Routledge and Kegan Paul, 1974.

Nodes, Daniel J. *Doctrine and Exegesis in Biblical Latin Poetry.* ARCA Classical and Medieval Texts, Papers and Monographs 31. Leeds: Francis Cairns, 1993.

Opelt, Ilona. "Der zürnende Christus in Cento der Proba." *Jahrbuch für Antike und Christentum* 7 (1964): 106–16.

Pavlovskis, Zoja. "Proba and the Semiotics of the Narrative Virgilian Cento." *Vergilius* 35 (1989): 70–84.

Roberts, Michael. *Biblical Epic and Rhetorical Paraphrase in Late Antiquity.* ARCA Classical and Medieval Texts, Papers and Monographs 16. Liverpool: Francis Cairns, 1985.

————. "The Latin Literature of Late Antiquity." In *Medieval Latin Studies: An Introduction and Bibliographical Guide*, edited by F. A. C. Mantello and A. G. Rigg, pp. 537–46. Washington, D.C.: Catholic University of America Press, 1996.

Shanzer, Danuta. "The Anonymous *Carmen contra paganos* and the Date and Identity of the Centonist Proba." *Revue des Études Augustiniennes* 32 (1986): 232–48.

Spinelli, Mario. "Proba Petronia." In *Enciclopedia Virgiliana,* edited by Francesco della Corte, vol. 4, cols. 283–85. Rome: Istituto della Enciclopedia Italiana, 1988.

Springer, Carl P. E. "Jerome and the *Cento* of Proba." *Studia Patristica* 28 (1993): 96–105.

Inscriptions on Fabia Aconia Paulina

Victoria Erhart

Fabia Aconia Paulina may be taken as representative of the role and function of aristocratic women in Roman society in the Late Antique period. She represents the finest attributes of traditional Roman religion, state-sponsored paganism, in its twilight in the later part of the fourth century C.E. An analysis of the information contained in inscriptions involving her gives a great deal of information about her class of women in Roman society. Immediately noticeable, even in inscriptions dedicated to her, as in Document 65, is the fact that she is primarily defined by her relationships to the significant male figures in her life, her father and her husband. Fabia Aconia Paulina was the daughter of a Roman senator and the wife of another, younger Roman senator. All three of them merit the honorific title "most distinguished." Each man is further defined by the addition of at least one major title relating to an important position he has held in the imperial civil service.

As a woman, Fabia Aconia Paulina could not play any public role in either political or social circles, these being male monopolies. Rather, she is defined by her religious titles, that is, by a list of her association with various matronal cults of both Roman and foreign origin, either Greek or Etruscan. As in the political and social realm, so too in the religious realm, women were banned from any public role, particularly if this involved the sacrifice of any live animals. In cults applicable exclusively to Roman matrons, that is, women still attached to their first husbands and with whom they have produced children, women could play a subservient role, but these cultic rites occurred only at infrequent intervals, at sites physically removed from the center of Roman power. They were essentially private rather than public cult acts and did not generally involve the sacrifice of live animals. Other types of votive offerings were used instead. Even though she came from the higher aristocratic circles of Roman society, Fabia Aconia Paulina could still hold positions of only marginal religious import.[1]

Of the deities with whose cults inscription Document 65 associates her, both Ceres and Hecate are foreign cults, originally Greek, that had later been "nationalized" into the Roman system. Ceres, in particular, was attractive to women because as an agricultural deity she was also associated with fertility. The cult of Isis, which had a reputation in male-dominated Latin literature as being religiously deviant, mere women's superstitions,[2] derives from Egypt and dates back to at least 2500 B.C.E. Worship of Isis was attractive to women because Isis had power equal to that of male deities.[3] Since women could take no autonomous part in Roman public cult functions, being a priestess or an initiate into a deity's cult perhaps meant that a woman then had some financial responsibility for the upkeep of that deity's temple and for the expenses associated with worship and sacrifice to it.

Document 66 gives evidence of Fabia Aconia Paulina's association with the ancient order of Vestal Virgins, priestesses at the temple of Vesta in the Forum in Rome, the seat of Roman identity and power. Vestals, unlike their patronesses, were required to remain virgin for their term of service, normally thirty years beginning when the girls were as young as seven or eight. Under the supervision of the Great Vestal Virgin, *virgo Vestalis maxima*, the Vestals tended the sacred fire in the temple of Vesta that represented the fire in the hearth of every Roman home. Severe penalties were imposed on Vestals who let the sacred fire die or who broke their vows of chastity (*pudicitia*). The Vestal initiation ceremony resembled a Roman marriage ritual in which the young girl was handed over by her father to the High Priest (*pontifex maximus*, a pagan title later taken over by the papacy). Vestals had an ambiguous gender identification. Since they were vowed virgins, they had neither husbands nor children. Their fathers gave up their authority over the girls when they were initiated into Vesta's service. Thus, they were neither matrons nor maidens. Although they did not sacrifice live animals in a public setting, Vestals did prepare the sacred flour to be sprinkled over all sacrificial animals, an item necessary for all sacrifices to be acceptable. They may have participated in the secondary or concluding rites of a public cult ceremony. Thus, they took on activities normally belonging only to adult male citizens. There were other categories of women who abrogated to themselves some of the secondary cultic activities of traditional Roman worship, but the cult of Vesta is the one with which Fabia Aconia Paulina was most closely associated, probably through a combination of social patronage and financial support.

Document 67, the joint funerary monument inscription, allows us to see beyond Paulina's religious duties and functions and glimpse her as an individual. This joint funerary monument is unusual in a number of respects, not the least of which is that it is a joint monument. In his analysis of the family relationship denoted in Late Antique funerary inscriptions, both pagan and Christian, Brent Shaw tabulated the dedication inscription of a wife to a husband as the rarest form of familial relationship depicted.[4] This joint funerary inscription also indicates that traditional Roman religious practices were still a viable option in the late fourth century C.E. despite the growing popularity and prestige of Christianity. Fabia Aconia Paulina's husband, noting the wealth the Christian Church in Rome was beginning to accumulate now that it could accept bequests, once remarked, "Make me bishop of Rome and I will become a Christian tomorrow." Yet both he and his wife remained participants in traditional cultic practices despite the inroads Christianity made in the thoughts and customs of Late Antique urban society. Both traditional Roman worship and Christianity preferred inhumation rather than cremation for burial beginning as early as the second century C.E. Pagan inscriptions, however, differed markedly from those memorializing Christians. Beginning in the early third century, Christian funerary inscriptions rarely mentioned secular relationships, even between members of the same nuclear family. Most important for a Christian was the individual's relationship to Christ, not who the various members of the family were and what posts in the imperial civil or military administration the deceased held. The deceased Christian was a son or daughter of Christ and a citizen of heaven, earthly relationships and positions being far secondary. Christian funerary inscriptions stressed Christian virtues, not secular relationships. This was not at all so for the funerary inscriptions of deceased practitioners of the traditional Roman cults. Their inscriptions eulogized the network of secular relationships and positions held by the deceased.

Both Fabia Aconia Paulina and her husband Vettius Agorius Praetextatus are also denoted by their formal patronymics. Late Antique Christian funerary inscriptions and most pagan funerary inscriptions of nonaristocratic persons denoted the deceased through the use of the single cognomen. What in traditional Roman funerary practice had been a sign of servile status, the use of only one name became more generally accepted in Late Antiquity except in aristocratic circles that were inclined to be more conservative in all traditional Roman practices, whether in life or in death. Aristocratic funerary inscriptions continued the memorial customs of the period of the principate, using all three formal names and denoting illustrious familial and political connections.[5] Thus, Vettius's initial commemoration on his monument stresses his aristocratic rank, his religious associations, and his positions within the civil administration of the Roman Empire.

Fabia Aconia Paulina is initially commemorated on the right side of the monument in rather formulaic terms that stress her participation in the traditional virtues of a respectable Roman matron. There is no indication of her individual personality. Rather she is commemorated as truthful, pure and chaste, obedient and loyal to her husband, a woman who excelled in the one area in Roman society open to her authority, the domestic household. Fortunately, Fabia Aconia Paulina is mentioned in other sources. None other than the famous pagan orator Symmachus mentions her in a letter written to her husband. From this letter, one learns that Fabia Aconia Paulina was that most fortunate of women. She had a loving marriage, rather than merely a contractual relationship undertaken in her name for the financial and political advantages of her male relatives. Disturbed by the lack of response to his previous letter to Vettius, Symmachus suggests that Vettius not concern himself entirely with Paulina's ill health, though he does state that he wishes her a swift and complete recovery.[6] Vettius apparently loved Fabia Aconia Paulina, a fact known to his acquaintances. His love for her is illustrated by the inscription on the left side of the monument. There Vettius stresses his real love for and gratitude to Fabia Aconia Paulina for the part she has played in his life.

The reverse side of the monument carries Fabia Aconia Paulina's inscription to her husband. A traditional Roman matron, she defines herself in relationship to her husband. He has brought her glory and respect, he has taught her, he is the reason why other women in Rome look upon her with favorable regard. Although the ideal-wife motif in traditional Roman culture stressed that a woman should not survive her one and only husband, she appears to be genuinely grieved that he has predeceased her. Thus Fabia Aconia Paulina continues the long line of Roman matrons who tried to live as the very embodiment of what the Romans considered their finest virtues.

NOTES

1. On the relegation of women to the margins of traditional Roman cult practices, see John Scheid, "The Religious Roles of Roman Woman," in *A History of Women in the West*, ed. Pauline Schmitt Pantel (Cambridge, Mass.: Belknap Press, 1992), pp. 77–108.

2. Juvenal *Satires* 6, in which he mocks matronal cult worship as *anilis superstitio*, "old women's superstitions."

3. For a brief history and explanation of the cult to Isis, see Sarah B. Pomeroy, *Goddesses, Whores, Wives and Slaves: Women in Classical Antiquity* (New York: Schocken Books, 1975), pp. 217–26.

4. For an analysis of Roman funerary inscriptions in Late Antiquity, see Brent D. Shaw, "Latin Funerary Epigraphy and Family Life in the Later Roman Empire," *Historia* 33 (1984): 457–97. See p. 465 for a brief discussion of the ratios of husband-to-wife to wife-to-husband dedications.

5. For a discussion of the connections between funerary art and architecture and social class in the Roman Empire, see Diana E. E. Kleiner, "Roman Funerary Art and Architecture: Observations on the Significance of Recent Studies," *Journal of Roman Archaeology* 1 (1988): 115–19, with extensive bibliography in the footnotes.

6. Symmachus *Epistle* 1.48 to Vettius Agorius Praetextatus [written prior to 385]: "Benevolent gods! How nothing is safe and certain for mankind! No doubt you have retired to Baiae to ease your mind. What evil eye has been cast on your intended repose? Has the health of Paulina, our shared concern, reached a crisis or is your fear for her so great that you consider all her inconveniences take on the

form of danger? Whichever of these it is, you should bear in mind the painful days and watchful nights you have passed. We are born doomed to endure frequent tribulation. Pleasures are fleeting and the enjoyment of every good is as brief as the experience is superficial. However, let these things be left to the arguments of philosophers. Let us now encourage our minds to a more joyful disposition when the peace of the gods has once again placed the health of our Paulina on a solid footing."

Inscriptions on Fabia Aconia Paulina

Document 65 (Corpus Inscriptionum Latinarum *6.1780* = Inscriptiones Latinae Selectae *1260); Rome*

[Letters shown within brackets are not present in the inscription.]
    FABIAE   ACONIAE PAVLINAE   C[larissima] F[emina]
    FILIAE ACONII CATVLLINI V[ir] C[larissimus] EX PRAEF ET
        CONSVLE ORD
    VXORI VETTI PRAETEXTATI V[ir] C[larissimus] PRAEF ET
        CONSVLIS DESIGNATI
    SACRATAE APVD ELEVSINAM DEO IACCHO CERERI ET CORAE
    SACRATAE APVD LAERNAM DEO LIBERO ET CERERI ET CORAE
    SACRATAE APVD AEGINAM DEABVS TAVROBOLIATAE ISIACAE
    HIEROPHANTRIAE DEAE HECATAE GRAECO SACRANEAE DEAE
        CERERIS

Document 66 (Corpus Inscriptionum Latinarum *6.2145* = Inscriptiones Latinae Selectae *1161); Rome*

    COELIAE CONCORDIAE VIRGINI
    VESTALI MAXIMAE FABIA PAV
    LINA C[larissima] F[emina] STATVAM FACIEN
    DAM CONLOCANDAMQVE
    CVRAVIT CVM PROPTER
    EGREGIAM EIVS PVDICI
    TIAM INSIGNEMQVE
    CIRCA CVLTVM DIVINVM
    SANCTITATEM TVM QVOD
    HAEC PRIOR EIVS VIRO
    VETTIO AGORIO PRAETEXTA
    TO V[ir] C[larissimus] OMNIA SINGVLARI
    DIGNOQVE ETIAM AB HVIVS
    MODI VIRGINIBVS ET SA
    CERDOTIBVS COLI STATV
    AM CONLOCARAT

Document 67 (**Corpus Inscriptionum Latinarum** *6.1779* = Inscriptiones Latinae Selectae *1259); Rome*

[This inscription from the joint funerary monument of Fabia Aconia Paulina and her husband, Vettius Agorius Praetextatus, is now in the Capitoline Museum in Rome.]

On the front of the monument:

VETTIVS AGORIVS PRAETEXTATVS
AVGVR PONTIFEX VESTAE
PONTIFEX SOLIS QVINDECEMVIR
CVRIALIS HERCVLIS SACRATVS
LIBERO ET ELEVSINIS HIEROPHANTA
NEOCORVS TAVROBOLIATVS
PATER PATRVM IN RE PVBLICA VERO
QVAESTOR CANDIDATVS
PRETOR VRBANVS
CORRECTOR TVSCIAE ET VMBRIAE
CONSVLARIS LVSITANIAE
PROCONSVLE ACHAIAE
PRAEFECTVS VRBI
LEGATVS A SENATV MISSVS V
PRAEFECTVS PRAETORIO II ITALIAE
ET ILLYRICI CONSVL ORDINARIVS
DESIGNATVS
ET ACONIA FABIA PAVLINA C[larissima] F[emina]
SACRATA CERERI ET ELEVSINIIS
SACRATA APVD EGINAM HECATAE
TAVROBOLIATA HIEROPHANTRIA
HI CONIVNCTI SIMVL VIXERVNT ANN XL

On the right side of the monument:

VETTIVS AGORIVS PRAETEXTATVS
PAVLINAE CONIVGI
PAVLINA VERI ET CASTITATIS CONSCIA
DICATA TEMPLIS ATQ AMICA NVMINVM
SIBI MARITVM PRAEFERENS ROMAM VIRO
PVDENS FIDELIS PVRA MENTE ET CORPORE
BENIGNA CVNCTIS VTILIS PENATIBVS
CALDASN ////// //////////// VS N/////

On the left side of the monument:

VETTIVS AGORIVS PRAETEXTATVS
PAVLINAE CONIVGI
PAVLINA NOSTRI PECTORIS CONSORTIO
FOMES PVDORIS CASTITATIS VINCVLVM
AMORQVE PVRVS ET FIDES CAELO SATA
ARCANA MENTIS CVI RECLVSA CREDIDI
MVNVS DEORVM QVI MARITALEM TORVM
NECTVNT AMICIS ET PVDICIS NEXIBVS
PIETATE MATRIS CONIVGALI GRATIA
NEXV SORORIS FILIAE MODESTIA
ET QVANTA AMICIS IVNGIMVR FIDVCIA
AETATIS VSV CONSECRANDI FOEDERE
IVGI FIDELI SIMPLICI CONCORDIA
IVVANS MARITVM DILIGENS ORNANS
COLENS

On the back of the monument (Paulina to Praetextatus):

SPLENDOR PARENTVM NIL MIHI MAIVS DEDIT
QVAM QVOD MARITO DIGNA IAM TVM VISA SVM
SED LVMEN OMNE VEL DECVS NOMEN VIRI
AGORI SVPERBO QVI CREATVS GERMINE
PATRIAM SENATVM CONIVGEMQ INL VMINAS
PROBITATE MENTIS MORIBVS STVDIIS SIMVL
VIRTVTIS APICEM QVIS SVPREMVM NANCTVS ES
TV NAMQVE QVIDQVID LINGVA VTRAQ EST PRODITVM
CVRA SOFORVM PORTA QVIS CAELI PATET
VEL QVAE PERITI CONDIDERE CARMINA
VEL QVAE SOLVTIS VOCIBVS SVNT EDITA
MELIORA REDDIS QVAM LEGENDO SVMPSERAS
SED ISTA PARVA TV PIVS MOVESTES SACRIS
TELETIS REPERTA MENTIS ARCANO PREMIS
DIVVMQVE NVMEN MVLTIPLEX DOCTVS COLIS
SOCIAM BENIGNE CONIVGEM NECTENS SACRIS
HOMINVM DEVMQVE CONSCIAM AC FIDAM TIBI
QVID NVNC HONORES AVT POTESTATES LOQVAR
HOMINVMQVE VOTIS ADPETITA GAVDIA
QVAE TV CADVCA AC PARVA SEMPER AVTVMANS
DIVVM SACERDOS INFVLIS CELSVS CLVES
TV ME MARITE DISCIPLINARVM BONO

PVRAM AC PVDICAM SORTE MORTIS EXIMENS
IN TEMPLA DVCIS AD FAMVLAM DIVIS DICAS
TE TESTE CVNCTIS IMBVOR MYSTERIIS
TV DINDYMENES ATTEOS QVI ANTISTITEM
TELETIS HONORAS TAVREIS CONSORS PIVS
HECATES MINISTRAM TRINA SECRETA EDOCES
CERERISQVE GRAIAE TV SACRIS DIGNAM PARAS
TE PROPTER OMNIS ME BEATAM ME PIAM
CELEBRANT QVOD IPSE ME BONAM DISSEMINAS
TOTVM PER ORBEM IGNOTA NOSCOR OMNIBVS
NAM TE MARITO CVR PLACERE NON QVEAM
EXEMPL VM DE ME ROMVLAE MATRES PETVNT
SVBOLEMQVE PVLCHRAM SI TVAE SIMILIS PVTANT
OPTANT PROBANTQVE NVNC VIRI NVNC FEMINAE
QVAE TV MAGISTER INDIDISTI INSIGNIA
HIS NVNC ADEMPTIS MAESTA CONIVNX MACEROR
FELIX MARITVM SI SVPERSTITEM MIHI
DIVI DEDISSENT SED TAMEN FELIX TV A
QVIA SVM FVIQVE POSTQVE MORTEM MOX ERO

TRANSLATION

Translated by Brian Croke and Jill Harries, in *Religious Conflict in Fourth-Century Rome: A Documentary Study* (Sydney: University of Sydney Press), 1982, pp. 105–108, Reprinted by permission of the authors. The notes are by Victoria Erhart.

Document 65 (**Corpus Inscriptionum Latinarum** *6.1780*)

To Fabia Aconia Paulina, c(larissima) f(eminia),[1] daughter of Aconius Catullinus,[2] v(ir) c(larissimus),[3] formerly Prefect and consul ordinarius.[4] Wife of Vettius

---

[1]*Clarissima femina*, literally "a most distinguished woman," was a semiofficial title of honor accorded to women of the senatorial class.

[2]Aconius Catullinus was a highborn Roman aristocrat. According to the *Theodosian Code* 16.10.3, he was prefect of the city in 342, at which time legislation was enacted to preserve from destruction places such as theatres and other temples where traditional pagan public amusements were held. For his brief biography, see A. H. M. Jones, J. R. Martindale, and J. R. Morris, *The Prosopography of the Late Roman Empire*, 1, A.D. 260–395 (Cambridge University Press, 197F), pp. 187–88.

[3]*Vir clarissimus*, literally "a most distinguished man," was a semiofficial title of honor accorded to men of the senatorial class.

[4]A consul was a senior Roman magistrate. His *imperium*, or authority, was valid not only in Rome, but throughout Italy and even in the provinces, where his mandate could override that of the provincial governor, provided the consul was acting according to law.

Praetextatus,[5] v(ir) c(larissimus), Prefect and consul designate,[6] consecrated at Eleusis[7] to the gods Iacchus, Ceres and Cora;[8] consecrated at Laerna to the gods Liber,[9] Ceres and Cora, consecrated to the goddesses at Aegina;[10] initiate of the taurobolium,[11] of Isis,[12] high priestess (*hierophantria*) of the Greek goddess Hecate,[13] of the sacred goddess Ceres.

Document 66 (Corpus Inscriptionum Latinarum 6.2145)

To Coelia Concordia, chief of the Vestal Virgins.[14] Fabia Paulina, c(larissima) f(emina), arranged to have this statue built and put in position because of her [Coelia's] scrupulous modesty and outstanding piety towards the divine ritual and because she had previously put up a statue to her [Paulina's] husband Vettius Agorius Praetextatus, v(ir) c(larissimus), outstanding in every way and worthy to be worshipped by the virgins and priests of that order.

---

[5]Vettius Praetextatus was a pagan aristocrat who had an illustrious public career in imperial service. For his brief biography, see *Prosopography of the Later Roman Empire*, vol. 1, pp. 722–24. He was also particularly known for his knowledge of Greek literature, an increasingly rare commodity among Latin aristocrats in Late Antiquity.

[6]A prefect had overall responsibility for the area under his jurisdiction, whether that area was a geographic entity, such as a province or a larger diocese, or a particular aspect of administration, such as finances or military matters.

[7]Eleusis in Greece was the main site dedicated to the worship of Ceres, the goddess of cereal grains, especially the corn supply. Her cult was secret.

[8]Iacchus, also called Liber or Bacchus, was the son of Ceres. In the Roman system of deities, Bacchus was identified with the Greek god Dionysus, whose cult was symbolized by wine and ecstatic excesses, including orgies. Ceres was a very old Italian-Roman earth goddess chiefly concerned with the production of cereals and other food stuffs. The temple dedicated to her on the Aventine side of the Forum Boarium was considered to be particularly beautiful. Cora is an alternative name for Proserpine, the daughter of Ceres by Jupiter.

[9]Liber is the Latin name of the god Bacchus / Iacchus, also known in the Greek pantheon as Dionysus.

[10]Aegina was the central location of the cult to the underworld goddess Hecate.

[11]*Taurobolium* is a rite connected with the veneration of Mithras and Cybele. During initiation, the initiate stood in a pit. Above the pit a bull was sacrificed so that the initiate would be drenched or baptized in its blood.

[12]Isis is a goddess from Egypt. She is the mother of Horus, and both the sister and wife of Osiris. After Osiris's murder and dismemberment, Isis wandered the known world seeking to find and restore the pieces of his body.

[13]Hecate was a daughter of Jupiter. She was a goddess of the underworld and thus merits special mention in a funerary inscription.

[14]Vestal Virgins were the six women who served in the special priesthood of the goddess Vesta. At age seven or eight, young girls were inducted into the priesthood to Vesta. They took a vow of chastity for the term of their service, normally thirty years. The chastity and purity of the Vestal Virgins served as the guarantee for the continued existence of the Roman Empire.

Document 67 (*Corpus Inscriptionum Latinarum* 6.1779)

[Funeral monument of Praetextatus and Paulina now in the Capitoline Museum, Rome.]

ON THE FRONT:

To the divine Shades, Vettius Agorius Praetextatus, augur,[15] priest of Vesta,[16] priest of the Sun,[17] *quindecemvir*,[18] curial of Hercules,[19] consecrated to Liber and the Eleusinian mysteries,[20] high priest, temple overseer (*neocorus*);[21] initiate of the taurobolium, Father of the Fathers [priest of Mithras],[22] but in public office: quaestor designate,[23] urban praetor,[24] governor (*corrector*) of Tuscia and Umbria,[25] governor (*consularis*) of Lusitania,[26] proconsul of Achaea,[27] Prefect of

---

[15]An augur was a priest whose duties involved divination. The College of Augurs usually numbered twelve men. Rather than serve as some type of fortune-teller, augurs kept manuals of instruction in order to interpret the objects and signs connected with a particular undertaking, such as a decision to go to war, to propose a new law, or other matters of state business.

[16]Vesta is a very ancient Roman goddess having no known image. So important was her cult that it was supervised by the pontifex maximus, the most senior priest of the Roman state religion. Her temple in the Forum Romanum was very old and held a perpetually burning flame.

[17]Sun worship persisted into the Late Antique period. Up to at least 312 C.E. and perhaps later, the nominally Christian emperor Constantine the Great (306–37 C.E.) issued coins in honor of the Unconquered Sun.

[18]*Quindecemvir*, one of only fifteen men at a time in charge of the books containing the Sibylline Oracles.

[19]Hercules, along with Mars and Silvanus, was considered to be a particularly virile deity. As such, he would have merited a set of devoted male priests and followers willing to offer sacrifice to him.

[20]Eleusinian mysteries were a secret cult centered at Eleusis in Greece. This cult was associated with the cult of Ceres.

[21]A temple overseer was in charge of the physical maintenance of the temple and supervised the sacrifices taking place there.

[22]Mithra or Mithras was a Persian god. His cult symbol was the bull. Mithraism became assimilated to the cult of the son god in the Roman army and was very popular.

[23]A quaestor was the lowest rung on the senatorial ladder. A man first had to be elected at least a quaestor before being elected to the Senate, usually about age thirty. A quaestor's duties usually involved financial matters with the treasury in Rome, helping to manage the finances of a province, or collecting port taxes.

[24]The urban praetor was responsible for the supervision of the law courts within the city of Rome. His decisions were enforceable up to a five-mile radius outside the limits of Rome. If both consuls of the city were absent, he was responsible for the defense of the city and had the power to summon the Senate into session on an emergency basis.

[25]A *corrector* was a type of official usually in charge of financial matters in a given area.

[26]Lusitania is equivalent to present-day Portugal. It was originally a part of the larger Roman Diocese of Spain.

[27]Vettius Praetextatus was proconsul, the official in charge, of Achaea in southern Greece on the Gulf of Corinth in 362.

the City,[28] seven times sent by the senate as ambassador,[29] twice Praetorian Prefect of Italy and Illyricum,[30] designated *consul ordinarius*, and Aconia Fabia Paulina *c(larissima) f(emina)*, consecrated to Ceres and the Eleusinian mysteries, consecrated at Aegina to Hecate, initiate of the taurobolium, high priestess. These two lived together for forty years.

ON THE RIGHT:

Vettius Agorius Praetextatus to his wife Paulina. Paulina, associate of truth and chastity, dedicated in temples and friend of the divine powers, putting her husband before herself, Rome before her man, modest, faithful, pure in mind and body, kind to all, a blessing to her household.

ON THE LEFT:

Vettius Agorius Praetextatus to his wife Paulina. Paulina, partner of my heart, nurse of modesty, bond of chastity, pure love and loyalty produced in heaven, to whom I have entrusted the deep hidden secrets of my heart, gift of the gods who bind our marriage couch with friendly and modest ties; by the devotion of a mother, the gratitude of a wife, the bond of a sister, the modesty of a daughter, and by all the loyalty friends show, we are united by the custom of age, the pact of consecration, by the yoke of the marriage vow and perfect harmony, helpmate of your husband, loving, adoring, devoted.

ON THE BACK:

[Paulina to Praetextatus] The glory of my parents gave me nothing greater than to have seemed already worthy of my husband; but all light and glory is my husband's name. Agorius, sprung of proud lineage, you illumine your country, the senate, and your wife by the integrity of mind, your character, and your scholarship all at once. By these you attained the highest peak of virtue, for by translating whatever is proclaimed in either tongue by the thought of the wise, to whom the gate of heaven lies open, both the poems which the learned have composed and the prose works recited aloud, you have improved upon what you have found written down. Yet these things are of little account. You, a holy man, and priest of the mysteries, conceal in the secret places of your heart what you discovered in

---

[28]Vettius Praetextatus was prefect of the city (of Rome) in 368. As such, he ranked immediately below a praetorian prefect, but his authority was supreme in the city of Rome itself. He was responsible for supervising all the other magistrates in the city who had been appointed for that year.

[29]The Roman Empire did not have a standing, professional department of foreign service. When an ambassador was necessary in order to represent the interests of the Roman Empire in treaty negotiations with foreign peoples, the man with the most political connections at that time was delegated to undertake the task.

[30]There is a record of Vettius Praetextatus serving as praetorian prefect of Italy and Illyricum only once, in the year 384. This appointment formed the pinnacle of his career in imperial service.

the secret initiations and with your manifold learning you worship the divine power, uniting with your kindness your wife as your associate with the sacred objects, confidante of men and gods, and in one mind with you as she was. What may I now say of the offices and powers, joys sought by men in their prayers, which you who regard yourself as a priest of the gods and are marked out by your priestly headbands,[31] always consider transient and trivial? You, O husband, deliver me pure and chaste from the lot of death by the goodness of your teaching, lead me into the temples and dedicate me to the gods as their handmaid. With you as witness I am initiated into all the mysteries. You, in your duty as husband, consecrate me as priestess of Didymenes [Cybele] and Attis[32] through the rites of the bull. You instruct me, as a priestess of Hecate, in the threefold secrets and you prepare me for being worthy of the rites of Greek Ceres. Because of you everyone proclaims me holy and blessed, since it is you who spread my goodness throughout the world. Although unknown, I am known to all. With you as my husband how could I fail to please? The matrons of Romulus'[33] city seek me as a model and regard their offspring as beautiful if it resembles yours. Men and women alike both seek after and acclaim the honors which you, my teacher, have given me. Now robbed of all this I, your grief-stricken wife, am wasting away. Happy would I have been had the gods granted that my husband had outlived me. Yet I am happy because I am yours, was yours, and soon shall be yours after death.

BIBLIOGRAPHY

Primary Sources
Corpus Inscriptionum Latinarum, vol. 6, part 1. Berlin: Georg Reimer, 1876.
Inscriptiones Latinae Selectae, ed. Herman Dessau, vol. 1. Dublin: Weidman, 1974.

Secondary Works
Croke, Brian, and Jill Harries. *Religious Conflict in Fourth-Century Rome: A Documentary Study.* Sydney: University of Sydney Press, 1982.
Jones, A. H. M. *The Later Roman Empire, 284–602.* Baltimore, Md.: Johns Hopkins Press, 1986.
————, J. R. Martindale, and J. Morris. *The Prosopography of the Later Roman Empire, I, A.D. 260–395.* Cambridge: Cambridge University Press, 1971.
Kleiner, Diana E. E. "Roman Funerary Art and Architecture: Observations on the Significance of Recent Studies." *Journal of Roman Archaeology* 1 (1988): 115–19.

---

[31]The various cults required different clothing for participants, each costume generally involving some sort of headgear. Women involved in the cult of the Bona Dea, the goddess of women, wore purple headbands. Vestal Virgins wore red headdresses.

[32]Didymenes [Cybele] was originally the Great Mother goddess from Asia Minor. Her cult was brought to Rome ca. 204 B.C.E. The rites of the cult of Attis, a male deity, were traditionally associated with those of Didymenes.

[33]Romulus is considered the traditional founder and first king of Rome, ca. 752 B.C.E.

Pomeroy, Sarah B. "The Roman Matron of the Late Republic and Early Empire." In *Goddess, Whores, Wives and Slaves: Women in Classical Antiquity*, pp. 149–89. New York: Schocken Books, 1975.

Scheid, John. "The Religious Roles of Roman Women." In *A History of Women in the West I: From Ancient Goddesses to Christian Saints*, edited by Pauline Schmitt Pantel, pp. 77–108. Cambridge, Mass.: Belknap Press, 1992.

Shaw, Brent D. "Latin Funerary Epigraphy and Family Life in the Later Roman Empire." *Historia* 33 (1984): 457–97.

Itinerarium Egeriae: A Pilgrim's Journey

Victoria Erhart

Itinerarium Egeriae is the name most commonly given to the surviving portion of a Latin narrative written late in the fourth century C.E., in which a woman writes to women friends about her experiences traveling through Egypt, Palestine, and Mesopotamia to visit sites with important biblical or early Christian associations. Although Egeria's *Itinerarium* is mentioned in a seventh-century text and quoted in Peter the Deacon's twelfth-century *De locis sanctis* (*Book of the Holy Places*),[1] not until the late nineteenth century was the manuscript of the *Itinerarium Egeriae* identified.[2] Dates for this pilgrimage range from late fourth century to mid–sixth century C.E., but the most commonly accepted dates are 381–83 C.E.[3] The surviving portion of the *Itinerarium Egeriae*, estimated to be approximately one-third of the entire text, falls into unequal sections. The first section records the places visited, their Christian significance, and the prayers and scriptural readings appropriate to each location. The second portion of the *Itinerarium Egeriae* consists of a detailed description of the manner in which the Christian liturgy was celebrated in Jerusalem late in the fourth century C.E.

Itinerarium Egeriae opens with a description of traveling to Mount Sinai, followed by a description of pilgrimages to various sites significant to the early development of Christian monasticism.[4] After visiting many of these Christian monks and hermits living near various oases that dotted the Egyptian desert in order to pray with them and secure their blessings, Egeria journeyed from Egypt through the Jordanian desert, where she climbed Mount Nebo, the traditional site of Moses' grave,[5] to Palestine. While in Palestine Egeria visited numerous biblical sites; the holy places in Jerusalem alone required a full three months' stay. She then traveled from Jerusalem, through Galilee into northern Mesopotamia. The extant narrative ends in Constantinople, the capital city of the eastern Roman

Empire, where Egeria considers extending her pilgrimage to include Christian sites in Asia Minor, particularly Ephesus, a city traditionally associated with the Apostle John. The sections of the narrative included in this volume are the beginning of Egeria's accounts of her departure from Jerusalem (17:1–3), her visit to Edessa and the shrine to St. Thomas (19:1–19), and her experiences at Holy Thecla's church in Seleucia (23:1–10).

The second section of *Itinerarium Egeriae* provides an invaluable source for descriptions of liturgical customs specific to the fourth-century Christian community in Jerusalem. She describes the six daily times of worship, when each occurred, and what hymns, Psalms, and scriptural readings were used. Thus, she provides not only a description of typical daily Christian worship but also descriptions of the annual major holidays: for the days of Lent and for Easter rites including Palm Sunday, Good Friday, Easter, and Pentecost. Since the Easter season was the traditional period when new adult members were accepted into the Christian community, Egeria also provides a description of the process of catecheses, or instruction, during the weeks prior to baptism at Easter.[6]

Because the surviving manuscript fragment of *Itinerarium Egeriae* contains virtually no personal information about Egeria, there has been a great deal of scholarly debate about her identity. At one time Egeria was (mis)identified with Silvia of Aquitaine, an aristocratic woman who also made a pilgrimage to the Holy Land in the late fourth century C.E.[7] Identification of the author of the *Itinerarium* with the name "Egeria" depends primarily on a letter the Spanish monk Valerius wrote around 680 and included in a compilation about the saints for the instruction of young monks.[8] There has been debate about whether she was a nun or a pious laywoman, her standing in society, where she was from originally, and, if she was not a nun, her marital status. Most scholars have concluded that Egeria was originally from Spain or Gaul. This conclusion is based on a rather fragmentary bit of information in *Itinerarium Egeriae* where the unnamed bishop of Edessa in northern Mesopotamia welcomes Egeria upon her arrival to the city: "My daughter, I can see what a long journey this is on which your faith has brought you—right from the other end of the earth" (19.5, included in this volume). Some scholars have interpreted *de extremis porro terris venires ad haec loca* quite literally. The farthest places away from Edessa would be those in the far west of the western Roman Empire, i.e., Galicia in Spain, bordering on the Atlantic Ocean, or Aquitaine in Gaul, also an Atlantic coastal province. If the phrase *de extremis porro terris* is interpreted as a rhetorical term, the bishop has merely indicated that Egeria has come from a place far away, remote either geographically or spiritually.

Egeria provides the only other helpful geographical clue when she travels along the Mesopotamian frontier and must cross the Euphrates River en route to the city of Batanis in northern Syria (18.2). Seeing the Euphrates for the first time, Egeria states: "It is very big, and really rather frightening since it flows very fast like the Rhone, but the Euphrates is much bigger" (*et quasi terribilis est; ita enim decurrent habens impetum sicut habet fluvius Rodanus, nisi quod adhuc maior est Eufrates*). Taking these two statements together, some scholars have concluded that Egeria was from Gaul, from one of the provinces along the Rhone River, most probably from an urban context such as Narbonne or Arles.[9]

Some scholars have assumed that Egeria was a nun or had monastic affiliation.[10] Evidence in the *Itinerarium Egeriae* is equivocal. Egeria's text is in the form of an informative but loosely written letter to a circle of female acquaintances whom she terms "my sisters," *dominae sorores*. However, this term could just as easily be used in the generic as in the technical sense, to refer either to a group of female friends or to officially enrolled female members of a monastic community. While it is clear that Egeria holds the intended recipients of her letter in close affection, there is no indication of the identity of these female associates nor of their relationship to Egeria. By the time she wrote in the late fourth century C.E., Christian women had begun to form communities centered on celibacy and ascetic self-discipline.[11] Women in some type of monastic community may, in fact, be the intended recipients of Egeria's letter. At the end of her letter to her female friends, Egeria states that she is considering lengthening her pilgrimage to include sites of Christian significance in Asia Minor. She does not ask for permission from her female acquaintances, something she might do if she were a nun and under a vow of obedience. Egeria nowhere mentions the cost of her pilgrimage, i.e., for transportation, food, accommodations, or charitable gifts. Surely financial considerations would have been of interest to her circle of female friends had she been a member of a religious community that was responsible for her financial support.[12]

Egeria mentions numerous times that she is going to visit a particular site of interest to Christian pilgrims and receive the blessings of the monks she would encounter there. Yet she does not mention any of these monks by name nor does she provide any information on the forms of eastern (Greek-speaking) monasticism encountered, information that would have been highly desirable to members of a monastic community in the western (Latin-speaking) Roman Empire. Likewise, there is no evidence to support the claim that Egeria was an abbess of an unnamed monastic community. It is unlikely that Egeria, if an abbess, could spend three years away from her monastic responsibilities. It is more probable that Egeria was a pious laywoman of indeterminate age who commanded enough financial resources to pay for her own pilgrimage. Though financially able to afford her pilgrimage, Egeria was probably not from the higher aristocratic segment of Gallic society.

Egeria was not by any means the only woman to make a pilgrimage to the Holy Land in the late fourth century C.E. Records survive indicating that numerous women from the aristocratic class did so. Accounts about the pilgrimages of Melania, Paula, and Eustochium, to name only the most well known, have been preserved in a variety of other sources, all written by men.[13] In the surviving fragments of their pilgrimage accounts preserved in other texts, the women provide ample evidence of the breadth and depth of the type of education female urban aristocrats received in the Late Antique period.[14] In each case, the aristocratic women refer frequently to other literary texts, both Christian and classical.

In contrast, Egeria provides no evidence that she received such an education. Though literate in Latin, she does not give any concrete evidence that she knew even rudimentary Greek. Egeria does not refer to any other text besides the Bible in her account, though this lack of reference could represent indifference to as easily as ignorance of other literary texts. Egeria does not show a particularly deep or thorough understanding of the Bible. She reads scriptural passages literally, rather than making any attempt at allegorical exegesis. What Egeria possesses is a highly developed sense of piety and devotion to Christianity. This has led her to leave familiar surroundings to travel in modest style on pilgrimage to sites mentioned in the Bible, there to read the appropriate scriptural passages accompanied by prayer, before moving on to the next site on the newly developing pilgrim tourist route.[15]

Egeria's account of her pilgrimage is not the first such account known in Latin-speaking Christian circles in the western Roman Empire. The text by the anonymous pilgrim of Bordeaux ca. 333 is approximately fifty years earlier than Egeria's account.[16] Unlike the Bordeaux pilgrimage text, which lists places for accommodations, distances between sites, and travel times, Egeria did not write a how-to guide. She deals almost exclusively with the scriptural and liturgical associations of significant pilgrimage sites. How a person got there was immaterial to the prayer experience once one arrived.

Egeria's text takes the form of an informal letter with little extraneous archaeological or historical material included. She has written so as to give her circle of female friends an avenue for participation in her pilgrimage of prayer and liturgical observance. Scholars have criticized Egeria's text because of the nature of her writing, her "too informal, at times downright slovenly, prose not easily mistaken for literary Latin."[17] But Egeria was not trying to write anything more than a letter to friends. Despite the fact that she frequently repeats herself and does not closely adhere to the rules of syntax for classical Latin, her letter preserves one of the earliest and most extensive examples of nonliterary Latin as it was being used in Late Antiquity.

NOTES

1. Peter the Deacon, a monk at the great Benedictine monastery of Monte Cassino in southern Italy, wrote *De locis sanctis*, his guide to the Holy Land, in 1137. He based his information on accounts from earlier travelers who had written in Latin, including Egeria. For a critical edition of the Latin text of Peter's work, see *Corpus Christianorum Series Latina* [*CCSL*], vol. 175, pp. 94–103. John Wilkinson includes an English translation of Peter the Deacon's abridgement, with archaeological drawings, in *Egeria's Travels* (Warminster, U.K.: Aris & Phillips, 1999), pp. 86–106.

2. The solitary manuscript of Egeria's text passed from the monastery at Monte Cassino to the monastery at Arezzo in Italy ca. 1599, where it remained unrecognized until it was rediscovered in 1884 and prepared for publication by G. F. Gamurrini, *S. Hilarii tractatus de Myusteriis et hymni et S. Silviae Aguitanae peregrinatio ad loca sancta,* vol. 4 (Rome: Biblioteca della Accademia storico-giuridica, 1887).

3. The most thorough analysis of the chronological possibilities for Egeria's pilgrimage is in Paul Devos, "La date du voyage d'Égérie," *Analecta Bollandiana* 85 (1967): 165–94.

4. One of the earliest texts describing the rise of monasticism in Egypt is Athanasius of Alexandria, *Life of St. Antony,* written ca. 356–57. Antony moved into the Egyptian desert ca. 285, at which time there was already a community of female monastics where his sister could live. Cf. *Life of Antony,* chap. 3: "Entrusting his sister to virgins who were well known and faithful, Antony placed her in a convent [Greek: *parthenon*] to be brought up." At the time Egeria made her pilgrimage through Egypt, several female penitents and monastics were living in the desert. A number of their stories are collected in Benedicta Ward, *Harlots of the Desert* (Kalamazoo, Mich.: Cistercian Publications, 1987).

5. Mount Nebo is three miles southwest of Heshbon on the opposite side of the Jordan River from Jericho. Moses climbed Mount Nebo to gain a view of the Promised Land. Cf. Deuteronomy 32:49–50: "That same day the Lord spoke to Moses and said, 'Go up this mount Abarim, Mount Nebo in Moab, to the east of Jericho, and look out over the land of Canaan that I am giving to the Israelites for their possession. On this mountain you shall die and be gathered to your father's kin.' "

6. Egeria's descriptions of liturgical practices in Jerusalem can be read with the catechetical instruction taught by Bishop Cyril of Jerusalem (349–87) in his *Mystagogical Catecheses,* a series of sermons designed for the instruction of potential converts. Taken together, these two texts form a rather complete picture of Christian worship in Jerusalem in the late fourth century C.E.

7. Silvia of Aquitaine is the subject of a chapter in a collection of stories about early Christian saints and ascetics in Egypt. Cf. Palladius, *Lausiac History,* chap. 55, in which Silvia's pilgrimage from Jerusalem to Egypt is mentioned. For an analysis of the theory of Egeria's (mis)identification with Silvia, now no longer accepted, see E. D. Hunt, "St. Silvia of Aquitaine: The Role of a Theodosian Pilgrim in the Society of East and West," *Journal of Theological Studies* 23 (1972): 351–73.

8. An English translation of Valerius's letter to the monks of the monastery of Vierzo is included in Wilkinson, pp. 200–204. Early in the letter Valerius says, "We revere the valorous achievements of the mighty saints who were men, but we are amazed when still more courageous deeds are achieved by weak womanhood, such deeds as are indeed described in the remarkable history of the most blessed Egeria, who by her courage outdid the men of any age whatever" (200). Valerius also makes a word play on Egeria's name, stating that Egeria will inherit the heavenly (*aetherea*) kingdom.

9. For a discussion of the available evidence for the various theories of Egeria's origins, see Hagith Sivan, "Who Was Egeria? Piety and Pilgrimage in the Age of Gratian," *Harvard Theological Review* 81 (1988): 59–72.

10. See Devos.
11. For an analysis of the different models Christian women used when they began to form ascetic or monastic communities in the later fourth century C.E., see Susanna Elm, *"Virgins of God": The Making of Asceticism in Late Antiquity* (Oxford: Clarendon Press, 1994).
12. See Sivan, pp. 70–71.
13. For example, St. Jerome's Letter no. 108 to the Lady Eustochium describes the Lady Paula's pilgrimage from Rome to the Holy Land in the later fourth century C.E.
14. On the level and type of education of Christian Roman aristocratic women, see Elizabeth Clark, *Jerome, Chrysostom and Friends: Essays and Translations* (New York: Mellon, 1979). St. Jerome's letters reveal a number of instances in which he conducted involved, theological discussions with various female correspondents.
15. Unlike Judaism and Islam, in which pilgrimage is a fundamental religious obligation, Christians were under no such obligation. Pilgrimage to the Holy Land became popular in the mid–fourth century after Empress Helena, the mother of Emperor Constantine the Great, made a pilgrimage to the Holy Land. She is credited in early Christian tradition with finding many significant Christian relics, including wood from the True Cross and the original site of Jesus' crucifixion.
16. John Wilkinson includes extracts from the Bordeaux Pilgrim text translated into English in *Egeria's Travels*, pp. 22–34.
17. Clifford Weber, *Itinerari Egeriae pars prior* (Bryn Mawr, Pa.: Bryn Mawr College, 1994), p. 2.

ITINERARI EGERIAE PARS PRIOR

17:1–3

17:1 Item in nomine Dei transacto aliquanto tempore, cum iam tres anni pleni essent, a quo in Ierusolimam venissem, visis etiam omnibus locis sanctis ad quos orationis gratia me tenderam, et ideo iam revertendi ad patriam animus esset: volui iubente Deo, etiam et ad Mesopotamiam Syriae accedere ad visendos sanctos monachos, qui ibi plurimi et tam eximiae vitae esse dicebantur ut vix referri possit: nec non etiam et gratia orationis, ad martyrium sancti Thomae apostoli, ubi corpus illius integrum positum est, id est apud Edessam, quem se illuc missurum, posteaquam in caelis ascendisset, Deus noster Iesus testatus est per epistolam quam ad Aggarum regem per Ananiam cursorem misit, quaeque epistola cum grandi reverentia apud Edessam civitatem, ubi est ipsud martyrium, custoditur.

    17:2 Nam mihi credat volo affectio vestra, quoniam nullus Christianorum est, qui non se tendat illuc gratia orationis, quicumque tamen usque ad loca sancta, id est in Ierusolimis accesserit; et hic locus de Ierusolima vicesima et quinta mansione est.

    17:3 Et quoniam de Anthiochia propius est Mesopotamiam, fuit mihi iubente Deo oportunum satis ut, quemadmodum revertebar Constantinopolim, quia per Antiochiam iter erat, inde ad Mesopotamiam irem, sicut et factum est, Deo iubente.

19:1–19

19:1 Ac sic denuo faciens iter per mansiones aliquot perveni ad civitatem. Cuius nomen in scripturis positum legimus, id est Batanis, quae civitas usque in hodie est. Nam et ecclesia cum episcopo vere sancto et monacho et confessore habet et martyria aliquanta. Ipsa etiam civitas habundans multitudine hominum est, nam et miles ibi sedet cum tribuno suo.

19:2 Unde denuo proficiscens, pervenimus in nomine Christi Dei nostri Edessam. Ubi cum pervenissemus, statim perreximus ad ecclesiam et ad martyrium sancti Thomae. Itaque ergo, iuxta consuetudinem factis orationibus et cetera quae consuetudo erat fieri in locis sanctis, nec non etiam et aliquanta ipsius sancti Thomae ibi legimus.

19:3 Ecclesia autem, ibi que est, ingens et valde pulchra et nova dispositione, ut vere digna est esse domus Dei; et quoniam multa errant, quae ibi desiderabam videre, necesse me fuit ibi stativa triduana facere.

19:4 Ac sic ergo vidi in eadem civitate martyria plurima nec non et sanctos monachos, commanentes alios per martyria, alios longius de civitate in secretioribus locis habentes monasteria.

19:5 Et quoniam sanctus episcopus ipsius civitatis, vir vere religiosus et monachus et confessor, suscipiens me libenter, ait michi: "Quoniam video te, filia, gratia religionis tam magnum laborem tibi imposuisse ut de extremis porro terris venires ad haec loca, itaque ergo, si libenter habes, quaecumque loca sunt hic grata ad videndum Christianis, ostendimus tibi," tunc ergo, gratias agens Deo primum et sic ipsi rogavi plurimum, ut dignaretur facere quod dicebat.

19:6 Itaque ergo duxit me primum ad palatium Aggari regis et ibi ostendit michi archiotepam ipsius ingens, simillimam, ut ipsi dicebant, marmoream, tanti nitoris ac si de margarita esset; in cuius Aggari vultu parebat de contra vere fuisse hunc virum satis sapientem et honoratum. Tunc ait mihi sanctus episcopus, "Ecce rex Aggarus, qui antequam videret Dominum, credidit ei, quia esset vere filius Dei." Nam erat et iuxta archiotipa similiter de tali marmore facta, quam dixit filii ipsius esse Magni, similiter et ipsa habens aliquid gratiae in vultu.

19:7 Item perintravimus in interiori parte palatii; et ibi erant fontes, piscibus pleni, quales ego adhuc nunquam vidi, id est tantae magnitudinis et vel tam perlustres aut tam boni saporis. Nam ipsa civitas aliam aquam penitus non habet nunc nisi eam quae de palatio exit, quae est ac si fluvius ingens argenteus.

19:8 Et tunc retulit michi de ipsa aqua sic sanctus episcopus dicens: "Quodam tempore, posteaquam scripserat Aggarus rex ad Dominum et Dominus rescripserat Aggaro per Ananiam cursorem, sicut scriptum est in ipsa epistola; transacto ergo aliquanto tempore superveniunt Persi et girant civitatem istam.

19:9 Sed statim Aggarus, epistolam Domini ferens ad portam cum omni exercitu suo publice oravit. Et post dixit: "Domine Iesu, tu promiseras nobis, ne aliquis hostium ingrederetur civitatem istam, et ecce nunc Persae inpugnant nos." Quod cum dixisset tenens manibus levatis epistolam ipsam apertam rex, ad subito tantae tenebrae factae sunt, foras civitatem tamen ante oculos Persarum, cum iam prope plicarent civitati, ita ut usque tertium miliarium de civitate essent: sed ita mox tenebris turbati sunt, ut vix castra ponerent et pergirarent in miliario tertio totam civitatem.

19:10 Ita autem turbati sunt Persae ut nunquam viderent postea qua parte in civitate ingrederentur, sed custodirent civitatem per giro clusam hostibus, in miliario tamen tertio, quam tamen custodierunt mensibus aliquod.

19:11 Postmodum autem, cum viderent se nullo modo posse ingredi in civitatem, voluerunt siti eos occidere, qui in civitate erant. Nam monticulum istum, quem vides, filia, super civitate hac, in illo tempore ipse huic civitati aquam ministrabat. Tunc videntes hoc Persae averterunt ipsam aquam a civitate et fecerunt ei decursum contra ipso loco, ubi ipsi castra posita habebant.

19:12 In ea ergo die et in ea hora, qua averterant Persae aquam, statim hii fontes, quos vides, in eo loco, iusso Dei a semel eruperunt; ex ea die hi fontes usque in hodie permanent hic gratia Dei. Illa autem aqua, quam Persae averterant, ita siccata est in ea hora, ut nec ipsi haberent vel una die quod biberent, qui obsedebant civitatem, sicut tamen et usque in hodie apparet; nam postea nunquam nec qualiscumque humor ibi apparuit usque in hodie.

19:13 Ac sic, iubente Deo, qui hoc promiserat futurum, necesse fuit eos statim reverti ad sua, id est in Persida. Nam et postmodum, quotienscumque voluerunt venire et expugnare hanc civitatem hostes, haec epistola prolata est et lecta est in porta, et statim nutu Dei expulsi sunt omnes hostes.

19:14 Illud etiam retulit sanctus episcopus eo quod hii fontes ubi eruperunt, ante sic fuerit campus intra civitatem subiacens palatio Aggari. Quod palatium Aggari quasi in editiori loco positum erat, sicut et nunc paret, ut vides. Nam consuetudo talis erat in illo tempore, ut palatia, quotiensque fabricabantur, semper in editioribus locis fierent.

19:15 Sed postmodum quam hii fontes in eo loco eruperunt, tunc ipse Aggarus filio suo Magno, id est isti cuius archiotipa vides iuxta patre posita, hoc palatium fecit in eo loco, ita tamen ut hii fontes intra palatium includerentur.

19:16 Postea ergo quam haec omnia retulit sanctus episcopus, ait ad me, "Eamus nunc ad portam, per quam ingressus est Ananias cursor cum illa epistola, quam dixeram." Cum ergo venissemus ad portam ipsam, stans episcopus fecit orationem et legit nobis ibi ipsas epistolas et denuo benedicens nos facta est iterata oratio.

19:17 Illud etiam retulit nobis sanctus ipse dicens eo quod ex ea die, qua Ananias cursor per ipsam portam ingresses est cum epistolam Domini, usque in praesentem diem custodiatur, ne quis immundus, ne quis lugubris per ipsam portam transeat, sed nec corpus alicuius mortui eiciatur per ipsam portam.

19:18 Ostendit etiam nobis sanctus episcopus memoriam Aggari vel totius familiae ipsius valde pulchra, sed facta more antiquo. Duxit etiam nos et ad illum palatium superiorem quod habuerat primitus rex Aggarus, et si qua preterea loca erant, monstravit nobis.

19:19 Illud etiam satis mihi grato fuit, ut epistolas ipsas sive Aggari ad Dominum sive Domini ad Aggarum, quas nobis ibi legerat sanctus episcopus, acciperem michi ab ipso sancto. Et licet in patria exemplaria ipsarum haberem, tamen gratius mihi visum est, ut et ibi eas de ipso acciperem, ne quid forsitan minus ad nos in patria pervenisset; nam vere amplius est quod hic accepi. Unde, si Deus noster Iesus iusserit et venero in patria, legitis et vos, dominae animae meae.

23:1–10

23:1 Nam proficiscens de Tharso perveni ad quandam civitatem supra mare adhuc Ciliciae, que appellatur Ponpeiopolim. Et inde iam ingressa fines Hisauriae mansi in civitate, quae appellatur Corico, ac tertia die perveni ad civitatem, quae appellatur Seleucia Hisauriae. Ubi cum pervenissem, fui ad episcopum, vere sanctum ex monacho, vidi etiam ibi ecclesiam valde pulchram in eadem civitate.

23:2 Et quoniam inde ad sanctam Teclam, qui locus est ultra civitatem in colle sed plano, habebat de civitate forsitan mille quingentos passus, malui ergo perexire illuc, ut stativa quam factura eram, ibi facerem. Ibi autem ad sanctam ecclesiam nichil aliud est nisi monasteria sine numero virorum ac mulierum.

23:3 Nam inveni ibi aliquam amicissimam michi, et cui omnes in oriente testimonium ferebant vitae ipsius, sancta diaconissa nomine Marthana, quam ego aput Ierusolimam noveram, ubi illa gratia orationis ascenderat; haec autem monasteria aputactitum seu virginum regebat. Quae me cum vidisset, quod gaudium illius vel meum esse potuerit, nunquid vel scribere possum?

23:4 Sed ut redeam ad rem, monasteria ergo plurima sunt ibi per ipsum collem et in medio murus ingens, qui includet ecclesiam, in qua est martyrium, quod martyrium satis pulchrum est. Propterea autem murus missus est ad custodiendam ecclesiam propter Hisauros, quia satis mali sunt et frequenter latrunculantur, ne forte conentur aliquid facere circa monasterium, quod ibi est deputatum.

23:5 Ibi ergo cum venissem in nomine Dei, facta oratione ad martyrium nec non etiam et lectus omnis actus sanctae Teclae, gratias Christo Deo nostro egi infinitas, qui mihi dignatus est indignae et non merenti in omnibus desideria complere.

23:6 Ac sic ergo facto ibi biduo, visis etiam sanctis monachis vel aputactitis, tam viris quam feminis, qui ibi erant, et facta oratione et communione, reversa sum Tharso ad iter meum; ubi facta stativa triduana, in nomine Dei profecta sum inde iter meum. Ac sic perveniens eadem die ad mansionem, quae appellatur Mansocrenas, quae est sub monte Tauro, ibi mansi.

23:7 Et inde alia die subiens montem Taurum et faciens iter iam notum per singulas provincias, quas eundo transiveram, id est Cappadociam, Galatiam, et Bithiniam, perveni Calcedona, ubi propter famosissimum martyrium sanctae Eufimiae, ab olim michi notum iam, quod ibi est, mansi loco.

23:8 Ac sic ergo alia die, transiens mare, perveni Constantinopolim agens Christo Deo nostro gratias quod michi indignae et non merenti praestare dignatus est tantam gratiam, id est ut non solum voluntatem eundi, sed et facultatem perambulandi quae desiderabam, dignatus fuerat prestare, et revertendi denuo Constantinopolim.

23:9 Ubi cum venissem, per singulas ecclesias vel apostolos, nec non et per singula martyria, quae ibi plurima sunt, non cessabam Deo nostro Iesu gratias agere, qui ita super me misericordiam suam prestare dignatus fuerat.

23:10 De quo loco, domnae, lumen meum, cum haec ad vestram affectionem darem, iam pospositi erat in nomine Christi Dei nostri ad Asiam accedendi, id est Efesum, propter martyrium sancti et beati apostoli Iohannis, gratia orationis. Si autem et post hoc in corpore fuero, si qua preterea loca cognoscere potuero, aut ipsa praesens, si Deus fuerit praestare dignatus, vestrae affectioni referam, aut certe, si aliud animo sederit, scriptis nuntiabo. Vos tantum, domnae, lumen meum, memores mei esse dignamini, sive in corpore, sive iam extra corpus fuero.

TRANSLATION

The translation is from John Wilkinson, *Egeria's Travels,* 3d ed. Warminster, U.K.: Aris & Phillips, 1999 is reprinted by permission of the publisher. The notes to the translation are by Victoria Erhart.

17:1–3

Some time after that, since it was already three full years since my arrival in Jerusalem, and I had seen all the places which were the object of my pilgrimage, I felt that the time had come to return in God's name to my own country. But God also moved me with a desire to go to Syrian Mesopotamia. The holy monks there are said to be numerous and of so indescribably excellent a life that I wanted to pay them a visit; I also wanted to make a pilgrimage to the martyrium of the holy apostle Thomas, where his entire body is buried.[1] It is at Edessa,[2] to which Jesus,

---

[1] See John 20:24–21:1 for information on the Apostle Thomas, who refused to believe in Jesus' Resurrection until Jesus appeared to him. Early Christian tradition states that Thomas journeyed to Parthia (Persia) to preach the Gospel after Jesus' death. Tradition also holds that Thomas was martyred and buried in Edessa. See Eusebius of Caesarea, *Ecclesiastical History* 3:1, notes 1 and 2, p. 137, for one version of the early Christian tradition involving Thomas's activities in Persian territory after Jesus' death and resurrection.

[2] Edessa, present-day Urfa in Turkey, is a city in northern Mesopotamia on the Euphrates River.

our God, was sending Thomas after his ascension into heaven, as he tells us in the letter he sent to King Abgar[3] by the messenger Ananias. This letter has been most reverently preserved at Edessa where they have this martyrium. And, believe me, loving sisters, no Christian who has achieved the journey to the holy places and Jerusalem misses going also on the pilgrimage to Edessa. It is twenty-five staging-posts away from Jerusalem. But Mesopotamia is not so far from Antioch. So, since my route back to Constantinople took me back that way, it was very convenient for me at God's bidding to go from Antioch to Mesopotamia, and that, under God, is what I did.

19:1–19

After several more staging-posts I came to Batanis,[4] a city mentioned in the Bible, and still there to this day. It has a church with a really godly bishop who is both monk and confessor. There are several martyria. And the city has a vast population, and a garrison with a tribune in charge. From there we set out again, and came, in the name of Christ our God, to Edessa.

As soon as we arrived, we went straight to the church and martyrium of holy Thomas;[5] there we had our usual prayers and everything which was our custom in holy places. And we read also from the writings of holy Thomas himself.[6] The church there is large and beautiful, and built in a new way—just right, in fact, to be a house of God. In this city there was so much I wanted to see that I had to stay there three days. I saw a great many martyria and visited the holy monks, some of whom lived among the martyria, while others had their cells further away from the city where it was more private.

The holy bishop of the city was a truly devout man, both monk and confessor. He welcomed me and said, "My daughter, I can see what a long journey this

---

[3]This is a reference to King Abgar Ucomo, "the Black," who ruled the principality of Edessa ca. 13–50 C.E. Despite the widespread belief in the existence of correspondence between King Abgar and Jesus, a pious tradition that lasted well into the medieval period, there is no historical evidence for any exchange of letters or other materials between the two. Most probably, this pious story was contrived by King Abgar IX, the first Christian King of Edessa (179–214 C.E.), to give himself an impressive Christian pedigree. Details of their purported correspondence will be discussed below.

[4]Also called Batnae and Serug, Batanis is located south of Edessa. Like Edessa, Batanis was a wealthy commercial city during Late Antiquity.

[5]For the location of the shrine of St. Thomas in Edessa, see J. B. Segal, "New Mosaics from Edessa," *Archaeology* 12 (1959): 151–57; see especially p. 152 for a simplified archaeological drawing of the main portion of early Christian Edessa.

[6]Early Christian tradition credits the Apostle Thomas as the author of a number of works. The non-canonical *Gospel of Thomas* survives in a fifth-century Coptic translation of the second-century Greek original. It is primarily a collection of sayings or parables attributed to Jesus. The *Infancy Narrative* by Thomas professes to record miracles performed by Christ in His childhood.

is on which your faith has brought you—right from the other end of the earth. So now please let us show you all the places Christians should visit here."[7] I gave thanks to God, and eagerly accepted the bishop's invitation. So first of all he took me to the palace of King Abgar, and showed me a huge marble portrait of him. People said it was an excellent likeness, and it shone as if it was made of pearl. The look on Abgar's face showed me, as I looked straight at it, what a wise and noble man he had been, and the holy bishop told me, "That is King Abgar. Before he saw the Lord he believed in him as the true Son of God." Next to this portrait was another of the same marble; he told me it was the king's son Magnus, and he too had a wonderful face.

Then we went inside the palace, and saw the pools with the fish in them.[8] I have never seen fish like them, they were so big, so brightly colored, and tasted so good.

The only water-supply which the city has inside its walls at the present day is this one which comes from the palace, and it is like a great river of silver.[9] The holy bishop told me this about it: "King Abgar wrote a letter to the Lord, and the Lord sent his answer by the messenger Ananias;[10] then, quite a time after, the Persians descended on this city and encircled it.[11] So at once Abgar, with his whole army, took the Lord's letter to the gate, and prayed aloud: 'Lord Jesus,' he said, 'You promised us that no enemy would enter this city. Look now how the Persians

---

[7]Scholars have used this phrase to argue that Egeria was from Spain or Gaul. For a critique of the various theories of Egeria's origins, see Andrew Palmer, "Egeria the Voyager, or the Technology of Remote Sensing in Late Antiquity," in Zweder von Martels, ed., *Travel Fact and Travel Fiction* (Leiden: E. J. Brill, 1994), pp. 39–53.

[8]All that survives of Abgar's palace are the pools for fish, now incorporated into the Pool of Abraham that forms part of the complex of the main mosque in Edessa. Long before the Christian era, a type of fish, most probably carp, were considered sacred by the northern Mesopotamian pagans and had been provided with pools within sacred precincts.

[9]For an analysis of Edessa's water-supply system in Late Antiquity, see John Wilkinson, *Egeria's Travels*, p. 199. See Palmer, "Egeria the Voyager," for a critique of the bishop of Edessa's story of the water-supply for the city, a story not supported by archaeological evidence.

[10]See Eusebius of Caesarea, *Ecclesiastical History* 1:6 for an early version of the Abgar-Jesus correspondence. Briefly stated, Abgar had heard that Jesus was a powerful healer and was having difficulties with the political authorities in Palestine. Abgar invited Jesus to be his guest in Edessa. He sent his invitation with the newly converted Christian Ananias. Jesus replied to Abgar that he himself could not visit Edessa but would shortly send one of his disciples who would heal Abgar's medical problem and explain Christianity to him. In some versions of the story, Jesus sent his portrait to Abgar, along with the promise that the city of Edessa would always be under divine protection as a reward for Abgar's faith in Jesus.

[11]It is difficult to know precisely what is meant by the phrase, "quite a time later." Shortly before Egeria visited Edessa in 384, the Persian Empire had made major inroads into Mesopotamian territory, forcing the Roman Empire to hand over the frontier city of Nisibis. In exchange the Persians allowed the army of the now dead Emperor Julian (361–63) to retreat back into Roman territory. For much of its history Edessa was a frontier city and subject to periodic raids by Persian troops.

are attacking us.' With that the king held up the letter, open in his hands, and immediately a darkness fell over the Persians, who were by then close outside the city walls. It made them retire three miles away, and the darkness was so confusing to the Persians that they found it difficult to pitch camp and carry out patrols even at three miles' distance from the city. They were too confused to discover how to enter the city, so for the next few months they stayed at a distance of three miles from the walls, leaving it with the gates shut, and besieging it. Then, since they could find no way of breaking into the city, they decided to kill the inhabitants by thirst. At the time, my daughter, the city had its water from the small hill you see up there. The Persians realized this, so they cut a channel to divert the water away from the city to the side where they had their camp. On the very day, and at the very moment they diverted the water, God brought water flowing out of the springs you can see here; and by God's grace it has continued to flow ever since. But at the same moment the water in the channel which had been made by the Persian besiegers dried up. They had not even enough water left for one day. And it is like that today, as you can see, for since then there has never been any water running in it. So, by God's will, they had to go home to Persis, as he had promised. And ever afterwards, if any enemy has come here and tried to overthrow the city, the letter is produced and read at the gate; and at once, by God's favor, he is driven away."[12] According to the holy bishop the springs had appeared lower down than Abgar's palace in a field which was inside the city. "Abgar's palace, as you can see, had been on higher ground, like the other palaces of those days. But after the springs began to flow, then Abgar built round them this palace for his son Magnus, the one whose portrait you saw next to the one of his father."

After the holy bishop had told me this, he said, "Now let us go to the gate where the messenger Ananias came in with the letter of which I have been telling you." When we got to the gate, the bishop stopped. He said a prayer and read the actual letters. Then he blessed us, and said another prayer. The holy man also told us this; from the day when the messenger Ananias brought in the Lord's letter through this gate until now neither has any one been allowed to pass through who is unclean or in mourning, nor has any dead body been taken out through it. The holy bishop also showed us the tomb of Abgar and all his family (which was beautiful but old-fashioned), and he took us up to Abgar's first palace, and showed us all the other things there were to see.[13]

One thing specially pleased me. I received from this holy man the copies of Abgar's letter to the Lord, and the Lord's letter to Abgar, which he had read to us. I have copies of them at home, but even so it is much better to have been given

---

[12]Belief in divine protection for Edessa lasted until the city was captured by al-Zingi in 1144 C.E.

[13]For archaeological information on fourth-century Edessa, see J. B. Segal, *Edessa "The Blessed City"* (Oxford: Clarendon Press, 1970).

them here by him. And it may be that what we have at home is not so complete, because what I was given here is certainly longer. So, dearest ladies, you yourselves must read them when I come home, if such is the will of Jesus our God.

23:1–10

Leaving Tarsus, but still in Cilicia[14] I reached Pompeiopolis,[15] a city by the sea, and from there I crossed into Isauria,[16] and spent the night in a city called Corycus.[17] On the third day I arrived at a city called Seleucia of Isauria,[18] and when I got there, I called on the bishop, a very godly man who had been a monk, and saw a very beautiful church in the city. Holy Thecla's[19] is on a small hill about a mile and a half from the city so, as I had to stay somewhere, it was best to go straight on and spend the night there.

Round the holy church there is a tremendous number of cells for men and women.[20] And that was where I found one of my dearest friends, a holy deaconess[21] called Marthana.[22] I had come to know her in Jerusalem when she was up there on pilgrimage. She was the superior of some cells of apotactites or virgins[23] and I simply cannot tell you how pleased we were to see each other again. But I must get back to the point. There are a great many cells on that hill, and in the middle a great wall around the martyrium itself, which is very beautiful.[24]

---

[14]Cilicia is a province in southeast Asia Minor on the Mediterranean Sea. The Apostle Paul was originally from Tarsus, the provincial capital of Cilicia.

[15]Pompeiopolis is also a city in the province of Cilicia.

[16]Isauria is a province in southern Asia Minor on the Mediterranean Sea.

[17]Corycus is the present-day Kizkalesi in southern Turkey. Christian-era archaeological remains from this site are all dated later than Egeria's visit in the late fourth century, though the site has not been completely excavated.

[18]Seleucia of Isauria was the provincial capital of Isauria. It is present-day Silifke.

[19]In early Christian tradition, St. Thecla was a young woman from Iconium who was converted to Christianity by the Apostle Paul's preaching. Basil of Seleucia wrote the *Life of St. Thecla*. Cf. J. P. Migne, *Patrologiae Graecae*, vol. 85.

[20]Until well into the fourth century C.E., mixed or double communities of male and female ascetics were the norm. Later these communities were segregated by sex. For the history of this development, see Susanna Elm, *"Virgins of God": The Making of Asceticism in Late Antiquity* (Oxford: Clarendon Press, 1994).

[21]For the history of the development of the office of deaconess, see Elm, *"Virgins of God,"* pp. 181–83.

[22]Marthana is the only person named in Egeria's text. She is mentioned by Basil in the *Life of St. Thecla* 2:30.

[23]The Greek word *apotaktikos* was used as a title to describe a religious person who no longer owned any material possessions. For the history of the use of this term in Christian ascetical theology, see Elm, *"Virgins of God,"* pp. 238–41.

[24]For archaeological information on Thecla's martyrium see John Wilkinson, *Egeria's Travels*, pp. 288–92.

The wall was built to protect the church against the Isaurians, who are hostile, and always committing robberies, to prevent them trying to damage the monastery which has been established there. In God's name I arrived at the martyrium, and we had a prayer there, and read the whole Acts of holy Thecla,[25] and I gave heartfelt thanks to God for his mercy in letting me fulfill all my desires so completely, despite all my unworthiness. For two days I stayed there, visiting all the holy monks and apotactites, the men as well as the women; then, after praying and receiving Communion, I went back to Tarsus to rejoin my route.

I stayed there three days before setting off to continue my journey, and then, after a day's traveling, I arrived at a staging-post called Mansucrene below Mount Taurus.[26] We stayed the night there, and the next day we climbed Mount Taurus, and continued along a road we already knew, since our outward journey had brought us along it. Passing through the same provinces of Cappadocia, Galatia, and Bithynia, I reached Chalcedon,[27] and I stayed there because it contains the renowned martyrium of holy Euphemia,[28] long known to me. Next day I crossed the sea and reached Constantinople,[29] giving thanks to Christ our God for seeing fit, through no deserving of mine, to grant me the desire to go on this journey, and the strength to visit everything I wanted and now to return again to Constantinople.

---

[25]*Acts of Thecla*, also called the *Acts of Paul and Thecla*, were written late in the second century C.E. Thecla was converted to Christianity and celibacy as a result of listening to Paul's preaching. Thecla's intended husband reported her to the authorities when she refused to marry him. Imprisoned along with the Apostle Paul, Thecla was given the chance to renounce Christianity and get married. Upon her refusal, she was sentenced to be burned to death. Divine intervention in the form of a rain cloud saved her life. She traveled with Paul to Antioch where she was again imprisoned and sentenced to be thrown to the wild beasts in the arena. The bears and lions instead lay down at her feet. Sentenced to be drawn and quartered by being attached to bulls, she was again saved through Divine Providence. Finally released from Roman custody, she returned to her home territory in Iconium to preach the Gospel. A partial translation of the *Acts of Thecla* is included in Wayne Meeks, ed., *The Writings of St. Paul* (New York: W. W. Norton, 1972), pp. 198–207.

[26]Mount Tarsus is in the province of Cilicia.

[27]Cappadocia is a province in central Asia Minor (Turkey). The provincial capital is Caesarea. Cf. Acts of the Apostles 2:9 for a mention of the Gospel being preached in Cappadocia. Galatia is a province in central Asia Minor. Cf. Acts of the Apostles 18:23 for a mention of the Apostle Paul's journey to Galatia. He wrote his Epistle to the Galatians to the Christian communities there. Bithynia is a province in northern Asia Minor along the Black Sea. The provincial capital is Nicomedia. Cf. 1 Peter 1:1 for a mention of the Christian communities in Bithynia. Chalcedon is a city on the Asian side of the Bosphorus Straits, opposite Constantinople.

[28]The Christian virgin Euphemia was martyred at Chalcedon ca. 303/4. The basilica of that city is named for her.

[29]Constantinople, present-day Istanbul, was the administrative and cultural capital of the Eastern Roman Empire. It was refounded by Emperor Constantine I after he became a Christian in the early part of the fourth century.

And in all the churches at Constantinople, in the tombs of the apostles, and at many martyria, I never ceased to give thanks to Jesus our God for his grace in showing me such mercy.

So, loving ladies, light of my heart, this is where I am writing to you. My present plan is, in the name of Christ our God, to travel to Asia, since I want to make a pilgrimage to Ephesus, and the martyrium of the holy and blessed Apostle John.[30] If after that I am still alive, and able to visit further places, I will either tell you about them face to face (if God so wills), or at any rate write to you about them if my plans change. In any case, ladies, light of my heart, whether I am "in the body" or "out of the body," please do not forget me.

BIBLIOGRAPHY

Primary Sources

Eusebius Pamphili. *Ecclesiastical History*, Books 1–5. Translated by Roy J. Deferrari. New York: Fathers of the Church, 1953.

Franceschini, E., and R. Weber. *Itinerarium Egeriae*. Corpus Christianorum Series Latina vol. 175. Turnhout: Brepol, 1965, pp. 27–90.

Gamurrini, G. F. S. *Hilarii tractatus de Myusteriis et hymni et S. Silviae Aguitanae peregrinatio ad loca sancta,* vol. 4 (Rome: Biblioteca della Accademia storicogiuridica, 1887).

Gingras, G. E. *Egeria, Diary of a Pilgrimage*. Ancient Christian Writers 38. New York, Newman Press, 1970.

Pétré, H *Éthérie. Journal de voyage. Texte latin, introduction et traduction*. Sources chrétiennes 21. Paris, 1948.

Weber, Clifford. *Itinerari Egeriae pars prior*. Bryn Mawr, Pa.: Bryn Mawr College, 1994.

Wilkinson, John. *Egeria's Travels*. 3d ed. Warminster, U.K.: Aris & Phillips, 1999.

Secondary Works

Devos, Paul. "La date du voyage d'Égérie." *Analecta Bollandiana* 85 (1967): 165–94.

Elm, Susanna. *"Virgins of God": The Making of Asceticism in Late Antiquity*. Oxford: Clarendon Press, 1994.

Hunt, E. D. "St. Silvia of Aquitaine: The Role of a Theodosian Pilgrim in the Society of East and West." *Journal of Theological Studies* 23 (1972): 351–73.

Palmer, Andrew. "Egeria the Voyager, or the Technology of Remote Sensing in Late Antiquity." In *Travel Fact and Travel Fiction*, edited by Z. von Martels. Leiden: E. J. Brill, 1994, pp. 39–53.

---

[30]Ephesus is on the west coast of Asia Minor (Turkey) opposite the island of Samos. There was an early Christian tradition that the Apostle John wrote his Gospel and Epistles while living in Ephesus ca. 65 C.E. There was also an early Christian tradition that Mary the mother of Jesus was buried at Ephesus. Cf. Acts of the Apostles 18:24–25 and 19:1 for Christian activity in Ephesus in the later half of the first century C.E.

Segal, J. B. "New Mosaic from Edessa." *Archaeology* 12 (1959): 151–57.

———. *Edessa "The Blessed City."* Oxford: Clarendon Press, 1970.

Sivan, Higath. "Who Was Egeria? Piety and Pilgrimage in the Age of Gratian." *Harvard Theological Review* 81 (1988): 59–72.

Wilkinson, John. *Jerusalem Pilgrims before the Crusades.* Warminster, U.K.: Aris & Phillips, 1977.

Appendix

Street Mysticism: An Introduction to *The Life and Revelations* of Agnes
Blannbekin
   Ulrike Wiethaus
Birgitta Birgersdotter, Saint Bride of Sweden (1303?–1373)
   Sandra Straubhaar

Appendix

Contributors

Volume 3. Early Modern Women Writing Latin

Angela Nogarola (ca. 1400) and Isotta Nogarola (1418–1466): Thieves of
Language
   Holt N. Parker
Costanza Varano (1426–1447): Latin as an Instrument of State
   Holt N. Parker
Cassandra Fedele (1465–1558)
   Diana Robin
Laura Cereta (1469–1499)
   Diana Robin
Conventual Life in Renaissance Italy: The Latin Poetry of Suor Laurentia
Strozzi (1514–1591)
   Jane Stevenson
Olympia Fulvia Morata (1526/7–1555): Humanist, Heretic, Heroine
   Holt N. Parker
Luisa Sigea (1522–1560): Iberian Scholar-Poet
   Edward V. George
Johanna Otho (Othonia) and Women's Latin Poetry of Reformed Europe
   Jane Stevenson
Elizabeth Jane Weston (1581–1612)
   Brenda M. Hosington
Bathsua Reginald Makin (1600–1675?)
   Anne Leslie Saunders
"*Alpha Virginum*": Anna Maria van Schurman (1607–1678)
   Pieta van Beek

Appendix

Contributors

Contributors

PHYLLIS R. BROWN is Associate Professor in the English Department and associated with the Program for the Study of Women and Gender at Santa Clara University, where she has taught since 1982. She has published articles on Louise Labé, Guillaume de Machaut, Heloise, and Anglo-Saxon poetry and is currently coediting a collection of essays on Hrotsvit of Gandersheim. Brown is also Faculty Director of the Peer Educator Program at Santa Clara University, and she edits *Chronica* for the Medieval Association of the Pacific.

LAURIE J. CHURCHILL is Associate Professor of Humanities-Classics at Ohio Wesleyan University, where she also coordinates the Women's Studies Program. She has been on the faculty at OWU since 1989. Churchill's academic research and publications focus on Ovid's erotic poetry and the representation of women in Latin poetry. Currently, she is working on a book with photographer Kippra Hopper on *Women Artists of West Texas*. She is on leave from academe while she considers reinventing her life in Truth or Consequences, New Mexico.

VICTORIA ERHART received her Ph.D. in early Christian studies from The Catholic University of America in Washington, D.C. Her area of expertise is the history of Christian Late Antiquity, particularly Syriac church history. She currently teaches in the Philosophy and Religion Department of Hood College in Frederick, Maryland.

JUDITH P. HALLETT is Professor and Chair of Classics at the University of Maryland, College Park. She has published widely on women in Latin literature, Roman sexuality, and the Roman family as well as on women and the classical tradition. She is author of *Fathers and Daughters: Women and the Elite Family* (Princeton, N.J., 1984) and coeditor of *Compromising Traditions: The Personal Voice in Classics Scholarship* (New York, 1997), *Roman Sexualities* (Princeton, N.J., 1998), and *Rome and Her Monuments: Essays on the City and Literature of Rome in Honor of Katherine A. Geffcken* (Wauconda, Ill., 2000).

JANE E. JEFFREY, Associate Professor of English at West Chester University, is the author of *Blicking Spirituality and the Old English Vernacular Homily: A Textual Analysis* (Lewiston, N.Y., 1989) and has published articles on Hrotsvit of Gandersheim and teaching medieval women.

BERNICE M. KACZYNSKI is Professor in the Department of History, McMaster University, Hamilton, Ontario, and a member of the graduate faculty of the Centre for Medieval Studies at the University of Toronto. She is author of *Greek in the Carolingian Age: The St. Gall Manuscripts* (Cambridge, Mass., 1988), as well as numerous other studies on manuscripts, language, and literacy in Late Antiquity and the Middle Ages.

JUDITH LYNN SEBESTA, Professor of Classics at the University of South Dakota, is a coeditor of *The World of Roman Costume* (Madison, Wis., 1994) and has written on gender and costume in the Roman world. She is currently editing a costume lexicon for the Website *Diotima: Women and Gender in the Ancient World*.

JANE STEVENSON was educated at Newnham College, Cambridge, where she studied Anglo-Saxon, Norse, and Celtic, specializing in Anglo-Latin. She has been a Research Fellow at Pembroke College, Cambridge, a Lecturer in Late Antique and Early Medieval History at the University of Sheffield, and a Senior Research Fellow in British and Comparative Cultural Studies at the University of Warwick. She is now Reader in English and Comparative Literature at King's College, Aberdeen. Her books include *The Laterculus Malalianus and the School of Archbishop Theodore* (Cambridge, 1995); *Early Modern Women Poets 1520–1700: An Anthology*, with Peter Davidson (Oxford, 2001); and the forthcoming *Women and the Language of Authority* (Oxford). She has also published a variety of articles and chapters on postclassical Latin and women's writing.

ELIZABETH WOECKNER is currently writing her dissertation at Princeton University in the Department of Classics. Her dissertation focuses on Roman social relations, specifically on Roman *amicitia*, "friendship", and explores the possibilities wherein at least one party in the relationship is female. Aside from her work on women's graffiti from Pompeii, her interests are epigraphy, numismatics, and the social history of the Roman Empire.